LI

2024

The Yearbook of
The Society for the Study of Midwestern Literature

MidAmerica (ISSN 0190-2911) is a peer-reviewed journal published
annually by The Society for the Study of Midwestern Literature.

This journal is a member of the Council of Editors of Learned Journals.

MidAmerica, a peer-reviewed journal of The Society for the Study of Midwestern Literature, is published annually. We welcome scholarly contributions from our members on any aspect of midwestern literature and culture. Except for winners of our annual poetry and prose contests, we do not publish poems, short stories, or creative nonfiction.

For submission guidelines, see ssml.org/publications/midamerica/submission. Please direct questions to the editor, Patricia Oman (poman@hastings.edu).

For permissions and back issues, please contact Marcia Noe (marcia-noe@utc.edu).

In honor of
Marcia Noe

Contents

Preface

Patricia Oman

MidAmerica LI is dedicated to Dr. Marcia Noe, who recently stepped down as the journal's editor. I am grateful for Marcia's mentorship and generosity over the years, first when I was a new member of The Society for the Study of Midwestern Literature and now as I become *MidAmerica*'s editor.

The first issue of *MidAmerica* was published in 1974 by Dr. David D. Anderson, SSML's founder. Marcia took over editorship of the journal officially in 2006, though she had been assisting for several years by that time. In *MidAmerica*'s first fifty years, Dave and Marcia kept the study of midwestern literature alive by encouraging and supporting scholars in the study of the region. Their legacies are cemented. My first goal as only the third editor in the journal's history is not to screw it up. My second goal is to lay the foundation for *MidAmerica*'s second fifty years.

The essays, book reviews, and bibliography in this issue, *MidAmerica*'s fifty-first issue, attest to the complexity and richness of midwestern literature and its study, particularly the continuous need to re-examine and re-evaluate how we see the region, its authors, and its literary and cultural productions.

Rosemary Erickson Johnsen's essay, "Marcie R. Rendon's Cash Blackbear Crime-Fiction Series and Nordic Settler Colonial Legacies in Minnesota's Red River Valley," for example, centers the perspectives of Indigenous people in the Midwest, whereas Gretchen Lida's Paul Somers Prize–winning nonfiction essay "Can Technical College Students 'Think Like a Mountain'?" and Alexandria Remm's essay "Green People in Dingess, Roberts, and Gieni's *Manifest Destiny: Flora and Fauna*" foreground nature, invoking the still-emerging field of ecocriticism to examine the relationship between humans and the natural environment in representations of the Midwest. (Christian Knoeller's review essay, "Restoring the Upper Midwest from Landscape to Literature," provides an overview of several recent publications on the relationship between people and the natural world in the Midwest.)

In their essays in this issue, Jefferson Storms, Madeline Bruessow, and Sherrin Frances excavate unknown midwestern voices. Storms's essay, "'An Antydote fer the Brute': Apocalyptic Imagination in *Farmer Hiram on the World's War*" (winner of the David Diamond Student Writing Prize) introduces the poet Lindley Grant Long to *MidAmerica* readers. Bruessow and Frances examine archival sources to reveal a new authoritative voice on the poet Theodore Roethke—his wife Beatrice Roethke, who took issue with published biographies on the poet.

And Janet Ruth Heller and Robert Dunne provide new insights into that staple of midwestern literature, Sherwood Anderson, Heller zooming in for a close reading of Anderson's story "An Awakening" and Dunne zooming out to provide a retrospective view of Anderson's critical reception since his death in 1941. Dunne's essay, "Anderson, Trilling, and the Influence of Powerful Critics: Score One for the Author," demonstrates the importance of re-evaluating literary criticism itself and is the winner of this year's James Seaton Midwestern Heritage Prize for Literary Criticism.

I look forward to working with members of SSML in the coming years to explore all the possible ways to study midwestern literature and culture.

Hastings College

Can Technical College Students "Think Like a Mountain"?

Gretchen Lida

I teach composition at a technical college in Kenosha, Wisconsin. It is the state's fourth largest city at just over 100,000 people and now infamous for being the place where teenage Kyle Rittenhouse killed two people in 2020 during a Black Lives Matter protest. Sitting squarely between Milwaukee and Chicago, the influence of the two cities looms large over Kenosha; many of my students have families in one or another. It is also a city with a lighthouse, which looks over Lake Michigan, and in the summertime, spear-headed Caspian Terns dive for fish. Their sharp white wings come together as they plummet in the waves.

While some of my students transfer to four-year schools, the majority will enter the workforce after they receive their associate's degrees or other certifications. They are studying to be mechanics, IT workers, nurses, and cops. But no matter their vocational choices, if they are in my class, they are going to read Aldo Leopold's "Thinking Like a Mountain," an essay he wrote in 1944.

Before we read it, I ask, "Have any of you been to the Wisconsin Dells?" Most of the hands go up when I mention the garish "Water Park Capital of the World" an hour or two north. "Leopold's essay was written in a shack really close to there. I got to sit in the exact spot where the author wrote it." I can only hold my fan girl in for so long.

I then gush unashamedly: how Leopold is considered the patron saint of American Conservation. Leopold was originally from Iowa but was transferred by the Forest Service to Wisconsin in 1924, when he began his career as the first game management professor at the University of Wisconsin and wrote the very first book on the subject. He also came up with a concept called the Land Ethic, which moved from the idea that land was simply there to serve us to the concept that we are in fact part of the ecosystem. We are a community with the living things around us.

I teach "Thinking Like a Mountain" partly for the midwestern connection and partly because its form and content suit the last unit of the class, where students are required to write a narrative essay. It is also mercifully short, perfect for our age of acutely limited attention spans and for students with educational trauma around reading. The essay also finds power in its brevity, with each sentence pulling as much weight as the next. And I confess: I include it in my lesson plan so I will make the time to read it again. Maybe this time I'll unearth its magic.

"Ok, we are going to read this out loud," I instruct as I pass around the single double-sided page that contains the essay. "I want you to underline two passages with sensory details, and two lines where the author reflects on what he is thinking."

The essay isn't a happy thing. It is simply a confession. As Leopold was working on his essay collection *Sand County Almanac*, which is mostly about the land along the Wisconsin River, his longtime friend Hans Albert Hochem, offering feedback, remarked that the wolf, an apex predator in all of North America, was absent from the work. In a letter to Leopold he wrote, "I think you'll have to admit you've got at least a drop of its blood on your hands." Leopold responded with "Thinking Like a Mountain," about a time in 1909 when, in the New Mexico mountains, 22-year-old Leopold killed a mother wolf. However, as the wolf died in front of him, his life changed forever:

> I was young then, and full of trigger-itch; I thought that because fewer wolves meant more deer, that no wolves would mean hunters' paradise. But after seeing the green fire die, I sensed that neither the wolf nor the mountain agreed with such a view.

Once we finish our read-around and I ask people to share, there is always someone who chooses this passage:

We reached the old wolf in time to watch a fierce green fire dying in her eyes. I realized then, and have known ever since, that there was something new to me in those eyes—something known only to her and to the mountain.

I used to tell students they could choose anything but this section. It is so famous that books and films about Leopold have had this in the title. I decided I would stop fighting the passage's magnetism. This iconic passage is famous for a reason—the darn thing is hard to forget.

"Man, Prof G, you are kind of obsessed with this guy, aren't you?" a student commented one semester.

I, of course, admit to my fandom. Teaching, I have learned, can be viewed in three parts: one-third knowledge, one-third actually liking students, and one-third enthusiasm. As we talk about the essay, I gush about how not a sentence is wasted, each working hard to convey more than one thing. I explain how wolves were reintroduced to Yellowstone in the 1990s, drastically improving the numbers of songbirds and beavers because there were fewer deers to eat the young trees. Then I say there are even a few wolves left in Wisconsin.

However, I do not tell them that every time I read "Thinking Like a Mountain" I think of spotting wolves in Yellowstone myself. How 16-year-old me screeched to my family and pointed out the window when we saw them. How we stood off the side of the road in the rain to watch the pack trot through the valley. As our t-shirts soaked through, we stared dumbstruck. A big black wolf with yellow eyes stared back at us. It was as if my teenage world of minivans and honor roll was shattered by something wilder.

My parents used to brag that I was a wildlife magnet. I wanted to see manatees in Florida; we saw at least a dozen. Humpbacks in both Maui and Cape Cod have breached endlessly, as though just for me. In Kenosha, I saw a snowy owl hunting in the morning snow outside the airport on my drive to work.

Even home in Chicago, an hour's drive from campus, I have seen bats, falcons, and night herons. One early morning, my breath caught when a coyote stood between me and my car. The yellow flames in the coyote's eyes were just as wild as the green fire Leopold described.

After we finish the read-aloud and if the weather is nice enough, I'll take my students outside with just a notebook and pen. I set a timer, and they write down what they see, hear, smell, and feel. Instead of birdsong, or the colors in the leaves, most of the students write about the concrete, the cars driving past, or the whir of the HVAC system. I realize now that many people, including the majority of students, are not taught to see the outside as a place of solace and wonder. They do not think that they are part of a larger world, that they are like a mountain. Instead, being outside is something to fear.

My students have a good reason to be afraid. Ignorance of things like poisonous plants, rip currents in Lake Michigan, and how to behave around wildlife makes the outside more dangerous. Most of my students of color have had the parental "talk" about the dangers of law enforcement; for them, loitering can be fatal. It was hard for me to be a woman alone in Kenosha. During the short spell that I lived there, I got harassed, and even chased, by strange men more than I ever did in Chicago. It is hard to want to birdwatch or identify native plants when people are simply trying to stay safe. Just like the mother wolf taught Leopold that fateful day, often people are the biggest thing to fear.

In the closing paragraph of "Thinking Like a Mountain," Leopold speaks to the condition of fear:

> We all strive for safety, prosperity, comfort, long life, and dullness. The deer strives with his supple legs, the cowman with trap and poison, the statesman with pen, and most of us with machines, votes, and dollars, but it all comes to the same thing: peace in our time. A measure of success in this is all well enough, and perhaps is a requisite to objective thinking, but too much safety seems to yield only danger in the long run.

The other fear, though, is rooted in Leopold's idea of "too much safety." I am a millennial, and I am one of the lucky few of my generation that got to play outside alone. I pretended I was Laura Ingalls Wilder in the green belt in my Denver suburb or hunted for cool rocks in the woods behind my grandparents' house up in the Rockies. Many of my cohort, even those in my neighborhood, were told to stay within earshot or, even more fear-inducing, to stay inside. Their parents, exhausted from work, were afraid of kidnappers and the judgment of strangers. So now, Gen Z and Gen Alpha have it even worse as the COVID-19 pandemic and political divisions generate more fear of the world beyond our doors and each other.

We have also been led to believe that wildness can be found only in places far from home. I do not tell my students about seeing wolves or whales, because it compounds the idea that wild things are inaccessible unless you live in the right place or have the money to get there. "There is no wilderness in the Midwest," is a common refrain. But the call of the Sandhill Cranes in the corn stalks by the highway and the fat raccoons having a party in the alley dumpster tell us that this is a lie. Even the deer in the graveyard and the flying squirrels who dive bomb the dogwalkers at night know to think like a mountain, that we are all part of the same thing.

"Perhaps this is behind Thoreau's dictum: In wildness is the salvation of the world. Perhaps this is the hidden meaning in the howl of the wolf, long known among mountains, but seldom perceived among men," Leopold continues in that last passage of "Thinking Like a Mountain."

I do not think one essay is going to turn an entire group of students into a group of naturalists, but I do believe that it may tear a small hole in the beliefs of a few and validate the sense of awe still held by several more.

After this exercise many of the individuals in my class tell me that they wish they sat outside more. In that last essay, the students write about a place that is important to them. After reading "Thinking Like a Mountain," their details become sharper and more visceral and their compassion just a bit more refined.

Gateway Technical College

ANDERSON, TRILLING, AND
THE INFLUENCE OF POWERFUL CRITICS
Score One for the Author

Robert Dunne

Sherwood Anderson died on March 8, 1941, from peritonitis after he had ingested a toothpick. A few short months later, Lionel Trilling, one of the most influential literary critics of his time, published his assessment of Anderson's body of work in the *Kenyon Review*, in essence attempting to strike the final nail in the coffin of Anderson's reputation. Six years later, Trilling expanded his essay, and in 1950 the essay "Sherwood Anderson" appeared as the second work in his influential book *The Liberal Imagination*.

Aiding and abetting Trilling in his take-down of Anderson, fellow New York Intellectuals Alfred Kazin and Irving Howe were also quite critical of Anderson after his death—Kazin dedicated most of a chapter to Anderson in his 1942 book *On Native Grounds*, and Howe published a biography of Anderson in 1951. Both authors were unequivocal in dubbing Anderson to be strictly a "minor writer"; however, the two did offer praise for Anderson's *Winesburg, Ohio* and a number of his other short stories.

But Trilling's *The Liberal Imagination* was regarded as a groundbreaking work and established Trilling as a preeminent literary critic for nearly the next two decades. And Trilling had nothing kind to say about *any* of Anderson's writings. In this same book, he also published an even more acerbic assessment of Theodore Dreiser and liberal critics who preferred Dreiser over Henry James. *The Liberal Imagination* perhaps did not have as much influence in American literary history as F. O. Matthiessen's seminal book *American Renaissance,* in which Matthiessen single-handedly established a canon of antebellum American authors (while relegating Edgar Allan Poe to a dismissive footnote). However, the sway that Trilling especially, as well as his fellow intellectuals, had in shaping the American canon cannot be overestimated, and it begs the question: Just *how* persuasive can a literary critic be? For Mark Krupnick, writing in 1986, "Sherwood Anderson['s] ... reputation has never recovered from Trilling's 1941 essay" (66). But has that been the case?

In 1923, with the publication of *Horses and Men*, a collection of short stories, Anderson was at the height of his reputation: *Winesburg, Ohio* came out in 1919, followed the next year by his best novel, *Poor White*, and then in 1921 by another short-story collection, *The Triumph of the Egg*. His novel *Many Marriages*, from 1922, was almost universally deemed a setback, but his 1925 novel *Dark Laughter* was his only commercially successful work (though not so successful with the critics). With the proceeds from *Dark Laughter*, he purchased a farm near Marion, Virginia, as well as two local newspapers. And from this time, until his death, his literary reputation progressively waned, in spite of some exceptional stories published in 1933's *Death in the Woods and Other Stories*.

Although he would go on to publish poetry, novels, and even plays in the late 1920s and '30s, Anderson more frequently turned his attention to nonfiction prose in the last decade of his life. Inspired by the social activism of Eleanor Copenhaver, who worked in the Industrial Division of the YWCA and would become his fourth wife in 1933, Anderson immersed himself in the labor movement, chronicling the lives of working men and women and the challenges they faced in industrial factory work during the Depression. He also dabbled in left-wing politics. (In fact, both he and Eleanor received entries by Elizabeth Dilling in her 1934 directory *The Red Network: A "Who's Who" and Handbook of Radicalism for Patriots* [262, 273].) Clearly, he was impassioned by this social activism, which also deepened his relationship with Eleanor. However, his many articles in the press on working conditions did not resuscitate his reputation, and the several books he published—not just the nonfiction exposés but also more artistic works—only advanced his decline in the literary arena. Describing his status in the mid-to-late 1930s, Kim Townsend states, "But not many readers were interested in Anderson anymore. The combined sale of the three books that Scribner's published, *Puzzled America, Kit Brandon,* and (in 1937) Anderson's *Plays,* was fewer than 6,500 copies" (301). And this list does not include the nonfiction works that bookend the 1930s, *Perhaps Women* (1931) and the last book published during his lifetime, *Home Town* (1940).

Throughout the 1930s, Anderson himself often questioned his writing abilities; starting and then shelving a number of writing projects, he was often depressed. Then taking a backward view of his life, he began composing his memoir. In his vast compilation of observations of his life, he noted, "Why what funeral orations have for example been preached over me. It has happened to all of us who have persisted in going on" (*Critical Edition* 4). He goes so far as to admit, "I have enough sense … in spite of my egotism to know that I am but a minor figure among the world's artists" (*Critical Edition* 11). And so, by the time he died in 1941, as if in affirmation of his own assessment of himself, Sherwood Anderson was widely regarded as a has-been.

For the rest of the 1940s, efforts were undertaken to revive Anderson's reputation, but with nominal success. In 1942, his long-time friend Paul Rosenfeld published *Sherwood Anderson's Memoirs,* a highly reworked text assembled from Anderson's incomplete autobiography. The next year, Maxwell Geismer dedicated a chapter to Anderson in *The Last of the Provincials.* In 1947, Rosenfeld edited *The Sherwood Anderson Reader,* a compendium of Anderson's short fiction, poetry, and nonfiction. And two years later, the Viking Press published *The Portable Sherwood Anderson,* edited by Horace Gregory. Surely, such publications as these should have placed Anderson back on the literary map. In his introduction, Gregory is confident enough to assert, "The decade following a writer's death provides, often enough, the severest test of his true vitality.… Sherwood Anderson has achieved his promise of 'immortality'" (1). Nevertheless, by the end of the '40s, the "true vitality" of Anderson's reputation remained on life support. As James Schevill observed in his 1951 biography of Anderson, "[T]he *Memoirs* was published, received a few nostalgic reviews, and vanished." Schevill cites the onset of World War II as one reason: "Perhaps even more significant was the low ebb of Anderson's reputation. He was regarded as a defeated writer and few critics took the time necessary to evaluate a new work" (340). But a year earlier, in 1950, Lionel Trilling had published an expanded version of his 1941 essay on Anderson in *The Liberal Imagination*, which seemed to be a death knell against any resurgent interest in Anderson.

Trilling was not an Americanist, although nearly half the essays in *The Liberal Imagination* are focused on American authors. René Wellek, for instance, states that, for Trilling, "The European novel [was] constantly preferred to the American" (38). However, as Thomas Bender points out, "During the 1940s, Trilling focused upon American literary history more than at any other time in his career. Between 1944 and 1951, he taught [at Columbia] his only specifically American literature course" (340). Nevertheless, the collected essays in *The Liberal Imagination* greatly steered the critical reception of American authors for a generation—in particular for the betterment of William Dean Howells and to the detriment of Theodore Dreiser and Sherwood Anderson.

Upon its publication, *The Liberal Imagination* had a galvanic influence on American literary criticism, selling 100,000 copies in paperback alone (Bender 324). In a retrospective essay on the book from 1986, Morris Dickstein, a younger contemporary of Trilling, recalls that "the book ... became an intellectual credo for the 1950s" (323). He continues, "Trilling's positions ... had been canonical so long that they seemed self-evident" (324), thus forming a "new consensus" into the early 1960s (331). He further summarizes Trilling's overall intention:

> Trilling's critical mission is to clear the cluttered scene of the Dreisers and Steinbecks and Sherwood Andersons to make room for a cosmopolitan European tradition that descends from Flaubert, James, and Conrad through the great modernists of the early twentieth century to Hemingway and Faulkner. (326)

Decades after Trilling's death in 1975, scholars like George Watson continued to acknowledge the impact of his book: he recalls that during the 1950s, the book "enjoyed in some literary households the authority of Holy Writ," and "[a]t that time Lionel Trilling was in midcareer … the most influential academic critic of the English-speaking world" (484).

In the first essay in the book, "Reality in America," Trilling dispatches literary historian Vernon Parrington for his three-volume *Main Currents in American Thought* chiefly because Parrington has no use for aesthetics and complexity in literature and prefers works that are rooted in "reality" (4). From there, Trilling makes a test case out of Dreiser, denigrating liberal critics who embrace his works while pooh-poohing the genius of Henry James. It is a thorough takedown of both Dreiser's reputation and liberal critics whose efforts to defend Dreiser verge on anti-intellectualism. Looking back over 35 years, Dickstein acknowledges the impact of Trilling's dissection of Dreiser: Trilling "encouraged a generation of students and critics to neglect the strong native tradition of American naturalism…. Trilling managed to ignore or belittle our principal social fiction" (327).

Trilling's dismissal of Dreiser in *The Liberal Imagination* has a whiff of the malicious to it; *if* he does not actually regard Dreiser himself as a malignant force in letters, then he does so the legion of critics who had propped up Dreiser during his career and after his death. In sharp contrast, in his essay "Sherwood Anderson," Trilling feels compelled, before the barbs come out, to offer a disclaimer of sorts that he was personally "much taken by Anderson's human quality" and that he admires his "innocence of heart" (22). And he repeats verbatim at the conclusion, after the barbs are put away, that he still has a "residue of admiration for him" (32). In between these confessions, however, is his methodical and condescending dismissal of Anderson—though not written with the kind of heat that he brought to Dreiser (perhaps because Dreiser still had outspoken champions of his work, and Trilling felt obligated to set them straight). He informs us that he has undertaken this revaluation "on the occasion of [Anderson's] death, or else I should not have undertaken it" (22). And so, this is a subtle admission that "now that I have gone back to his books again and have found that I like them even less than I remembered," *this*, presumably, will be his final word on Anderson. (Well, it would not be. One year later, Trilling published a short essay,

"Dreiser, Anderson, Lewis, and the Riddle of Society," in which he dubs the trio of authors "[t]hree lonely men" for whom "society is the last thing in the world they were really interested in" [39].)

In brief, Trilling regards Anderson as a faux mystic, literally befitting the status of a grotesque, as Anderson described the term in *Winesburg*, a man of limited intellect best suited for an adolescent audience. Variations of the word "adolescence" pervade the essay: "Anderson's greatest influence was probably upon those who read him in adolescence"; "[i]t is not surprising that Anderson should have made his strongest appeal, although by no means his only one, to adolescents" (23); and this trifecta:

> Most of us will feel now that this world of Anderson's is a pretty inade-
> quate representation of reality and probably always was. But we cannot
> be sure that it was not a necessary event in our history, like adolescence
> itself; and no one has the adolescence he would have liked to have had.
> But an adolescence must continue beyond its natural term, and as we
> read through Anderson's canon what exasperates us is his stubborn, sat-
> isfied continuance in his earliest attitudes. (24)

Perhaps for Trilling adolescence also connotes impulsivity or acting on one's "gut," because he takes Anderson to task for continually being rebellious towards society and believing that "feeling is understood as an answer" (26): "Anderson is connected with the tradition of the men who maintain a standing quarrel with respectable society and have a perpetual bone to pick with the rational intellect" (24). Continuing a thread spun in his essay on Dreiser, Trilling chides Anderson for failing to capture the "reality" of his characters and their actions: "[J]ust as there is no real sensory experience in Anderson's writing, there is also no real social experience"; "[h]is people have passion without body" and they speak in "no idiom" (28). Ultimately, for Trilling, after revisiting Anderson's works immediately after his death, he now sees no reason to ever return to them—even *Winesburg*: "As for the Winesburg stories themselves, they are as dangerous to read again, as paining and as puzzling, as if they were old letters we had written or received" (23).

Published originally in 1941 and then expanded and reprinted in *The Liberal Imagination* in 1950 to a far wider audience, Trilling's "Sherwood Anderson" essay hardly represented a lone voice crying out in the wilderness decrying Anderson's worth as a writer. Two of Trilling's fellow New York Intellectuals, Alfred Kazin and Irving Howe, were also highly critical of Anderson's body of work, although they each had praise for *Winesburg* and a handful of his other short stories. Although published nine years apart, Kazin's *On Native Grounds* (1942) and Howe's 1951 biography of Anderson share assessments of and even vocabulary about Anderson's career. Anderson was unequivocally a "minor writer" whose life eventually was both a "tragedy" and a "humiliation."

The tenor of both their works parallels my outline above charting the decline in the quality of Anderson's work from the late 1920s until his death: both critics spend an *undue* amount of time on this decline. As Kazin posits sympathetically,

> It is a terrible thing for a visionary to remain a minor figure; where the other minor figures can at least work out a minor success, the visionary who has not the means equal to his vision crumbles into fragments. Anderson was a minor figure, as he himself knew so well; and that was his tragedy. (216)

And, in mistakenly aligning Anderson with Sinclair Lewis as a proponent of the "revolt from the village," Kazin asserts that both authors were heralded as "light-bringers," "cultural influences" with their calls for freedom from gentility and small-town mores; however, they also suffered the "humiliation of being remembered as 'cultural influences' rather than as serious and growing artists; the humiliation of knowing that they had ceased to be significant, or even interesting" (218). It seems, in other words, that their talents were outdated before they knew it.

Irving Howe, in contrast, was a bit more upbeat in his assessment of Anderson's career. However, like Kazin, Howe seems utterly preoccupied with judgment labels. In his biography of Anderson, Howe concludes the book leading with Anderson's own admission that he was "but a minor figure" (243). And, as if to prove that he was resolute in his opinion after fifteen years, in an "Author's Note" to the 1966 reissue of his biography, he begins with, "It is hard to be a minor writer—hard perhaps in any country, but especially in the United States" (vii). And in his 1951 conclusion, Howe adopts Trilling's condescending belief that Anderson's work "suggests something of the quality of adolescence" and that "[i]t is precisely this quality of adolescence … which has caused most of the uncertainties and difficulties in our response to Anderson's work" (250). At the very least, though, Howe parts company with Trilling's trenchant criticism of Anderson's failure to capture "reality":

> And when we say—this is the favorite gambit of hostile critics—that Anderson's work deals not with reality but with adolescent gropings, we ignore the reality of those very gropings; we ignore, as well, the fact that from these gropings none of us is or should be exempt. (251)

And yet, tapping into the vocabulary that Kazin used nine years earlier, Howe nonetheless feels that tragedy eventually overshadowed Anderson's life: "It was his tragedy that after the early 1920's he was trapped between two worlds: he could find sustenance neither in the deep kinships of the folk bard nor in the demanding traditions of the sophisticated artist" (254). But, departing from Kazin's and especially Trilling's final assessment, he does concede that "in his masterpiece, *Winesburg, Ohio*, as in a half dozen stories and the first part of *Poor White*, [Anderson] wrote with a purity of voice, a loveliness of tact, a sweetness of compassion, such as few Americans have ever reached" (ix). Perhaps this shines but a faint spotlight on Anderson's reputation ten years after his death, but critical attention over the next twenty years would go far in resurrecting that reputation.

In the ensuing years of the 1950s, the prospects for any kind of resurgence seemed fairly dim, however. Published in the same year as Howe's tepid biography, James Schevill's biography of Anderson attempted to elevate Anderson's stature, but in comparing the two biographies, prominent critics, such as Henry Nash Smith and Frederick J. Hoffman, definitively sided with Howe's. While acknowledging that Schevill "presents a fuller biographical narrative" of Anderson, Smith provides a ready rejoinder: "But Mr. Howe ... has a deeper insight into the meaning of Anderson's baffled career, and he is a much better critic of Anderson's work" (472). For Hoffman, there is no comparison: "[Schevill] seems almost entirely to have given in to a spell under which critics of Anderson and Dreiser have come." Failing to recognize that perhaps *he* has fallen under the spell of the Trillings and Howes, Hoffman declares, of Anderson, "[H]e was, in fact, never more than a minor artist, occasionally successful"; and he commends Howe for his ability to discern the few gold nuggets of Anderson's work from the dross: "The sense of Anderson's limitations is given brilliantly well by Irving Howe.... A critic with Howe's sharpness of discrimination can rescue the values of Anderson's work from the wreckage of his failures" (159–60).

However, the seeds had been planted, by the likes of Rosenfeld, Geismer, and Schevill, and it would take some time before Anderson's work would garner a fresh revaluation from newer generations of critics. Not a remarkable development at the time, in 1947 Anderson's wife Eleanor donated her husband's manuscripts to the Newberry Library, and John T. Flanagan prophesied that this robust collection of materials "may well stimulate a revaluation of the position of the author himself" (170). Indeed, Howe acknowledged gratitude that Anderson's archives were now available, and the collection was essential to Howard Mumford Jones and Walter B. Rideout's *Letters of Sherwood Anderson*, which came out in 1953. Another early beneficiary was William L. Phillips, whose 1950 doctoral dissertation focused on Anderson's composition of *Winesburg*. Another dissertation, completed earlier, in 1943, by William A. Sutton, provided a detailed groundwork of Anderson's early life. Although neither dissertation was published in its entirety, both would become invaluable sources for subsequent scholars.

Late in the decade, 1958, five years after he had published an appreciation of Anderson in the *Atlantic*, William Faulkner again added fuel to the flames of an Anderson resurgence when, at a talk at the University of Virginia, he proclaimed that Anderson "has never been given his rightful place in American literature. In my opinion he's the father of all my generation…. Sherwood Anderson has still to receive his rightful place in American letters" (qtd. in Burbank 141). In the same year, writer and activist Josephine Herbst published an essay, "Ubiquitous Critics and the Author," that was an impassioned and perceptive critique of the runaway influence that literary critics had in stifling any constructive reapprais-als of Anderson's career. It is impossible to gauge what—if any—impact this had in the academic community (it was published in the *Newberry Library Bulletin*), but it reads like a manifesto decrying the undue sway of critics and demanding that fresh attention be paid to Anderson's career. Oddly, she does not identify Trilling by name, but critics like him are definitely in her sights. She begins her attack, "For more than a decade, the writings of critics, their editing, their com-mentaries, their down-grading and their up-grading of past and present works have more or less dominated the literary scene" (1). Characterizing the 1950s as a "period of critic-supremacy" (2), she bemoans the fact that such an influence of critics was prevalent even when Anderson was alive: "In the case of Sherwood Anderson, the carping of his critics took a sharp edge some fifteen years before the end of his career" (4). She thus ponders that "[o]ne may speculate on how much the shifting fads and fancies affected Anderson" (8). Herbst's essay is a re-sounding call-to-action for scholars to do an end-run around the powerful critics and evaluate Anderson's work with fresh eyes. And this is what happened begin-ning in the 1960s.

The decade began with *Sherwood Anderson: A Bibliography*, edited by Eu-gene P. Sheehy and Kenneth A. Lohf. Although hardly an exhaustive reference work, it was the first book-length study to list the publications by Anderson, as well as over 350 secondary sources about him (116). In 1962, Maxwell Geis-mer edited a collection of Anderson's stories. In his introduction, he sound-ed what seems like a battle cry: "Mr. Lionel Trilling's commiserative essay on

Sherwood Anderson's presumed literary destruction after *Winesburg*, and Mr. Irving Howe's book on the same theme, are, in Mark Twain's phrase, grossly exaggerated. The rumor was premature; it was also not true" (xii). The floodgates were now opened. In 1964, two short biographies were published, one by Rex Burbank and the other by Brom Weber. A new generation of scholars, not raised under the sway of the New York Intellectuals, was teaching in universities and publishing new critical studies of Anderson's works. The first (and still significant) collection of critical essays on Anderson, *The Achievement of Sherwood Anderson*, came out in 1966. Edited and including an excellent introduction by Ray Lewis White, the book was a judicious compendium of older and newer critical assessments, including Trilling's and Howe's negative reviews, as well as contributions by younger scholars like White and David D. Anderson, who would greatly expand critical attention to Anderson for the next twenty years. In his introduction, White recognizes the growing critical output on Anderson in the previous ten years, and ends with a question:

> These volumes and the large number of articles on Sherwood Anderson that now appear frequently in popular and learned journals seem to disprove the wisdom of those critics who apparently wrote Anderson's literary epitaph in the early 1940's. Why did these leaders in literary affairs fail to foresee the coming renaissance of interest in Sherwood Anderson, and, more importantly, what is the extent and significance of this renaissance? (7)

And, in the last essay of the collection, David Anderson, in a commemorative overview of Anderson's career marking the twentieth anniversary of his death, offers an honest appraisal of his reputation while also arguing why the author demands continuing scholarly attention: "Critical opinion generally has relegated Anderson to a minor position in American literary history, and yet that history has not only been unable to ignore him but has continued to give him more attention than it accords to many figures considered to be major" (246). And the next year, 1967, David Anderson would go on to publish one of the first critical overviews of Anderson's works, *Sherwood Anderson: An Introduction and Interpretation*. Thus, by the end of the 1960s, it was becoming more commonplace for critics to recognize Anderson's achievements and not dwell on the supposed "tragedy" and "humiliation" of his career. For the next thirty years, in fact, this resurgence would be in full force via numerous published collections of Anderson's previously unpublished letters, as well as many new editions of his novels and short stories, and the burgeoning growth of critical essays and books about his works. Indeed, the tide had begun to turn.

Meanwhile, during this same decade, the tide had also begun to turn for Lionel Trilling's reputation, but for the worse. John Rodden posits that after the success of *The Liberal Imagination*, Trilling became more widely known outside of academe, as demonstrated by his frequent recommendations to several nation-wide book clubs (14). And with this growing popularity he was regarded as a tastemaker: "Trilling gradually assumed the lofty twin roles of cultural sage and arbiter of public taste…. Although his fame increased, he became less well-regarded in advanced literary-intellectual circles" (14). Whether he liked it or not, Trilling became an Establishment figure. This certainly did not bode well for him as the civil rights movement and student protests against the Vietnam War gained traction from the mid-1960s onward. Recognizing the impact of student protests on college campuses like Columbia, Trilling, in a 1965 book *Beyond Culture*, warned about a growing "adversary culture," which Edward Alexander describes thusly: "Its bastions of power were the universities, where it aggrandized and perpetuated itself, cultivating to the nth degree the conformity of dissent…. In place of the old order it sought to confer an ideological status upon 'sex, violence, madness, and art'" (46). In 1968, the organization Students for a Democratic Society was a frequent disruptive presence at Columbia. Tom Hayden (not a Columbia student) went so far as to post photographs of Trilling around the Morningside Heights campus with an all-caps warning: "WANTED DEAD OR ALIVE. FOR CRIMES AGAINST HUMANITY" (Alexander 47).

Although their friendship had been strained due to political differences for much of the decade, Trilling and Howe each adopted a form of trench warfare against the radicalization of college campuses, which no doubt accelerated Trilling's reputational decline. Bemoaning the apparent intellectual deficiencies of his late-1960s students, Trilling concluded that they were "much less literate, much less intellectually curious, and much less intelligent" than previous generations (qtd. in Alexander 48). Alexander summarizes the demoralized state Trilling found himself in at the start of the 1970s: "The lethal combination of Stalinism and … American know-nothingism was finding a cozy reception within the universities, most especially the English departments" (61).

But putting aside the vicissitudes of the turbulent 1960s, what *emphatically* made Trilling a dated figure in literary criticism consigned to the 1950s and early '60s was the two-fold rise to prominence of postmodern and more politicized literary theories that have been the mainstay in academe for the last several decades. As Rodden has observed about Trilling's reputation since the 1990s, "For many readers, Trilling's inattention to the issues that dominate the American literary academy today—most of them having to do with race, class, and gender—makes him little more than a curiosity of literary history, a period piece" (17). He adds, "And because the literary academy has turned toward theory and postmodern modes of criticism since the 1980s, college students rarely encounter Trilling in their literature courses" (18). As if anticipating the changing tide in literary criticism, Howe had asked Trilling, shortly before his death in 1975, "What do you say when people ask what your critical method is?" Trilling replied that the question made him anxious, "since I don't even know whether I have a critical method" (qtd. in Alexander 65). But as early as 1979, William M. Chace could already detect a decline in Trilling's reputation:

But what was adulation of Trilling in some quarters of American intellectual life was condescension or disregard elsewhere. Many literary intellectuals believed that he was old-fashioned, weak because untheoretical, tiresome in his suspicion of the new, and laborious as a prose stylist. When he died, many younger-generation critics saw him as the last representative of a form of criticism deserving of decline. (50–51)

Ten years later, Thomas Bender would conclude, "Trilling lacked an adequate rhetoric for the diverse public he confronted in the 1960s. He had no rhetorical approach, no form of address, that could reach outside of the homogeneous middle class he had defined as his audience in the 1940s" (343). And, almost thirty years later, in 2019, Michael C. Kimmage would reaffirm these earlier assessments:

> Thus, forty-three years after his death, Trilling is doubly an anachronism. The academic world has dismissed the great books foundation on which his career was built. Its preferred politics challenge the establishment to which Trilling belonged.... English departments have replaced the personalized essay at which Trilling excelled with the impersonal apparatus of theory. (90)

Even those still championing Trilling's reputation in recent decades, such as Adam Kirsch in his 2011 book *Why Trilling Matters*, have taken a backward-looking, almost nostalgic view of him. Kirsch declares that the current state of literature, the current state of studying or just reading literature, has been in a "long term crisis" (2), whereby literature no longer matters in America's current "consumer culture." For Kirsch, Trilling still "matters" because he "had been accustomed to treating literature as *the* medium of experience" (164, emphasis added), and so "the cure for the decline and fall of literature is a return to Trilling's ideal of literary education" (4). Wishful thinking?

Perhaps literary criticism does not have the same kind of staying power as literary *works* may enjoy: there are usually virtual start-up dates and virtual end-dates when this or that school of criticism runs its course and is eventually supplanted by newer schools of criticism. Such has been the case with Lionel Trilling, whose word was gold for about twenty years in the mid-twentieth century, but whose overall influence on American literary history has clearly eclipsed. And so, how has Sherwood Anderson's reputation fared over the last thirty or so years, after his critical resurgence started in the 1960s and grew steadily throughout the 1980s?

Well, he remains a lasting and significant subject of study to this day because of sustained scholarly interest. Let us count the ways. Because his works are now out of copyright, there are voluminous editions of his writings available. Founded in the early 1970s by David Anderson, the Society for the Study of Midwestern Literature, with its publications *MidAmerica* and *Midwestern Miscellany* and its annual symposium, has for over fifty years provided fertile ground for Anderson studies. In 1985, David Stouck was the first scholar to approach Anderson's work from a postmodern lens, in "Sherwood Anderson and the Postmodern Novel." Kim Townsend's 1987 biography of Anderson was probably then the most expansive treatment on Anderson's life (even earning high praise by *People* magazine! [Vespa 17–18]). In 1990, John Crowley edited a collection of essays, *New Essays on* Winesburg, Ohio, that introduced additional contemporary approaches to Anderson. In 1994, Judy Jo Small published the comprehensive and invaluable reference work *A Reader's Guide to the Short Stories of Sherwood Anderson*. In 1996, Charles Modlin and Ray Lewis White edited the first Norton Critical Edition of *Winesburg*. An updated second edition, edited by Marc Dudley, came out in 2023.

Entering the twenty-first century, I published the first book-length study of Anderson's early fiction from a postmodern standpoint, *A New Book of the Grotesques*, in 2005. Using Herman Melville's reputation as a comparison to Anderson's, I assert that

> Throughout the twentieth and into the twenty-first century, each generation of critics has found a "new" Melville who merits his preeminent place in the canon…. Melville's works have of course remained the same, yet the *reasons* for his secure standing in the canon have been as varied as the critical temperament of each generation that has examined him. (xi–xii)

In the book I declare a call to action that would not only sustain but strengthen Anderson's place in American literary history: "Anderson's canonical status could very well be the beneficiary as current literary theory … begins to consider matters of race, class, gender, and postmodern conceptions of language and power" (xvi). Hence, a "new" Sherwood Anderson awaits to be discovered. And indeed, such a movement has taken place since then.

Perhaps an added catalyst for this movement was the magisterial two-volume Anderson biography by Walter Rideout, posthumously published in 2006–07. Recognizing the potential impact of the book on the scholarly community, Charles Modlin writes in the introduction to the first volume, "All writers go in and out of fashion, but the best writers always weather the passing literary mode, and Anderson is due for the kind of rousing rediscovery that Rideout's book should help launch" (xi).

Since 2000, over seventy-five journal essays, over thirty articles in collections of essays, and over half a dozen book-length critical studies of Anderson have been published, according to the *MLA International Bibliography* ("Sherwood Anderson"). This wide range of scholarship has studied Anderson's works—novels, short fiction, poetry, and non-fiction—from multiple theoretical approaches, including those grounded in postmodernism, race, gender, class, and the environment. And yet, as so many critics (and the author himself) have observed since he was alive, Sherwood Anderson is not a pedestal figure in the American canon; he remains a minor author, if gauged by the long-standing critical consensus of his creative output as compared to that of the likes of Faulkner and Hemingway. However, many of his writings have sustained the test of time and are indeed classics—they are the gifts that keep on giving, they reward a diverse array of critical approaches, and there continue to be "new" Andersons being recognized. To add to these accomplishments, his influence on writers of his generation—Hemingway, Faulkner, Jean Toomer, Thomas Wolfe—as well as many established authors long since then further cements his reputation as a writer never to be forgotten.

Appraising his reputation during his decline in the 1930s, Anderson wrote in his *Memoirs*, "The time will come when … [t]here will be a renaissance and then my own work and my own life will be appreciated" (*Critical Edition* 554). After a slow but persistent start after his death, that renaissance took flight in earnest in the 1960s thanks to a younger generation of scholars untethered to the dictates of the looming midcentury sway of critics like Trilling and others, and has continued with little interruption to the present day.

So, to return to my question posed at the beginning of this essay about Mark Krupnick's assertion that "Sherwood Anderson['s] … reputation has never recovered from Trilling's 1941 essay" (66): Has that really been the case? I say with complete confidence, No, not at all.

Score one for the author.

Central Connecticut State University

Works Cited

Alexander, Edward. "Lionel Trilling and Irving Howe: A Literary Friendship." *New England Review*, vol. 25, no. 3, summer 2004, pp. 20–75.

Anderson, David D. *Sherwood Anderson: An Introduction and Interpretation.* Holt, 1967.

———. "Sherwood Anderson after 20 Years." 1962. *The Achievement of Sherwood Anderson*, edited by Ray Lewis White, U of North Carolina P, 1966, pp. 246–56.

Anderson, Sherwood. *Letters of Sherwood Anderson.* Edited by Howard Mumford Jones and Walter B. Rideout, Little, Brown, 1953.

———. *The Portable Sherwood Anderson.* Edited by Horace Gregory, Viking, 1949.

———. *The Sherwood Anderson Reader.* Edited by Paul Rosenfeld, Houghton Mifflin, 1947.

———. *Sherwood Anderson: Short Stories.* Edited by Maxwell Geismer, Hill and Wang, 1962.

———. *Sherwood Anderson's Memoirs.* Edited by Paul Rosenfeld, Harcourt, Brace, 1942.

———. *Sherwood Anderson's Memoirs: A Critical Edition.* 1942. Edited by Ray Lewis White, U of North Carolina P, 1969.

———. *Winesburg, Ohio.* Edited by Charles Modlin and Ray Lewis White, Norton Critical Edition, W. W. Norton, 1997.

———. *Winesburg, Ohio.* Edited by Marc K. Dudley, Norton Critical Edition, W. W. Norton, 2023.

Bender, Thomas. "Lionel Trilling and American Culture." *American Quarterly,* vol. 42, no. 2, June 1990, pp. 324–47.

Burbank, Rex. *Sherwood Anderson.* Twayne, 1964.

Chace, William M. "Lionel Trilling: The Contrariness of Culture." *The American Scholar,* vol. 48, no. 1, winter 1979, pp. 49–59.

Crowley, John W., editor. *New Essays on* Winesburg, Ohio. Cambridge UP, 1990.

Dickstein, Morris. "Lionel Trilling and *The Liberal Imagination.*" *The Sewanee Review,* vol. 94, no. 2, spring 1986, pp. 323–34.

Dilling, Elizabeth. *The Red Network: A "Who's Who" and Handbook of Radicalism for Patriots.* Elizabeth Dilling, 1934.

Dunne, Robert. *A New Book of the Grotesques: Contemporary Approaches to Sherwood Anderson's Early Fiction.* Kent State UP, 2005.

Flanagan, John T. "The Permanence of Sherwood Anderson." *Southwest Review,* vol. 35, no. 3, summer 1950, pp. 170–77.

Geismer, Maxwell. Introduction. S. Anderson, *Sherwood Anderson: Short Stories,* pp. ix–xxiii.

———. *The Last of the Provincials: The American Novel, 1915–1925.* Houghton Mifflin, 1943.

Gregory, Horace. "Editor's Introduction." S. Anderson, *The Portable Sherwood Anderson,* pp. 1–31.

Herbst, Josephine. "Ubiquitous Critics and the Author." *Newberry Library Bulletin,* vol. 5, no. 1, Dec. 1958, pp. 1–13.

Hoffman, Frederick J. "Sherwood Anderson: A 'Groping, Artistic, Sincere Personality.'" *Western Review,* vol. 18, no. 2, winter 1954, pp. 159–62.

Howe, Irving. *Sherwood Anderson: A Biographical and Critical Study*. 1951. Stanford UP, 1966.

Kazin, Alfred. *On Native Grounds: An Interpretation of Modern American Prose Literature*. 1942. Harcourt Brace Jovanovich, 1982.

Kimmage, Michael C. "Trilling's Tutelage." *National Interest*, no. 159, Jan./Feb. 2019, pp. 88–96.

Kirsch, Adam. *Why Trilling Matters*. Yale UP, 2011.

Krupnick, Mark. *Lionel Trilling and the Fate of Cultural Criticism*. Northwestern UP, 1986.

Matthiessen, F. O. *American Renaissance: Art and Expression in the Age of Emerson and Whitman*. Oxford UP, 1941.

Modlin, Charles. Introduction. *Sherwood Anderson: A Writer in America*, vol. 1, by Walter B. Rideout, U of Wisconsin P, 2006, pp. xi–xvii.

Phillips, William L. "Sherwood Anderson's *Winesburg, Ohio*: Its Origins, Composition, Technique, and Reception." 1950. U of Chicago, PhD dissertation.

Rideout, Walter B. *Sherwood Anderson: A Writer in America*. 2 vols. U of Wisconsin P, 2006, 2007.

Rodden, John. "Introduction: Lionel Trilling's Opposing Selves." *Lionel Trilling and the Critics: Opposing Selves*, edited by John Rodden, U of Nebraska P, 1999, pp. 1–29.

Schevill, James. *Sherwood Anderson: His Life and Work*. U of Denver P, 1951.

Sheehy, Eugene P. and Kenneth A. Lohf. *Sherwood Anderson: A Bibliography*. Talisman, 1960.

"Sherwood Anderson." *MLA International Bibliography. Ebscohost.com*.

Small, Judy Jo. *A Reader's Guide to the Short Stories of Sherwood Anderson*. G. K. Hall, 1994.

Smith, Henry Nash. "The Liberated Artist." *Nation*, vol. 172, no. 2, 1951, pp. 472–73.

Stouck, David. "Sherwood Anderson and the Postmodern Novel." *Contemporary Literature*, vol. 26, no. 3, autumn 1985, pp. 302–16.

Sutton, William A. "Sherwood Anderson's Formative Years (1876–1913)." 1943. Ohio State U, PhD dissertation.

Townsend, Kim. *Sherwood Anderson*. Houghton Mifflin, 1987.

Trilling, Lionel. "Dreiser, Anderson, Lewis, and the Riddle of Society." *The Reporter*, vol. 5, Nov. 1951, pp. 37–40.

———. "Reality in America." *The Liberal Imagination: Essays on Literature and Society*. 1950. Harcourt Brace Jovanovich, 1979, pp. 3–20.

———. "Sherwood Anderson." *Kenyon Review*, vol. 3, no. 3, summer 1941, pp. 293–302.

———. "Sherwood Anderson." *The Liberal Imagination: Essays on Literature and Society*. 1950. Harcourt Brace Jovanovich, 1979, pp. 21–32.

Vespa, Mary. Review of *Sherwood Anderson*, by Kim Townsend. *People*, vol. 28, no. 17, Oct. 1987, pp. 17–18.

Watson, George. "The Empire of Lionel Trilling." *The Sewanee Review*, vol. 115, no. 3, summer 2007, pp. 484–90.

Weber, Brom. *Sherwood Anderson*. U of Minnesota P, 1964. University of Minnesota Pamphlets of American Writers.

Wellek, René. "The Literary Criticism of Lionel Trilling." *New England Review*, vol. 2, no. 1, autumn 1979, pp. 26–49.

White, Ray Lewis. Introduction. *The Achievement of Sherwood Anderson*, edited by Ray Lewis White, U of North Carolina P, 1966, pp. 3–18.

"An Antydote fer the Brute"
Apocalyptic Imagination in *Farmer Hiram on the World's War*

Jefferson Storms

Lindley Grant Long's 1920 midwestern-dialect epic *Farmer Hiram on the World's War* recounts the Great War through the voice of Hiram, a plainspoken farmer who sets out to narrate "a true history of the great conflict" (Long iii). As Tim Dayton notes in *American Poetry and the First World War*, Long's interpretation of the war's events is pervaded by a mood of skepticism both toward the Central Powers (especially Germany) and the Allies (especially the United States). From cover to cover, Long—through Hiram—rejects the logic of the dominant ideological framework that legitimated US involvement in the war, a logic on display in US president Woodrow Wilson's millenarian narration of the war as a precursor to world redemption. *Farmer Hiram* resists this millenarian vision that legitimates the war and, indeed, any ideological interpretation of the war that frames its violence as necessary or justified.

Long's rejection of common justifications for the war is not unique, as rejections of justifications for the war proliferate in post-war modernism. The significance of Long's rejection of Wilson's justifications for entry into the war lies, I argue, in the fact that his critique draws heavily on elements of the same Jewish/early Christian apocalyptic literatures on which the legibility of Wilson's wartime rhetoric depends. For Long, the images and themes of Jewish/early Christian apocalyptic literatures, far from underwriting US involvement in the war and its violence, provide resources for questioning the legitimacy of US involvement in the war—and, indeed, for questioning whether the violence of any of the belligerent powers is justifiable. Long's apocalyptic imagination produces in *Farmer Hiram* a notable alternative to prominent modes of condemning or legitimating the war present in American literature of the period—and, for that matter, to contemporary ways of naturalizing violence by narrating it in apocalyptic registers. Because, to my knowledge, Tim Dayton offers the only scholarly engagement with *Farmer Hiram on the World's War*, this essay builds consciously on his work in order to consider the ways in which Jewish/early Christian apocalyptic literature offers resources for criticizing and resisting ideologically justified violence—both in Long's day and in ours.

In *American Poetry and the First World War*, Dayton considers the ideological character of First World War poetry; that is, he attends to the work poetry does to "place events within a meaning-giving framework that translates them into terms conformable to the cultural patterns characteristic of a given society" (43). He notes that much pro-war poetry echoes a particular American ideology that "manifests itself as a collection of cultural-symbolic and rhetorical patterns that define the United States in terms of a redemptive mission of global and ultimately transcendental import" (Dayton 21). Thus, as he notes, "under Wilson's guidance, American intervention in the First World War was understood through and articulated often in millennialist terminology, nearly always with the narrative trajectory of an American mission to universalize democracy, end aristocratic rule, and redeem a fallen world" (Dayton 26). This can be seen, for example, in the conclusion of Wilson's "Fourteen Points" speech: "The moral climax of the culminating and final war for human liberty has come" (qtd. in Dayton 16). On another occasion, Wilson speaks of the potential that the redemption, liberation, and salvation of the world will come about through the war and its aftermath (qtd. in Dayton 17). In short, "in Wilson's reckoning, the War was a redemptive crusade which would usher in a new era of peace and democracy" (Dayton 220). American poetry that echoed this millenarian vision interpellated its readers into just such a way of conceptualizing the war, with its attendant legitimation of US involvement in the war and the larger American hegemonic project.

Such millenarian framings of the War did indeed contribute to many American Christians' pro-war attitudes. For instance, leadership of the Methodist Episcopal Church and the Methodist Episcopal Church (South)—described by

Cindy Wesley as "the most mainstream of mainstream Protestants"—ardently supported Wilson's claim that "the Great War was a noble effort to crush the German forces of autocratic villainy and promote the good of worldwide democracy" (Wesley 183). Gordon Heath affirms that "Americans, Canadians, and Britons all would have been familiar with the vivid metaphors and passionate language of 'holy war,' for Christian leaders in these states often used similar language to frame the conflict as a battle against the 'barbarous hordes of the German Kaiser'" (6). Moreover, apocalyptic framings of the war imbued an already "holy" war with a cosmic quality: according to Philip Jenkins, "apocalyptic ideas boomed as the United States entered the war, with Germany or the Kaiser as the Antichrist. Revivalist Billy Sunday characterized the war simply: 'It is Bill [Kaiser Wilhelm] against Woodrow [Wilson], Germany against America, Hell against Heaven'" (140). Thus, one might expect that a typical American Protestant of the period would align with pro-war visions like those present in Wilson's wartime rhetoric.

Lindley Grant Long was one such Protestant who might be expected to align with the majority of American Protestantism in viewing the war as sanctified violence that would culminate in a sort of democratic millennium.[1] Yet, in *Farmer Hiram on the World's War* Long rejects the apocalyptic narration of the war that was a hallmark of Wilson's wartime rhetoric. For Dayton, *Farmer Hiram* is "what might be called a minimally epic poem: narrative, wide in scope, objective in presentation, and with a few nods to, or winks at, the classical epic" (183). If placing this work in a generic category is difficult, situating the work in relation to major aesthetic movements of the day is even trickier; the poem is "part of neither the literary modernism that became enshrined after the war, nor the aesthetically defeated but still socially powerful remnants of the sentimental and Genteel elements in American culture" (Dayton 208). Hiram, in conveying the "plain, unvarnished story of the tragic affair" (Long iii), presents a more-or-less objective overview of the war, which, as "epic," aims to provide the reader with a coherent view of the war's events.

As Dayton observes, this overview of the war serves a didactic purpose: Hiram "felt it an impelling duty to write a true history of the great conflict, and thereby render a service to mankind by rescuing it from a perverted and improper conception of the same" (Long iii). Hiram's voice, "descended from Mark Twain by way of James Whitcomb Riley,"[2] has according to Dayton a deflationary effect, "whereby the otherwise world-historical events of the poem often feel petty, familiarized by the language of the poem" (210).[3] Such a voice is in keeping with Hiram's consistent refusal to treat the war's major actors—Allied or otherwise—with the same seriousness with which they treat themselves; so, naturally, he refuses to take their proffered justifications for the war at face value (210–11). Rather, Hiram sees the role of these major actors' economic interests—over and against national self-defense or Wilsonian world-redemption—as determinative for their involvement in the war (211). Thus, for Hiram, the war "amounts to little but waste and ruin," which "lacks the profound meaning that many found in it" (218). *Farmer Hiram* does not thereby degenerate into hopeless cynicism. The work ends hopefully, as Hiram envisions the possibility of postwar peace. However, Hiram's vision of peace differs from the millenarian visions of peace articulated by Wilson. He concludes, "You've got to git *Christ,* and *the things he stands for,* / Wrot into men's *conscience* before you'll end *war*! / If *Right* you'd hev reign, and cam *Reason* to boot, / You've got to find some antydote fer the *brute*" (Long 277–78, italics in original). Dayton quite rightly asserts that "unlike most of the writers of the disillusionment, Long (through Hiram) appears to reject pro-war visions not on the basis of any first-hand experience of the war … but rather from a cultural-ideological complex that predates the war" (220). It is to the reasons for this rejection that we now turn.

As noted above, the mere fact that Long rejects justifications for the war that frame it as necessary or legitimate is not unique; rather, Long's rejection of such pro-war sentiment is unique because of his reasons for this rejection. The cultural-ideological complex from which Long's response to the war emerges is, like Wilson's, shaped by the images and themes of Jewish and early Christian apocalyptic literature; both Long and Wilson narrate the war in apocalyptic registers.[4] In contrast to Wilson's apocalyptic vision of the war and its aftermath, which came to ring hollow for many Americans, Long draws on apocalyptic symbols and themes in ways that allow him both to bear unflinching witness to the moral horror of the conflict—including the pretensions of the powers involved—and to conceive of a hopeful way forward for humanity after the war's end.

As mentioned, the apocalyptic elements of the book of Daniel—particularly Daniel's vision of the four beasts (Dan. 7.1–27)—heavily influence Long's narration of the war.[5] *Farmer Hiram*, like the book of Daniel, grapples with the apparent reality that violent human powers, rather than the peaceable reign of God, ultimately decide the fate of the world. In Daniel's vision, kings and kingdoms appear as ravenous beasts, destructive forces of chaos: three beast-kings rise up in quick succession to wreak havoc on the earth. Daniel sees a lion with eagles' wings, a bear with three ribs between its teeth, and a winged leopard (Dan. 7.2–6). A mysterious fourth beast appears, "terrifying and dreadful and exceedingly strong. It … was devouring, breaking in pieces, and stamping what was left with its feet. It was different from all the beasts that preceded it" (Dan. 7.7). John Collins explains that "the vision of terrible beasts rising out of the sea does not merely give factual information that four kings or kingdoms will arise. It paints a picture of these kingdoms as monstrous eruptions of chaos, in order to convey a sense of terror far beyond anything suggested by the flat statement of [its] interpretation" (106). In other words, Daniel's vision of the kings and their empires as beasts unveils the nature of these imperial beast-kings as pretenders to glory. Matthew Michael argues that "by describing political kingdoms or kings as predators and ferocious animals, the apocalyptic author of Daniel polemically also suggests the oppressive and predatory character of these human political institutions" (11).[6]

Ultimately, these destructive human powers are revealed for what they are; they face divine justice for the violence they unleash on the world and are stripped of their authority to do violence any longer (Dan. 7.9–12). As John Goldingay notes, "the narratives of Daniel promise that the cynicism and deceit which often characterize politics will not have the last word … [the stories of Daniel] affirm that the pretensions of the state to be the embodiment of all that keeps life going will be exposed, but that the powers that be are ordained by God and are in his hand" (114–15).

Long draws on Daniel's apocalyptic characterization of imperial powers as ravenous beasts to articulate, through Hiram, what he takes to be their true motivations for involvement in the war. Though Farmer Hiram "make[s] no pretense to be prophet, er seer" (Long 287), his work—like Daniel's—is that of unveiling the pretensions of the powers that seek to justify the violence they unleash: "I've tried to onveil a slight bit uv the woe / That tyrants, and traitors, and scoundrels, let go" (Long 261). This characterization of powers as beasts is consistent from the beginning to the end of the poem; in narrating the start of the war, Hiram writes, "When once the thing started, each let out a roar / And frothed at the mouth like a razor-back boar. / *He shouted aloud that the uthers had sinned, / And all he cud do was to strike, and defend* (Long 33, emphasis added). Seen in light of Daniel 7, the beastly character of belligerent parties undermines each's claim to innocence over the other, even as those very claims are being made.

As Hiram sees it—contrary to the powers' stated justifications for entering the war—the belligerents are, like the beasts of Daniel 7, eager to devour the earth, having entered the war with eyes turned toward acquisitions they can make through the fighting[6]: "Frum what I kin learn, standin' on the outside, / They all are durn rascals, and every one lied. / The hul trubble wuz that the world is too small, / And each one was achin' to gobble it all / There wasn't a country uv Alley er Hun,' / But held aspirations ez big as the sun" (Long 33). Long, through Hiram, draws on apocalyptic symbolism to expose and critique the incongruities between the belligerent parties' purported innocence and their underlying motives for entering the war.

While Hiram does not insist that parties involved in the war bear equal responsibility for its horrors, he does see them as equally characterized by the same beastly qualities. Germany most resembles the fourth and most terrible beast to appear in Daniel 7,[7] and Germany is finally confronted by the other nations in a showdown resembling the New Testament book of Revelation's final clashes between the forces of light and darkness. Hiram, describing the powers arrayed for combat, sees that

> Earth's crimson-browed nations, bedrunken with power,
> Hev marshalled their forces fer this final hour.
> They glare at each uther like beasts frum their cage,
> Prepared to onleash all their inhuman rage.
> They tremble like bloodhounds at sight uv their game,
> A-strainin to leap to a glorious fame.
> Republics and empires, all races uv men,
> All faiths and religions, all colors and kin—
> A hotchpotch uv passion, a cauldron uv hate,
> Mixed up in one batch and tost boldly to Fate. (Long 227)

Here at the end of the war, it is clear that all the powers—not just Germany—are like the beasts of Daniel 7 (and Revelation, which draws heavily on Daniel). The powers are all driven by "inhuman" rage, violence, and hatred (Long 227). In contrast to American rhetoric, which demonized Germany while upholding Allied innocence, the difference between powers is for Hiram not one of kind but of degree, since all alike embody the beastliness that animates and intensifies the conflict. The ability to see this emerges from an apocalyptically informed "cultural-ideological complex which predates the war" (Dayton 220).

Hiram reserves some of his harshest criticism for the United States—particularly as regards the incongruity between its justifications for entering the war and what he perceives to be the reality behind its participation in the conflict. Hiram sees the "pretensions" with which the United States entered the war—and which justified its involvement—as inconsistent with its wartime actions:

> Sam's husky fer Liberty, Jestice, and Right—
> And that was his slogan on enter'n' the fight.

His grandest pretensions it seems, were fergot

Before he had scase dumpt his goose in the pot …

He shet every mouth up that dared utter fac's,

And jumpt on his statesmen, and broke all their backs.

The things he wuz fightin' fer, over the foam,

He wudn't permit fer a minute round home. (Long 194)

In his final assessment, the United States disappointingly (if unsurprisingly) reveals itself to be like the other beastly empires; its wartime actions belie motives that fly in the face of the high-minded ideals employed to justify US involvement in the war. Indeed, one of the most damning popular critiques of Wilson's propaganda was its inadequacy for making sense of the conflict or its aftermath. Those for whom Wilson's millenarian visions of a redeemed world after the war rang hollow were justifiably disillusioned and distrustful of the authorities who were considered to have lied to their people (Dayton 28).

Thus far, we've seen the ways in which Long appropriates the resources of Jewish/early Christian apocalyptic literature to critique the powers involved in the war by unveiling the beastly values and dispositions that prolong and intensify the conflict—contrary to these nations' pretensions to innocence. Yet despite the carnage that blots its pages, *Farmer Hiram*, like Daniel 7, ends (as Dayton observes) in hope. In *Farmer Hiram*, as in Daniel 7, the beastly powers are not allowed free rein to bring ruin and chaos on the world. In Daniel's vision, the final beast is judged for its arrogance and destruction of the world and is itself destroyed, whereas the other beasts are judged and allowed to live a short while longer (Dan. 7.11–12). Germany—the "final beast"—is destroyed by the Allies. However, Germany is not the only beastly power that is called to account:

Stand up, all ye monarchs, ye sultans and czars,

Ye flaunters of feathers and flashers uv stars,

Ye Kaisers and junkers, ye presidents proud

That sit in high places deceivin' the crowd …

Ye soul-shriveled wolves that oppress humankind,

And crush out its spirit and darken its mind,

Ye slayers uv innocents, makers uv war,

Pretenders fer peace, but adorers uv Thor— (Long 260)

Hiram calls presidents and kaisers alike to bear witness to the suffering they are responsible for, and for which they will receive divine judgment. Thus, while Germany is defeated in the conflict, the rest of the powers share in its condemnation.

In Daniel's vision, authority to rule the earth is taken from the beasts and is given to one who is truly human, who assumes an everlasting kingship (Dan. 7.13–14). Hiram, similarly, has a vision for who should inherit the earth, were authority stripped from the rulers he holds responsible for the war:

Once *peoples* wake up, and take hold uv the reins,

The earth will soon cast all her sorrows and pains.

If all the war-mongers were sewed in one sack,

And launched on a boat that wud never cum back,

And leave none behind except duffers like *us*—

It wudn't take long to forestall every fuss!

But while earth is curst with ambition and greed,

There'll always be ways to make *common mutts* bleed. (Long 261, italics in original)

Hiram's democratic vision of the future is one in which violence is curtailed not by the will of autocrats, but by common people: "Once Peoples take Givernments right by the snoot, / And say *"We're the dubs must decide when to shoot!"* / The killin's all over, and war is no more, / And Hope will hang garlands on every front door" (Long 273, italics in original).

In order for this democratic vision to come to fruition, however, these common people must embody an alternative politics to those of the beasts, animated by alternative values: "You've got to git *Christ*, and *the things he stands for*, / Wrot into men's *conscience* before you'll end *war*! / If *Right* you'd hev reign, and cam *Reason* to boot, / You've got to find some antydote fer the *brute* (Long 277–78, italics in original). For Hiram, these things Christ stands for are an "antydote fer the *brute*" that enable a way of ruling and reigning by common people, characterized by "Right" and "cam Reason" (Long 278). Put another way, Hiram believes in democratic rule by those who are animated by the values of the Human One rather than rule by autocrats who devour their own and one another. Hiram's narration of the war thus ends with a sort of millenarian vision—but it is not the vision of Wilson, in which redemption comes through violence; human violence is not prescribed as an "antydote fer the *brute*." Thus, Long's imagination is resourced by Jewish/early Christian apocalyptic literature, such that he can name and criticize the forces that drive the conflict. This literature also provides Long with a grammar for articulating a hopeful and peaceful vision of the postwar world that does not necessitate human violence for its realization.

In the same vein as the Jewish and early Christian apocalyptic literature on which it draws, *Farmer Hiram on the World's War* attempts to make meaning of violent suffering while encouraging its readers with a hopeful vision of the future. Thus, for Hiram the war can be both unspeakably evil and, in some sense, comprehensible. This comprehensibility, however, does not emerge from a vision of the war as redemptive violence, but from attempting to rightly see and critique the war and its major actors. While literary modernism came to reject common justifications of the war as hollow,[8] and while the sentimental and genteel literary traditions underwrote Wilson's apocalyptic vision of peace through the violence of the war,[9] Long's work presents a notable alternative to these perspectives that is seldom, if ever, found in other literature of the period. Though Long, like the modernists, rejects common justifications for the war, his hopeful vision of a world after the war is not one predicated on human violence, as was the hopeful vision of the traditional literary culture.

In closing, I note that Long's use of Jewish/early Christian apocalyptic literature does not contrast with uses of these literatures to underwrite violence only in his own day. Long's nonviolent apocalyptic imagination is markedly different from that of contemporary American Christians who would draw on apocalyptic literatures to reinforce what Walter Wink calls the "myth of redemptive violence."[10,11] Such violent, apocalyptic ways of storying the world form Christians—for example, white evangelicals in the United States—toward violence. In the case of US evangelicals, dispensationalist, "end-times" stories about the state of Israel continue to hamper the effectiveness of US foreign policy[12] for fostering peace in the region; "end-times" predictions of QAnon, treated as credible by an alarming number of evangelicals, fomented religio-political violence during the last US presidential election cycle.[13] Thus, Long's apocalyptic storying of the world contrasts, in his day and ours, with those readings of apocalyptic literatures that hamper our ability to tell the truth about the world around us, which in turn primes us to toward violence to defend that which is founded on our untruths.[14] In *Farmer Hiram on the World's War*, we glimpse the potential of apocalyptic literature for resourcing nonviolent ways of seeing and being in the world—ways we learn as we become able to tell the truth.

Kansas State University

Notes

1. A brief sketch of Lindley Grant Long's background, as well as his writing, provides some interpretive clues for understanding the critique of the War present in *Farmer Hiram*. Long was born and educated in Ohio. Law was his primary profession; he practiced in his home state—primarily in Dayton—for three decades (Coyle 392). Though he published other volumes of poetry, Long's religious prose includes his 1948 *Layman's Look at Prophecy* (Coyle 392). That he wrote such a work not only evidences familiarity with Jewish and early Christian "prophetic" literature, including the apocalyptic literature of Daniel and the book of Revelation, but also attests to his concern for interpreting history through the lens of biblical "prophecy." Thus, Long's framework for making meaning of historical events—informed by the Jewish apocalyptic imagination—contributes to the view of the War he advances through the mouth of Hiram.

2. While future readings of this poem might investigate the significance of Twain's potential influence on this work, I think that Long is alluding more clearly to Riley. Long dedicates *Farmer Hiram on the World's War* to "those Good Old-Fashioned People who Refuse to Accept War as the Best Means of Perfecting the Happiness of their Fellow-Beings" (Long vi); this allusion to a well-known title of Riley's, and Long's use of the persona of the farmer—often employed by Riley—suggest to me that we are meant to read this poem as being informed by Riley more than by Twain. For more on the persona of the farmer, as well as the significance of dialect in Riley, see David Robertson, "Re-Forming Frontier Values."

3. In addition, given the trope of the Midwest as the American "heartland," the use of midwestern dialect works to underscore the internal nature of Long's/Hiram's critique of the war. This criticism emerges not from outside the United States, but from within.

4. John Collins, taking up and expanding the work of the Society of Biblical Literature Genres Project (1979), defines an "apocalypse" as "a genre of revelatory literature with a narrative framework, in which a revelation is mediated by an otherworldly being to a human recipient, disclosing a transcendent reality which is both temporal, insofar as it envisages eschatological salvation, and spatial insofar as it involves another, supernatural world" (Collins 14). According to Collins, apocalyptic literature is meant to reveal a divine perspective on the true nature of events, ordinarily concealed from human eyes; problems taken up in apocalyptic literature are "not viewed simply in terms of the historical factors available to any observer. Rather, [they are] viewed in light of a transcendent reality disclosed by the apocalypse, or, to put it differently, an apocalyptic vision facilitates an alternate experience of reality" (Collins 42). As Collins notes, this alternate experience of reality not only serves a critical purpose but also works to encourage its readers.

5. Revelation is a close second to Daniel in terms of Jewish/early Christian apocalyptic works that influence this poem, though I will attend primarily to the influence of Daniel on *Farmer Hiram*.

6. "The Bear had its eye on the bright Golden Horn / And had had it there ever since he was born. / The Lion was achin' to gobble the Sphinx, / And looked on Baghdad with the eye uv a lynx" (37).

7. "They'd watched the grim Monster crawl over the earth, / Devourin' all things that had value er worth. / Before his approach, nations trembled and fell; / And when he passed over Hope plunged into hell. / It seemed that no power cud stand in his path; / And nuthin' cud sate his insatiable wrath ..." (236).

8. This rejection is exemplified by Ezra Pound in "Hugh Selwyn Mauberly" I.IV (534).

9. See, for example, Lynn Howard Hough, *The Clean Sword* and Henry van Dyke, *The Red Flower*.

10. Gerald J. Mast, borrowing from Methodist minister and theologian Walter Wink, defines "the myth of redemptive violence" as "the recurring ancient plot by which safety and order are secured from chaos through the violent eradication of an externalized enemy" (70).

11. Long's attention to the nonviolent thrust of much Jewish/early Christian apocalyptic literature resonates with a similar impulse among prominent biblical scholars and theologians who contest the use of apocalypse to underwrite violence. See, for instance, Michael Gorman, who claims in *Reading Revelation Responsibly: Uncivil Worship and Witness: Following the Lamb into the New Creation*, "Revelation conveys a spirituality and ethic of nonviolence" (183). See also Richard Hays, *The Moral Vision of the New Testament*: "A work that places the Lamb that was slaughtered at the center of its praise and worship can hardly be used to validate violence and coercion. God's ultimate judgement of the wicked is, to be sure, inexorable ... But these events are in the hands of God; they do not constitute a program for human military action" (175). In the same vein, John Howard Yoder writes in *The Politics of Jesus* that "when read carefully, none of the biblical apocalypses from Ezekiel through Daniel to Mark 13 and John of Patmos, is about either pie in the sky or the Russians in Mesopotamia. They are

about how the crucified Jesus is a more adequate key to understanding what God is about in the real world of empires and armies and markets than is the ruler in Rome, with all his supporting military, commercial, and sacerdotal networks … in Jesus we have a clue to which kinds of causation, which kinds of community-building, which kinds of conflict management, go with the grain of the cosmos, of which we know, as Caesar does not, that Jesus is both the Word (the inner logic of things) and the Lord ('sitting at the right hand')" (246).

12. See Daniel G. Hummel, "American Evangelicals and the Apocalypse."

13. See Jason Springs, "QAnon, Conspiracy, and White Evangelical Apocalypse."

14. On the relationship between truthfulness and nonviolence, see Stanley Hauerwas, *The Peaceable Kingdom*, pp. 14–15, 114–15.

Works Cited

Collins, John J. *The Apocalyptic Imagination: An Introduction to Jewish Apocalyptic Literature*. William B. Eerdmans, 2016. *ProQuest EBookCentral*.

Coyle, William, editor. *Ohio Authors and Their Books: Biographical Data and Selective Bibliographies for Ohio Authors, Native and Resident, 1796–1950*. World Publishing Co., for the Ohioana Library Association, 1962. babel.hathitrust. org/cgi/pt?id=cub.u183025255329&seq=422&q1=lindley+grant+long.

Dayton, Tim. *American Poetry and the First World War*. Cambridge UP, 2018.

Goldingay, John. "The Stories in Daniel: A Narrative Politics." *Journal for the Study of the Old Testament*, vol. 12, no. 37, 1987, pp. 99–116. doi. org/10.1177/030908928701203706.

Gorman, Michael J. *Reading Revelation Responsibly: Uncivil Worship and Witness: Following the Lamb into the New Creation*. Wipf and Stock, 2011. *ProQuest Ebook Central*.

Hauerwas, Stanley. *The Peaceable Kingdom: A Primer in Christian Ethics*. U of Notre Dame P, 1983.

Hays, Richard B. *The Moral Vision of the New Testament: A Contemporary Introduction to New Testament Ethics*. HarperCollins, 1996.

Heath, Gordon L., editor. Introduction. *American Churches and the First World War*. Pickwick Publications, 2016, pp. 1–14.

The Holy Bible: New Revised Standard Version. Thomas Nelson Publishers, 1989.

Hough, Lynn Howard. *The Clean Sword*. Abingdon Press, 1918. *Internet Archive*.

Hummel, Daniel G. "American Evangelicals and the Apocalypse." *The Cambridge Companion to Apocalyptic Literature*, edited by Colin McAllister, Cambridge UP, 2020, pp. 288–315.

Jenkins, Philip. *The Great and Holy War: How World War I Became a Religious Crusade*. HarperOne, 2014.

Long, Lindley Grant. *Farmer Hiram on the World's War*. Christian Publishing Association, 1920. *Internet Archive*.

Mast, Gerald J. "The Myth of Redemptive Violence." *Evangelical Christians and Popular Culture*, edited by Robert H. Woods, Jr., vol. 2, Praeger, 2013, pp. 70–85.

Michael, Matthew. "Yahweh, the Animal Tamer: Jungles, Wild Animals and Yahweh's Sovereignty in the Apocalyptic Space of Daniel 7:1–28." *Scriptura*, vol. 119, no. 1, Feb. 2020, pp. 1–16. doi.org/10.7833/119-1-1696.

Pound, Ezra. "Hugh Selwyn Mauberly." *American Poetry: The Twentieth Century*, edited by Robert Haas et al., vol. 1, Penguin Putnam, 2000, pp. 532–45.

Robertson, David. "Re-Forming Frontier Values: The Dialect Poetry of James Whitcomb Riley." *Thalia*, vol. 19, no. 1, 1999, pp. 14–27.

Springs, Jason. "QAnon, Conspiracy, and White Evangelical Apocalypse." *Contending Modernities*, 16 June 2021, contendingmodernities.nd.edu/theorizing-modernities/qanon-evangelical-apocalypse.

Van Dyke, Henry. *The Red Flower: Poems Written in War Time*. Charles Scribner's Sons, 1917. *Internet Archive*.

Wesley, Cindy. "Making the Bible Safe for Democracy: American Methodists and the First World War." *Journal of the Bible and Its Reception*, vol. 4, no. 2, 2017, pp. 181–92. doi.org/10.1515/jbr-2017-0015.

Yoder, John Howard. *The Politics of Jesus*. 1972. Wm. B. Eerdmans, 1994.

Multiple Awakenings in Sherwood Anderson's Story "An Awakening"

Janet Ruth Heller

Sherwood Anderson's story "An Awakening"—written from 1915 to 1917 and published first in *The Little Review* in December 1918 and then in Anderson's 1919 collection *Winesburg, Ohio*—has three main characters: the young newspaper reporter George Willard; the woman he dates, Belle Carpenter; and the older man whom Belle loves, the bartender Ed Handby, who wants to marry Belle. *Merriam Webster's Dictionary* online defines "awakening" as "a coming into awareness" (definition 3). The story's title emphasizes the theme of reaching a new awareness or insight about one's life. As the plot progresses, all three characters wake up to realize their desires, their true power, and their place in Winesburg's society. Anderson creates empathy for these characters and raises questions about traditional norms and constricting gender roles.

The third-person omniscient narrator of "An Awakening" begins by introducing the three main characters and analyzing their views of power and the types of power that they have. Belle's father Henry Carpenter, the bookkeeper at the local bank, used to dominate and bully her. His abuse has left her confused about her power: "When black thoughts visited her she grew angry and wished she were a man and could fight someone with her fists" ("An Awakening" 102). This fantasy foreshadows the fight between George and Ed later in the story. Belle's transgendered desire to be a man also emphasizes the problematic status of women in early twentieth-century America when gender roles were rigid and society considered women inferior to men. Women did not obtain suffrage until 1920, a year after Anderson published *Winesburg, Ohio*. These limitations create difficulties for Belle in her relationships with men.

However, when Belle has matured and has a job as a milliner, the new power dynamic of an aging father and his adult daughter reverses their roles. Anderson explains, "When she was a young girl Henry Carpenter made life almost unbearable for Belle, but as she emerged from girlhood into womanhood he lost his power over her" (103). Henry now fears his daughter (103). Obsessed with having his business clothes wrinkle-free, Henry has invented a special press made of boards that he keeps spotlessly clean. To torment him and to get revenge for his previous bullying of her, Belle secretly smears the boards of his press with soft mud from the road (103).

She has more trouble dealing with men her age, like Ed Handby, who want a serious relationship with her. Belle loves the bartender; however, she feels that he is socially beneath her and worries that she will not be able to control him. The narrator emphasizes Belle's "anxiety" over how to handle Ed (103). He is strong and powerfully built. The narrator describes Ed as "a tall, broad-shouldered man of thirty" with large fists (103). This description also foreshadows the fight near the conclusion of "An Awakening."

When Belle and Ed spend one evening together, he finds himself unable to talk with her romantically about his desire. Instead, he expresses his longing physically: "Taking the milliner into his arms and holding her tightly in spite of her struggles, he kissed her until she became helpless" (104). Such conduct scares Belle, but Ed has no idea how to resolve the situation. This impasse creates problems for both Belle and Ed.

To relieve her longing for physical contact with Ed, Belle sometimes takes evening walks with George Willard, whom the narrator describes as "the *young* reporter," and lets him kiss her (103, emphasis added). While Ed engenders anxiety in Belle, "She felt that she could keep the *younger* man within bounds" (103, emphasis added). Her father's abuse has made Belle nervous about relationships with mature men, but she feels that she can control the adolescent George. The narrator of "An Awakening" repeatedly emphasizes how young and immature George is.

In contrast to Ed, George has some verbal ability. George can talk and write easily about any subject; however, he believes that he has verbal mastery when he is really quite immature. The budding author is obsessed with words and books. Anderson portrays George with other Winesburg "boys" at the local pool room, where he talks about his theory concerning relationships between men and women (104). He insists that "women should look out for themselves, that the fellow who went out with a girl was not responsible for what happened" (104). Because George has very little experience with such relationships, his proclamations seem naïve, ironic, and somewhat silly. Clarence Lindsay views George as following the "infatuation-with-self script" (14–15).

Another young man at the Winesburg pool room, Art Wilson, tells a story about visiting a house of prostitution. To punish a prostitute for being "fresh" with him, Art sits in her lap and kisses her (104–05). Lindsay comments that this tale reveals "a witless masculine bravado unaware of its little-boyness" (143). Both Art and George consider themselves knowledgeable and mature, but they are really quite naïve.

Restless, George leaves the pool room and walks around under the January stars and the new moon. He pretends that he is drunk, then imagines himself a soldier and an inspector (105). He talks to himself about the importance of order in human life and feels "[h]ypnotized by his own words" (105). He realizes that he has much to learn, and this is also obvious to the reader. George "said words without meaning" as he walks along (106). To him, uttering language is more important than constructing meaningful thoughts.

In "Nobody Knows," an earlier story in *Winesburg, Ohio*, when George is much younger than he is in "An Awakening," Anderson also emphasizes the reporter's intoxication with his own grandiosity and verbosity before a sexual encounter with Louise Trunnion: "A flood of words burst from George Willard … Doubt left him … He became wholly the male, bold and aggressive." He assures Louise Trunnion that no one will "know anything" about their tryst ("Nobody Knows" 29). Nervous, George repeats that phrase to himself at the end of "Nobody Knows" (30). But whether anyone knows about two people having intercourse begs the question of whether their experience grows out of any deep commitment to one another or is just an impulsive fling.

In "An Awakening," George feels excited and powerful because of what seem to him profound meditations (105). He walks through the dilapidated section of Winesburg where day laborers and their domesticated animals live (105–06). As he strolls, George remembers stories from the books that he has been reading and feels "oddly detached and apart from all life." He begins to feel "unutterably big and remade" (106).

At this point, George longs to be with a woman and decides to go to Belle's home to display his newfound power to her. In the past, he had felt "used" by Belle, but now he thinks that he can change their power dynamic. He believes that he "had suddenly become too big to be used" (107). His journey resembles the quest of heroes in traditional stories. However, the rest of "An Awakening" disproves this young reporter's claim that he is a fully mature man.

The omniscient narrator informs us that while George was walking, Ed had visited Belle's home, intending to propose marriage to her. Instead, the nervous bartender commands Belle to "stay away from that kid" and threatens, "If I catch you together I will break your bones and his too" (107). Again, Ed finds himself tongue-tied and unable to express his love to Belle. Rebecca Sanchez contends that the "inability to communicate with one another … most strongly links the characters in *Winesburg*." Furthermore, Sanchez finds that in Winesburg, Ohio, the "prescribed modes of communication do not accommodate the diverse needs of its population" (31–32). Similarly, David T. Humphries emphasizes the misunderstandings at the heart of some stories in *Winesburg*. He concludes, "Rather than accepting existing gender roles or offering a programmatic model for how they might be changed, Anderson calls attention to the limits of language in *Winesburg*" (54).

Predictably, Belle has no intention of cooperating with Ed's rude powerplay. When George arrives at her home, Belle "greet[s] him effusively" and goes out to walk with the reporter in order to irritate her lover and to make Ed jealous (107). She knows that Ed will follow them and confront George eventually.

As the reporter and the milliner stroll, George feels mature, masculine, and confident. He tells Belle, "You've got to take me for a man or let me alone" (107). But the narrator describes them as "the woman and the *boy*" (107, emphasis added), which deflates the young man's pretensions. Also, inexperienced George does not understand why Belle fails to pay attention to his fancy words (108). The reader and the narrator know that she is watching for Ed to see how he will react to her manipulative little drama. But this dramatic irony escapes confused and self-centered George, who assumes "that Belle Carpenter was about to surrender herself to him" (108). He grips her shoulder and turns her around to face him. Then he kisses her, and "she leaned heavily against him and looked over his shoulder into the darkness." Unaware of her preoccupation, George embraces Belle tightly (108). He fails to do a sophisticated transactional analysis of her behavior.

The narrator now flashes forward to a scene in which the depressed reporter is alone in his room, full of anger and hatred for Belle. Then Anderson flashes back to the hillside and tells the reader what has made George so upset. The adolescent has led Belle to a clearing and dropped to his knees beside her, feeling very powerful. But Ed Handby appears and roughly shoves George into some bushes. The reporter does not want to give up, so he springs at Ed three more times, only to be sent sprawling back into the bushes. The fourth time, George's head hits a tree root, which leaves him unconscious for a while (108–09).

Although Ed's strong hands could severely injure George, the narrator tells readers, "The bartender did not want to beat the *boy*.... He knew that beating was unnecessary, that he had the power within himself to accomplish his purpose without using his fists" (108, emphasis added). Despite George's illusion that he possesses a "new force" and "a new power in himself" (108), the most potent male in "An Awakening" is Ed, and Anderson emphasizes this with the last name *Hand*by (emphasis added) and by the ease with which Ed overcomes George. The young reporter uses a stream of words to build up his confidence while he walks with Belle, and George convinces himself that she will "surrender herself to him" (108) as Louise Trunnion did. But this is a delusion: Belle has no intention of having sex with George.

During the fight, Ed finally tells Belle his true feelings: "I'd let you alone if I didn't want you so much" (108). After the struggle with George, Ed marches Belle away (109). The older man has triumphed: he has defeated George in a fight, he has declared his love to Belle, and she has chosen to spend her evening with Ed.

The concluding paragraph of "An Awakening" focuses on George's overwhelming emotions of humiliation and self-hatred. He feels "sick," disillusioned, and completely deflated (109). He needs to face the reality that his inflated meditations and boastful words have masked.

Each of the three main characters has a different awakening in this story. Ed Handby learns that he needs to tell the woman he loves about his desire for her without threats of violence. Because of social mores of the early twentieth century, Belle cannot simply tell Ed that she loves him. Instead, she stages a scene in which she pretends to enjoy a romantic evening with George. Aware that Ed is following them on their walk, Belle manipulates the bartender to provoke him to commit himself emotionally to their relationship. As usual, Belle "uses" George in her little drama, but she does not love him or care about his hurt feelings.

David D. Anderson points out that Sherwood Anderson met pioneering psychoanalyst Trigant Burrow in 1915, and the two men became friends. Sherwood Anderson used insights from psychology in works like *Winesburg, Ohio*. David D. Anderson views the "isolation of the individual" as the theme of this collection of stories. By 1916, he writes, "Increasingly, Anderson was becoming interested in the inner nature of human life—the twists, the quirks, and the secrets that make communication between individuals so difficult." *Winesburg, Ohio* creates empathy and compassion for its struggling characters (D. Anderson 35–37, 39–40).

In a letter to a Russian translator in 1923, Anderson wrote, "With the publication of *Winesburg* I felt I had really begun to write out of the repressed muddled life about me" (*Letters* 93). Because of his own awareness of repression, the author conveys the problems that social constraints place on his characters.

In "The Book of the Grotesque," a short story which prefaces *Winesburg, Ohio*, Anderson defines what he means by the term "grotesque." The old man in this story believes that when a person focuses on only one truth and "trie[s] to live his life by it, he bec[omes] a grotesque, and the truth he embrace[s] bec[omes] a falsehood" (7). In general, the grotesque characters in *Winesburg*,

Ohio obsess about certain issues, and this trait distorts their lives. Belle's narcissism and her obsession with power over men make her grotesque. Daniel Davis Wood views *Winesburg, Ohio* as "an example of the literary formalization of obsession in a small-town setting" (43). He argues that the narrator, whom Wood terms the "focalizing consciousness" of this work of fiction, shares the characters' obsessed perspective (43–44). David D. Anderson observes that when Sherwood Anderson uses the word *grotesque* in *Winesburg, Ohio*, this term "does not connote revulsion or disgust…. [T]he spiritual ills of his people merely intensify their need for understanding and love" (41). Sherwood Anderson wanted to create such empathy in his readers.

Deborah Tannen contends in *You Just Don't Understand: Women and Men in Conversation* (1990) that women's culture emphasizes connection, support, and intimacy. In contrast, men's culture focuses on issues of power, independence, and hierarchy: who is one-up, and who is one-down (24–25)? Belle differs from this definition of women in her obsession with control over men.

Marilyn Judith Atlas finds evidence of discomfort with women in Anderson's publications, writing "[H]e was frightened of women. Most of all, he was frightened of needing them, losing his independence, of somehow being seduced by sexuality into being corporeal rather than creative" (254). Atlas points out that although Anderson "questioned some of the traditional myths" about women in *Winesburg, Ohio*, he "embraced others." For example, he believes that women "long to be subsumed in a man" (256). Although Helen White, who appears in several stories including "Sophistication" and "The Thinker," has the potential to become George Willard's partner in a fully egalitarian relationship, Atlas emphasizes that Anderson does not allow this to happen: "He is not ready, even fictionally, to create a liberated woman with whom his protagonist must relate on equal terms." Atlas finds that *Winesburg, Ohio* "portrays the women whose lives are limited because they live within a system which was never created for their benefit" (264). Similarly, William M. Etter contends, "*Winesburg, Ohio* constitutes a complex reinforcement, rather than an undermining, of a conservative sense of modern 'manhood'" (80).

However, other literary critics find that Anderson questions traditional gender roles. John W. Crowley argues that in *Winesburg, Ohio*, Anderson wants "to explore the boundary between 'man' and 'woman,' to expand the horizon of his own masculinity" (13). Celia C. Esplugas insists that the narrator in *Winesburg, Ohio* strongly criticizes "women's psychological suffering at the hands of patriarchal tyranny" and foregrounds "social injustice and the interrogation of traditional gender roles" (167). Similarly, Peter Nagy argues that Anderson depicts "a patriarchal social order in which men shape women into grotesques by denying their subjectivity" (784; see also Esplugas 167). So Belle is not entirely responsible for her conduct because her society constricts her behavior.

Humphries contends that Anderson uses the text of *Winesburg, Ohio*, which is full of misunderstandings among characters, to stimulate readers: "*Winesburg* challenges readers to play a particularly active role in making sense of its interstitial silences and the repeated misunderstandings of its characters, so that *Winesburg* can serve as one of the forward-looking 'thoughtful books' that Anderson describes" in the story "Godliness, Part Three—Surrender" (Humphries 55). Humphries finds a "fundamental lack of communication between men and women" in *Winesburg, Ohio* (55–57). Some stories in this book "expose the shortcomings of conventional language and gender roles in establishing a functioning community" (64). *Winesburg* "gradually reveals how conventions of language and gender rely on vague generalities and prohibitions which act more to censure than promote individual expressions and desires" (71).

Clarence Lindsay observes that nine of the twenty-five stories in *Winesburg, Ohio* focus on women, including "An Awakening." Lindsay finds these women as "grotesque" as their male counterparts in the stories that center on men (174–75).

Note that Belle says nothing in this story. The men talk, but she is silent and voiceless. If "An Awakening" had been written in 2024, Belle would have more power in her society, and she would not feel obligated to repress her feelings about Ed. She could openly talk to the man she loves. Rather than manipulating George and Ed, Belle could exercise her contemporary power to communicate clearly to them. She could avoid becoming grotesque in an era when women have more agency and power than they did in 1919.

George's awakening is the most complex and multifaceted. He revels in his power to speak fluently and meditate about important issues. He feels mature and wants a sexual relationship with Belle, but he finally realizes what the narrator has repeatedly brought to the readers' attention: George is too young and inexperienced to handle Belle, and she does not really love him or want to have a serious commitment to him. The young reporter does not love Belle either and misunderstands her. Walter B. Rideout points out that George "feels no more sympathy for her, has no more understanding of her needs than he had for Louise Trunnion" in the story "Nobody Knows" (153). Furthermore, Ed keeps throwing the reporter out of his way, bruising both George's body and his premature self-confidence. Early in "An Awakening," George declares that women in relationships "should look out for themselves" (104), but by the end of the story, he learns that men, especially inexperienced young men, also have to be careful in relationships.

George finds a more comfortable relationship when he accompanies Helen White in "Sophistication." Their interaction is playful and mutual, in contrast to Belle's manipulative and controlling behavior. George seeks "understanding" from Helen (136). Instead of hurling a stream of words at her, George walks and frolics with Helen. The narrator emphasizes their "silence," repeating this word and related words like "silently" and "silent" (140–41). Because George avoids his usual verbosity, he experiences their relationship on an intuitive and profound level: "The presence of Helen renewed and refreshed him," and he feels a "reverence" for her (140). Both feel "[m]utual respect" for one another (141). This evening of quiet fulfillment means a lot to George and Helen, and the narrator comments at the end of the story that both have become more "mature" (142).

James M. Mellard argues that Anderson parodies "the romantic quest" in "An Awakening," using the pattern of taking a journey, engaging in a battle, facing defeat, and experiencing rebirth (1306). Earlier in this story, George thinks that he is a young hero; however, he discovers that he is not ready and not mature, so this quest ends in failure. Anderson portrays George later in *Winesburg, Ohio*, in "Sophistication," as "realizing his own insignificance in the scheme of existence" (140). To have a fulfilling life, individuals need to understand their talents, their desires, and their true place in society. Individuals also need to fully understand the people around them. Though George gets bruised both physically and psychologically, he achieves valuable insight into his real situation. He realizes that human relationships are complicated and sometimes difficult to navigate.

In addition to depicting the characters' new realizations, Sherwood Anderson tries to awaken readers to make them more sensitive to ways that our society represses individuals of both sexes, makes communication difficult, stunts our development, and causes unnecessary frustration and suffering. He implies that we readers can work to make our environments less constricting by allowing more variation in people's interactions and loosening the bonds of rigid gender roles.

Michigan College English Association

Works Cited

Anderson, David D. *Sherwood Anderson: An Introduction and Interpretation.* Edited by John Mahoney, Barnes & Noble, 1967. American Authors and Critics Series.

Anderson, Sherwood. "An Awakening." *Winesburg.*

———. "The Book of the Grotesques." *Winesburg.*

———. *Letters of Sherwood Anderson.* Edited by Howard Mumford Jones, Little, Brown, 1953.

———. "Nobody Knows." *Winesburg.*

———. "Sophistication." *Winesburg.*

———. *Winesburg, Ohio.* Edited by Marc K. Dudley, Norton Critical Edition, 2nd ed., W. W. Norton, 2023.

Atlas, Marilyn Judith. "Sherwood Anderson and the Women of Winesburg." *Critical Essays on Sherwood Anderson*, edited by David D. Anderson, G. K. Hall, 1981, pp. 250–66.

"Awakening." *Merriam Webster's Dictionary*, www.merriam-webster.com/dictionary/awakening.

Crowley, John W. Introduction. *New Essays on* Winesburg, Ohio, edited by John W. Crowley, Cambridge UP, 1990, pp. 1–26.

Esplugas, Celia C. "Marìa Luisa Bombal and Sherwood Anderson: Early Twentieth-Century Pan-American Feminism(s)." *College Literature*, vol. 40, no. 2, spring 2013, pp. 155–70.

Etter, William M. "Speaking of Manhood in *Winesburg, Ohio*." *Sherwood Anderson's* Winesburg, Ohio, edited by Precious McKenzie, Brill Rodopi, 2016, pp. 77–105. Dialogue 20.

Humphries, David T. "Failed Adventures and Imagined Communities in Sherwood Anderson's *Winesburg, Ohio*." *Sherwood Anderson's* Winesburg, Ohio, edited by Precious McKenzie, Brill Rodopi, 2016, pp. 51–76. Dialogue 20.

Lindsay, Clarence. *Such a Rare Thing: The Art of Sherwood Anderson's* Winesburg, Ohio. Kent State UP, 2009.

Mellard, James M. "Narrative Forms in *Winesburg, Ohio*." *PMLA*, vol. 83, no. 5, Oct. 1968, pp. 1304–12.

Nagy, Peter. "The Woman in the Man: Male Modernism and Cross-Gender Identification in Sherwood Anderson's *Winesburg, Ohio*." *College Literature*, vol. 45, no. 4, fall 2018, pp. 773–800.

Rideout, Walter B. "The Simplicity of *Winesburg, Ohio*." *Critical Essays on Sherwood Anderson*, edited by David D. Anderson, G. K. Hall, 1981, pp. 146–54.

Sanchez, Rebecca. "Shattering Communicative Norms: The Politics of Embodied Language in *Winesburg, Ohio*." *Modern Language Studies*, vol. 43, no. 2, winter 2014, pp. 24–39.

Tannen, Deborah. *You Just Don't Understand: Women and Men in Conversation*. Ballentine Books, 1990.

Wood, Daniel Davis. "Winesburg, Elsewhere: George Willard and the Literary Formalization of Obsession in Small-Town America and Abroad." *Sherwood Anderson's* Winesburg, Ohio, edited by Precious McKenzie, Brill Rodopi, 2016, pp. 23–49. Dialogue 20.

Beatrice Roethke's Marginalia
Unseen Narratives about a Pulitzer Poet's Legacy

Madeline Bruessow and Sherrin Frances

In 1968, Allan Seager published *The Glass House: The Life of Theodore Roethke*, the seminal biography detailing the life and legacy of Pulitzer Prize–winning poet Theodore (Ted) Roethke. Roethke and Seager were colleagues at the University of Michigan, the same school where the two had met as undergraduate students. They developed a friendship as classmates and colleagues, and they shared similar backgrounds—both being writers, professors, and having been raised in small Michigan cities—rendering Seager the ideal author to undertake the biography. For over thirty years, scholars have relied on the content of Seager's text. Yet the perspective of Beatrice Roethke, Ted Roethke's wife of ten years and one of the people who knew him best, is missing.

Seager was invited by Beatrice to write the biography, a decision she later came to regret. Twenty-five years later, she would add extensive annotations to her personal copy of Seager's book, which is now held in the archives at Saginaw Valley State University's Zahnow Library.[1] They illuminate her views of Roethke's life and Seager's portrayal of it, providing a unique lens through which to reread *The Glass House*. While the majority of these annotations have to do with factual accuracy and elaboration of detail, about one-fourth of them concern expressions of doubt or corrections regarding the claims Seager makes throughout the book. With her marginalia, not only does Beatrice provide a critical analysis of Seager's biography approximately thirty years after Roethke passed, but her insights and corrections also draw back the narrative curtain to provide a personal, and at times emotional, reflection on her relationship with Roethke.

Contextualizing Theodore Roethke

Born in 1908 in Saginaw, Michigan, Theodore Roethke grew up amidst the greenhouses of his family's floral company, a setting that deeply influenced the themes of his poetry. Despite the traumatic losses of his father and uncle during his adolescence, Roethke excelled academically and creatively. He earned degrees from the University of Michigan and briefly attended Harvard University before embarking on a dual career as a poet and professor at several prestigious institutions, including Lafayette College, Michigan State College (now Michigan State University), Pennsylvania State College, Bennington College, and the University of Washington. His dynamic presence and charismatic style made him a memorable figure both in the classroom and in literary circles. He was awarded the Pulitzer Prize for Poetry in 1954 for his volume *The Waking*, solidifying his status as a prominent literary figure.

Despite his successes, however, Roethke struggled tremendously with mental health. In 1935, the year in which he began teaching at Michigan State, he suffered a severe breakdown, the first in a series of several major manic depressive episodes throughout his life, which resulted in hospitalization. Michigan State declined to rehire Roethke after this, and he ultimately settled down at the University of Washington, where he would teach and write for the rest of his career. Roethke's writing often delved into themes of nature, identity, and the human experience, reflecting his deep connection to the natural world and his personal struggles. His influence extended beyond his own works, shaping the landscape of American poetry in the mid-twentieth century.

Beatrice Heath O'Connell met Roethke in the 1940s while she was a student at Bennington College in Vermont. They reconnected a decade later in New York, and despite their significant age difference—she was eighteen years younger—they married in 1953. Although they traveled extensively together, they eventually settled down in Seattle, Washington. Similarly to her husband, Beatrice was an educator and taught French at Bellevue High School in Washington. They remained married until Theodore Roethke's sudden passing in 1963, when he died from a cardiac event while swimming in a friend's pool on Bainbridge Island. Beatrice remarried in 1972 to Stephen Lushington, a British teacher, and relocated to England.

Contextualizing Beatrice's Comments

In 1967, Beatrice and June Roethke, Theodore Roethke's sister, exchanged a series of letters that included discussion of Seager's text. Beatrice reviewed a draft of the manuscript in 1967 and sent Seager "fifteen pages of criticism" on chapters one through eleven. She wrote to June, "I don't think Seager's mind is suited to biography: it seems better suited to fiction" (B. Roethke, "Letter" 30 Apr. 1967). She felt that the chapters on Roethke's childhood were the best, while the last chapters left her "bored by the account of our marriage which had tragic, comic and poetic sides that Seager misses." Ultimately, Beatrice refused to grant him permission to include any of Roethke's poetry in the biography and at one point even sought legal advice to prevent him from publishing it (B. Roethke, "Letter" 26 Sept. 1967).

Twenty-five years later, Beatrice would add 294 comments throughout her copy of *The Glass House*. The comments begin toward the end of chapter five, "Trouble," on page 105. Of these comments, about 25% correct or confirm factual data, about 43% elaborate on Seager's content, and about 27% correct or cast doubt on claims made by Seager.[2] The content of each annotation is generally very short, often a single word or phrase. The precise timing of these annotations is unclear. In one comment, in reference to a 1959 copyright request, she notes "9/91 I am still getting the royalties." This complicates a definitive timeline because the edition she wrote in was published in 1994.

The consistency of the ink color and handwriting throughout the book indicate she likely made the majority of her comments in one sitting. However, occasional comments in slightly darker blue ink and some in red or black ink suggest multiple passes through the book. Furthermore, there are some pages where the handwriting is shakier, indicating that her situation had somehow changed—maybe she was in a moving vehicle, or perhaps she had aged since writing prior comments. For instance, on page 106 of the biography, Beatrice writes in blue ink "Untrue" in neat handwriting (see Figure 1). However, we see another instance of this word in more shaky handwriting on page 123 of the text (see Figure 2).[3]

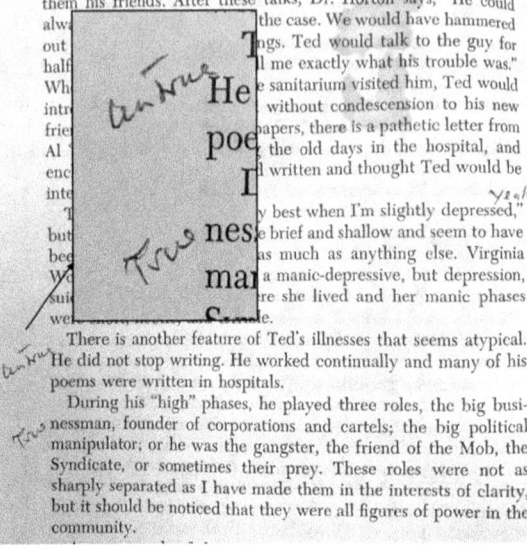

them his friends. After these talks, Dr. Horton says, He could
alw[...]the case. We would have hammered
out[...]ngs. Ted would talk to the guy for
half[...]l me exactly what his trouble was."
Wh[...]e sanitarium visited him, Ted would
intr[...]without condescension to his new
frie[...]apers, there is a pathetic letter from
Al [...]the old days in the hospital, and
enc[...]l written and thought Ted would be
inte[...]
[...]y best when I'm slightly depressed,"
but[...]e brief and shallow and seem to have
bee[...]as much as anything else. Virginia
y[...]a manic-depressive, but depression,
sui[...]re she lived and her manic phases
we[...]e.

There is another feature of Ted's illnesses that seems atypical.
He did not stop writing. He worked continually and many of his
poems were written in hospitals.

During his "high" phases, he played three roles, the big busi-
nessman, founder of corporations and cartels; the big political
manipulator; or he was the gangster, the friend of the Mob, the
Syndicate, or sometimes their prey. These roles were not as
sharply separated as I have made them in the interests of clarity,
but it should be noticed that they were all figures of power in the
community.

Figure 1. Marginalia by Beatrice Roethke on p. 106 of *The Glass House*. Photograph by Madeline Bruessow, 2022.

the only thing that could have happened. [...]
truggling in the quotidian humdrum, the f[...]
murky. By the time he was at Penn State, [...]
t, that, despite illness, lapses in confidence[...]
, his life would be devoted to it, and he ha[...]
mple of that life. What he did not yet kno[...]
t he would be. Yet to the later observer, [...]
ccitement of life lay within himself, not ou[...]
ast but his own. What struck him throu[...]
rmed at once into signs of his own states of[...]
himself he had to sing, not the circuman[...]
sed that.

ley Kunitz says he was not a really close observer, and, of
he did not need to be since everything around him was
to him only as signatures of himself. Lyne Hoffman says [...]
seemed to want to go everywhere, experience everything,[...]
s seems a temporary aberration for, again, he did not need[...]
e he already had nearly all the pertinent experience he was[...]
o use in his work. (Ted was not a traveler, a sightseer. He
vent anywhere he did not have to and the rare times he did,
to see people, not the monuments or the natural beauties.
er his marriage, with Auden's villa at Ischia lent him for
eymoon, Ted dug his heels in and nearly refused to go.[...]
e of his letters to me did he ever mention how anything
but he always wrote about people.) To his contemporaries
n seemed merely selfish but to one who is looking for the
seems that he was guarding his heart. But at this time he
yet aware of this.

Figure 2. Marginalia by Beatrice Roethke on p. 123 of *The Glass House*. Photograph by Madeline Bruessow, 2022.

Seager's narrative flair makes the biography engaging, though it contains factual inaccuracies likely due to his deteriorating health during its completion. He was still proofreading drafts of the book from his hospital bed before he succumbed to lung cancer in 1968, resulting in several errors such as incorrect names, addresses, and dates. Many of Beatrice's corrections are minor. She tells us that on a visit home, Roethke found his coonskin coat in the attic and not hanging in a closet (262); that Roethke graded her cooking not as a B but a B+ (219); and that the name of a vacation spot was not Orchis (244) but "Oreas Island." Some errors are more significant, for example, when Seager writes that June Roethke was at the University of Michigan in 1936 (110) and Beatrice corrects that to Michigan State. Later, Seager writes Roethke last visited his mother, Helen, during Christmas vacation in 1953 and that she died in February of 1954 (221). The text reads, "In February, 1954, Helen Roethke died of a heart attack." In fact, Helen died in 1955. Beatrice corrects Roethke's visit to 1954 and supplements the sentence to read, "Helen Roethke [in hospital for exploratory operation—lump in throat—cancer had spread but she] died of a heart attack."

The last three chapters—"Marriage and the Pulitzer Prize," "The Prizes, the Awards," and "The Last Years"—most directly discuss Beatrice's life with Roethke. That almost half of Beatrice's comments appear on only fifty of 250 total pages makes sense. She adds embellishment and elaboration to many of the anecdotes and details that Seager includes. For example, Beatrice's parents did not just send her "some furniture" (244), they sent her "some [antique] furniture." Seager includes an anecdote that mentions a "sweet-tasting banana concoction that she cooked herself, having consulted a cookbook" (275), and Beatrice clarifies, "never. I learned 'Bananes Flambées' from restaurants in Geneva in 1946-7." And when Seager talks about the Roethkes living in the University district and playing *bocce* in the yard (238), she notes, "not here but at 3802 E. John Street where we had a home in 1956." Her comments alongside Seager's text add a new narrative layer, and one gets the sense that she is rather enjoying reading and commenting on these memories.

Beatrice often takes a wry, casual tone in her comments. For example, she responds to Seager's claim that "Mrs. Roethke is quite a well-known linguist and is also versed in Italian," by noting, "Delighted to hear it." And when Seager makes some general claims about Roethke's students at Bennington College (141), Beatrice writes, "For god's sake, we weren't all debutantes."

When she speaks directly to or about Seager, one can see most acutely how her voice is outside of Seager's text. In one paragraph that begins, "The strains of the marriage began to tell on Beatrice," Seager elaborates on the many ways in which "Ted almost unconsciously demanded so much of her time and attention" (238). He was a finicky eater, he snored, he sweated, he needed eight or nine blankets every night (Beatrice corrects this to five), he changed pajamas so often there were "often eighteen or twenty pairs of pajamas a week in the laundry" (Beatrice says this is a "gross exaggeration, 2-3 more like it"). He ends with, "If he had finished a poem or paragraph of good lines, she wanted to listen." Beatrice responds directly to Seager with, "Ye gods, Allan, it wasn't listening to poems that was a strain!" All of the notes in these last chapters lend a feeling of intimacy to the story of Roethke's life—or now, Roethke and Beatrice's life.

On Roethke's "Gnawing Doubts"

The biography paints Roethke as a complex figure balancing multiple personas—a tough, charismatic public speaker who sometimes presented a gangster-like facade to mask a person with deep-seated insecurities and plagued with a deep lack of confidence. Beatrice's annotations cast some doubt on this. When Seager writes that Roethke "was ridden by gnawing doubts that his work was any good at all and that his career, such as it was, was only an elaborate deception" (179), Beatrice notes, "Nonsense!" When Seager writes that at a conference, "the sight of so many academics all in one place filled him with rage and contempt which he dared not display and the exercise of the necessary hypocrisy was a strain" (132), Beatrice responds that this statement was "Inaccurate & Seager's sentiments projected onto TR." And in Seager's description about Roethke's pursuit of a Guggenheim Fellowship in 1942, he writes that Roethke

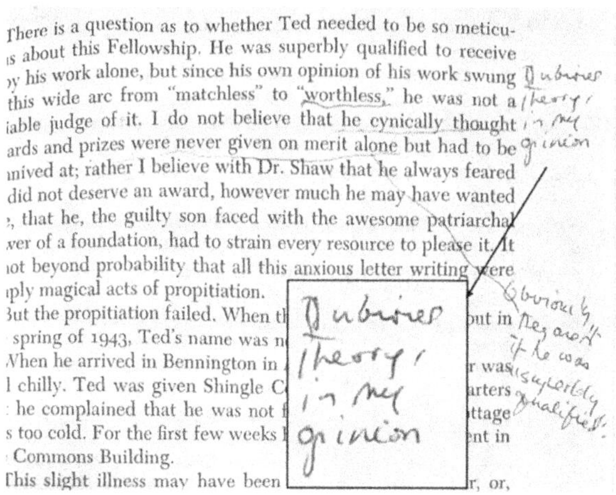
There is a question as to whether Ted needed to be so meticu-
is about this Fellowship. He was superbly qualified to receive
by his work alone, but since his own opinion of his work swung
this wide arc from "matchless" to "worthless," he was not a
iable judge of it. I do not believe that he cynically thought
ards and prizes were never given on merit alone but had to be
mived at; rather I believe with Dr. Shaw that he always feared
did not deserve an award, however much he may have wanted
:, that he, the guilty son faced with the awesome patriarchal
wer of a foundation, had to strain every resource to please it. It
not beyond probability that all this anxious letter writing were
mply magical acts of propitiation.
But the propitiation failed. When th … out in
spring of 1943, Ted's name was n
When he arrived in Bennington in … r was
l chilly. Ted was given Shingle C … arters
he complained that he was not … ttage
s too cold. For the first few weeks … ent in
Commons Building.
This slight illness may have been … r, or,

Figure 3. Marginalia by Beatrice Roethke on p. 135 of *The Glass House.* Photograph by Madeline Bruessow, 2022.

"was superbly qualified to receive it by his work alone, but since his own opinion of his work swung in the wide arc from 'matchless' to 'worthless,' he was not a reliable judge of it" (135). Beatrice underlines "worthless," and comments, "Dubious theory, in my opinion" (see Figure 3). Even in these very short phrases, she is actively crafting a narrative distinct from Seager's.

On Roethke's "Episodes"

Throughout *The Glass House,* Seager makes speculative claims about what Donald Hall describes in the introduction as "the relationship between Roethke's mental illness and his genius" (Hall xi), eliciting some of Beatrice's most important annotations. Seager is "willing to believe" that Roethke brought the Michigan State episode upon himself and that he was so driven to find "a new place to stand, a new way of looking at things" he was "willing to abuse his body to refresh his spirit" (105). Beatrice does not respond directly to anything in this paragraph, but at the start of the next paragraph when Seager writes, "Since, in Ted's individual case, there were obvious strains and pressures, both inner and outer, that preceded the later episodes …" (106), Beatrice simply challenges, "examples?," that one word casting doubt on the entire passage.

Two pages later, Seager considers that Roethke might have viewed hospital stays as a respite, writing, "It is conceivable that after a stretch of hard work at poetry or a period of domestic or social strain, he wanted a vacation, that a hospital or sanitarium where he would be taken care of by strangers to whom he owed nothing, where he could take off his mask, where he could be utterly irresponsible, looked good to him" (108). Beatrice vigorously denies this claim, writing, "He fought like hell to stay <u>out</u> of hospitals. Ran away on 2 occasions during our marriage." Later, when Seager writes, "Thus the Albany episode might be regarded not as an interruption in his life but perhaps as a spur to a new psychic synthesis of Ted's creative energies" (288), Beatrice responds, "Rubbish!" And when Seager claims that "Ted always said, 'I'm at my best when I'm slightly depressed'" (108), she responds, "Oh yeah?"

Beatrice also adds some details that make Seager's hospital descriptions more vivid. In 1953, the first year Roethke and Beatrice were married, Beatrice experienced Roethke having an episode for the first time. In the margin next to Seager's recounting of the event (220), she writes, "This hospitalization still vivid to me. Sheer terror—disappeared, phone calls, sleeplessness, bought me a blue Buick convertible!" When Seager concludes with, "However, it was not a serious episode," Beatrice writes, "Yes, it was! He was far from 'right' when he emerged," and continues, "but the worst was before and during time at Columbus Hospital; a Catholic institution. Parties, nude in corridor (I was told)." In a passage describing another hospitalization in 1957, Beatrice clarifies not only that was he taken to Harborview Hospital but that he was "put in restraints" (246). Three years later, they were visiting Ireland when another episode came on. Seager simply writes, "Ted realized he was getting ill and he wanted treatment. He entered Ballinasloe, a hospital not far from Galway" (267). It sounds very calm, almost routine by this point. Beatrice's experience was quite different, more frantic: "I took him to hospital in a priest's VW with the *garda* on our heels. It had been called by the Inishbofin priest—got to Cleggan Pier just as we left!"

At one point in the biography, Seager notes a "curious" entry from Roethke's journal: "Why do I wish for an illness, something I can get my teeth into" (142). He mentions it just after discussing an incident in the fall of 1945 when the parent of a Bennington student claimed Roethke had proposed to her daughter. The

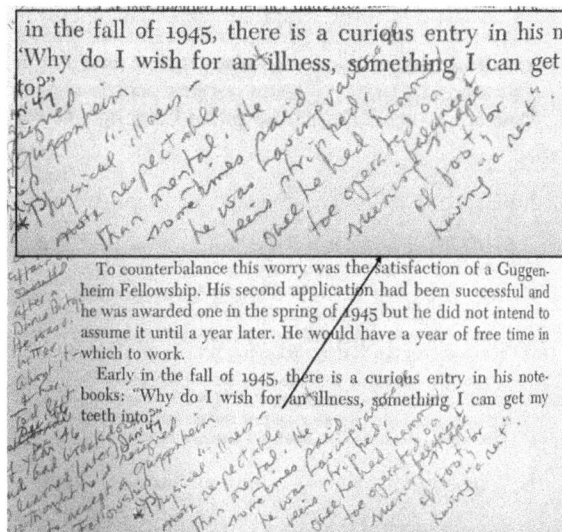

Figure 4. Marginalia by Beatrice Roethke on p. 142 of *The Glass House*. Photograph by Madeline Bruessow, 2022.

president decided not to rehire Roethke because of it. The quote from Roethke was written in his notebook at about the same time, but Seager does not otherwise elaborate on why he includes this quote here. He seems to be supporting his earlier claim that Roethke wanted to be hospitalized as a way to relieve stress. However, Beatrice clarifies that he means "'Physical' illness—~~more~~ respectable than mental. He sometimes said he was having varicose veins stripped. Once he had hammer toe operated on" (see Figure 4). In the context of Beatrice's other comment, it seems less likely that he is wishing for an illness as an excuse to go to hospital for a vacation, and more logical that he is longing to swap the bipolar disorder with something concrete, easily understandable, and socially acceptable as an ailment. Her comment points to the stigma around mental illness during Roethke's time and its profound effect on his life.

On Roethke's Hometown and Family

Beatrice helps us better understand Roethke's feelings about having grown up in the small town of Saginaw, Michigan. Seager describes Roethke's complex feelings towards Saginaw and suggests a disdain for—and even shame of—his hometown. Seager writes, "Who was he, a Saginaw Valley boy, the son of an immigrant greenhouse-keeper, to aspire to the grandeur of writing poetry?" (180). Beatrice counters this by stating Roethke did not look down on or feel ashamed of Saginaw, attributing such views to Seager's own biases. She writes, "This seems very unlike Ted."

Later, in "The Prizes, the Awards," Seager notes that rage appears often enough in Roethke's work to be considered one of his "poetic moods" (222). Seager speculates that this stems, in part, from "his angry stupefaction when he discovered that the greenhouse and the field where he had played happily as a child lay in a setting as banal and inimical as Saginaw …" (222). Beatrice responds without ambiguity: "He did not look down on or feel ashamed of Saginaw, in my opinion. This is Seager's view of provincial Mich[igan] town." Seager's portrayal of Roethke as someone plagued by self-doubt and imposter syndrome due to his Saginaw roots is an important point of contention for Beatrice. She dismisses this characterization, arguing that it is not reflective of Roethke's true sentiments.

Beatrice makes it clear that Roethke was not ashamed of where he came from, and she even points out that "Ted's mother approved of his being a poet— no mention of this in entire biog[raphy]" (126). However, she does note his wish for some secrecy surrounding his relationship with his mother and sister, particularly regarding his health. Speaking of Roethke's connections with his family, Seager writes, "One thing that emerges from this incident is the relations of the Roethke family one to another. They were always, each of them, trying to spare the others" (120). Beatrice corrects Seager here, claiming, "I am not sure they always want secrets kept, 'tho Ted did NOT want his mother + sister to know when he was having a breakdown," indicating that Roethke intentionally concealed his mental health struggles from his immediate family. This concealment suggests a man who, despite his public bravado, was deeply concerned with maintaining a certain image for his family.

Additionally, Seager makes statements regarding writer Katherine (Kitty) Stokes, close friend to Roethke and the Roethke family, claiming, "Kitty sent a night letter to Saginaw which would reach Ted's mother the next morning" (120). Beatrice elaborates on Seager's claims, writing, "Much later Typical / June R. would tell Kitty not to tell me she'd broken her femur, or been to look at my parents [sic] house in Va, but K.S. would tell me. I am not sure they always want secrets kept." This suggests a pattern of selective information-sharing within the family. These quotes also illustrate a familial culture of secrecy that likely influenced Roethke's own habits of concealment and disclosure. This intricate web of secrecy and selective honesty within his family adds another dimension to Roethke's identity, complicating the narrative of his public and private lives.

Conclusion

The Glass House is the seminal book about Roethke's life. Roethke scholars have been influenced by it, and Seager's claims have taken root as the definitive story of Roethke's life. Edward Hirsch writes in his own Roethke biography that Roethke was an "extremist of the imagination" and that "he purposefully seemed to disorder his senses." He cites Seager's anecdote of Roethke telling Beatrice his "first episode had been self-induced 'to reach a new level of reality'" (Hirsch xvii). William Barillas invokes Seager in his essay "House, Field, Stones, and Stars: An Introduction" when he writes, "Seager suggests that Roethke partly brought [manic episodes] on himself in a search for mystical insight and dopetic expression" (6). And Seager appears more subtly in pieces like John Rohrkemper's analysis of Roethke's poem "Root Cellar." Here, Rohrkemper echoes Seager's sentiments when he suggests, "Roethke felt that his creativity was intricately tied to the demons of his own mental illness" and that "the mature poet's realization that his creativity, the procreative energy of his imagination, might arise from the terrifying energy of his illness" (80). One must wonder: How would these scholars' interpretations change had they read Beatrice's reactions to a text from which she was undeniably excluded by the author?

Reading Beatrice's annotations alongside Seager's biography raises questions about many parts of Roethke's life that readers currently take for granted. This article discusses just a few of these parts, including the nature of Roethke's mental state, his self-confidence, and his family. But Beatrice addresses many more. Her annotations prompt a deeper contemplation of what defined Roethke's identity, and more broadly what defines any writer's identity. How do public perception, personal relationships, and the texts one creates shape one's legacy? For Theodore Roethke, his identity appears to be a mosaic of these elements, continuously evolving as new facets of his life and work are examined. Beatrice Roethke's annotations in *The Glass House* provide a personal, nuanced perspective on her husband's life and legacy. Her insights ask readers and scholars of Roethke to challenge Seager's interpretations and may allow Roethke scholars to shed new light on Roethke's multifaceted identity.

Saginaw Valley State University

Notes

1. Our initial research on this artifact was funded in 2022 by the Saginaw Valley State University Undergraduate Research Program.

2. The remaining 5% are attributed to notes in which Beatrice added a mark such as an underline or brackets, or she rewrote a word from the text, but did not include any explanatory text.

3. The almost 300 handwritten comments provide a high level of confidence in the transcription accuracy. All comments were reviewed multiple times and by both authors, and the final transcriptions discussed in this essay reflect Beatrice's exact words, punctuation, and capitalization. Illegible words are noted as such.

Works Cited

Barillas, William. "House, Field, Stones, and Stars: An Introduction." *A Field Guide to the Poetry of Theodore Roethke*, edited by William Barillas, Ohio UP, 2021, pp. 1–27.

Hall, Donald. Introduction. *The Glass House: The Life of Theodore Roethke*, by Allan Seager, U of Michigan P, 2011, pp. ix–xiv.

Hirsch, Edward. Introduction. *Theodore Roethke: Selected Poems*, edited by Edward Hirsch, The Library of America, 2005, pp. xii–xxv.

Roethke, Beatrice. Annotations in *The Glass House: The Life of Theodore Roethke*, by Allan Seager, 1968, U of Michigan P, 1994. Beatrice Roethke Papers, Saginaw Valley State University, Zahnow Library, Special Collections.

———. Letter to June Roethke. 30 Apr. 1967. The Friends of Theodore Roethke Collection, Saginaw, MI.

———. Letter to June Roethke. 26 Sept. 1967. The Friends of Theodore Roethke Collection, Saginaw, MI.

Rohrkemper, John. "All the Small, Unlovely Things: 'Root Cellar.'" *A Field Guide to the Poetry of Theodore Roethke*, edited by William Barillas, Ohio UP, 2021, pp. 78–82.

Seager, Allan. *The Glass House: The Life of Theodore Roethke*. 1968. U of Michigan P, 2011.

Marcie R. Rendon's Cash Blackbear Crime-Fiction Series and Nordic Settler Colonial Legacies in Minnesota's Red River Valley

Rosemary Erickson Johnsen

That Indians have been living in, been shaped by, and in turn have shaped the modern world [is] news to most people…. Indians are not little ghosts in living color, stippling the landscape of the past and popping up in the present only to admonish contemporary Americans to behave.
—David Treuer (Leech Lake Ojibwe), The Heartbeat of Wounded Knee

Marcie R. Rendon (White Earth Ojibwe) sets her Renee "Cash" Blackbear crime-fiction series in the Red River Valley of the 1970s, a strategic choice of setting and genre to illuminate complex entanglements such as those of settler colonialism and its legacies during a period of national attention to civil rights. As 19-year-old Cash moves among the sugar beet fields, Minnesota's public university at Moorhead, pool-table dive bars in Fargo, North Dakota, and area reservations to investigate crimes, the region's settler colonial descendants are pushed to the margins of the action. The socioeconomic agenda they set for the region is still visible, but seen through a different lens, one that foregrounds Native populations.

Rendon is an accomplished writer of drama, poetry, and children's literature, and her publication record reflects her continuing productivity in multiple genres. Her Cash Blackbear crime-fiction series launched with *Murder on the Red River* in 2017, followed by *Girl Gone Missing* (2019) and *Sinister Graves* (2022), with the fourth series entry, *Broken Fields*, scheduled for release in 2025. In Rendon's hands, the criminal investigative core of the genre brings to life Indigenous history in the Red River Valley of Minnesota and North Dakota from her young Indigenous protagonist's perspective, and in so doing illuminates historical continuities into the late twentieth and early twenty-first centuries. Not only does her series portray the important presence of the region's tribal nations, but it also offers a different historical narrative. As Cassandra Krauss observes, "North American history, told from a settler-colonizer point of view, absolves itself from violence, instances of the same reduced to exceptions, reactions necessary to protect and promote freedom and democracy" (204).

Because crime fiction calls for a way of reading that is attentive to detail—anything might be a potential clue—it puts its own spin on the purpose and value of historical knowledge as the plots unfold. Cash's process of investigation melds Indigenous forms of knowing with traditional crime-fiction sleuthing, and the interplay of civic and legal jurisdictions thematizes the ongoing struggles over the land and its assets. The crime plots reward attention as individual, fictional examples of structural injustices that have permeated the region's history, and Cash brings to life the Indigenous assertion of reality offered in my essay's epigraph.

The Red River Valley

In her contribution to *Concurrent Imaginaries, Postcolonial Worlds*, Gunlög Fur asks, "what if place is the holder or owner of history instead of, or at least alongside, people? It would make historians rethink borders and agency, advancing metaphors of leaching and metamorphosis rather than progress and development" (48). The Red River Valley (RRV) setting of the Cash Blackbear series is particularly ripe for such an approach, and Rendon offers a sophisticated understanding of the region. Cash Blackbear's investigations illuminate borders—not only geographical, but also jurisdictional, both types of which overlap in different ways—and the challenges of agency for a young Indigenous woman in the RRV of the 1970s.

Some historical context for Rendon's presentation of the RRV helps explain the basis for these geographical and jurisdictional borders. The Ojibwe bands of the western Great Lakes region migrated westward from Atlantic coastal regions and settled in the upper Midwest, a process completed by the seventeenth century. For a couple of centuries after they had settled, the Ojibwe in the RRV were primarily trappers and traders. The RRV, not technically a valley because it is not deep enough, has rich black soil due to its origin as the lakebed of the ancient Lake Agassiz. The economic potential of this fertile soil would change the region's landscape and population dramatically, as it is "particularly well suit-ed for farming, unlike the sandy uplands to the east and west. Between 1849 and 1850, before Minnesota statehood, Zachary Taylor resolved to open up the area to settlement," and two treaties with the Pembina and Red Lake Bands of Ojibwe were signed ceding Indian rights to the RRV in 1863 and 1864 (Treuer 258). Relevant to the RRV is the fact that while most of the Ojibwe had settled in the forested lake areas of present-day Minnesota, "some had continued pushing farther west and wound up in the Red River valley [which] was a buffer zone of sorts between the rest of the Ojibwe and the Dakota, whom the Ojibwe had gradually pushed into the Plains" (Treuer 258).

This "buffer zone" created as a border bears an unexpected resemblance to the border-seeking habits of the nineteenth-century Nordic immigrants who came to present-day Minnesota and North Dakota for land. The RRV's white settlers came mainly from Norway and from French-speaking Canada. The Norwegian immigrants, in particular, prioritized economic and ethnocentric motivations in their settlement patterns, as noted by historian Odd Lovoll's book *Norwegians on the Prairie*. "More than other Nordic groups, Norwegians sought land on the farthest edge of settlement," Lovoll observes, where "their rural communities were regularly based on old-country localism and cen-tered on the Lutheran church" (75). Similarly, Caitlin Sackrison explains that "though many Norwegians had left their family farm and land behind in Nor-way, they sought to recreate that connection to the land in Minnesota" (3). These tendencies extended into decisions about national citizenship, with concomitant issues created regarding legal jurisdictions. In Bodil Stenseth's study of the Muus case in late nineteenth-century Minnesota, for example, in addition to ethnocentricity and adherence to Norwegian Lutheranism, the feuding couple's decades-long maintenance of their Norwegian citizenship raised jurisdictional questions about whether "Norwegian or American law should apply" to their litigation over Oline Muus's inheritance (238).[1] The cultural tenacity of this immigrant group is explored in crime fiction by the twentieth-century Norwegian-American Minnesota writer Mabel Hodnefield Seeley (1903–1991).[2] Seeley published novels set in Minnesota for several decades beginning in the late 1930s, and her characters' relation to the world of work and real property are inextricably connected to their immigrant status. As S. L. Clark observes, Seeley "sees the Midwest as providing a rich ethnic heritage coupled with an upwardly mobile economic sensitivity" (31). While Seeley was largely silent on the Indigenous communities supplanted by real and/or fictional Norwegian-Americans, the Norwegian combination of priorities named by Clark are viewed from a different perspective in Rendon's crime fiction.

Rendon infuses her crime fiction with accurate and assured historical knowledge, and nearly every point she makes about the region from its geological formation to the series' present time can be confirmed and explored further by readers interested in learning more. The first Cash book opens with two sections entitled "Fargo, the North Dakota Side of the Red River" and "Moorhead, the Minnesota Side of the Red River." The novel's opening is rich in atmosphere and scene; it is also factual on the region's geography and agricultural character. Fargo encompasses her rented efficiency apartment, her local pool-shooting bar, and casual lover Jim Jenson; it introduces Cash herself, the Scandinavian locals, and the ever-present backdrop of the Vietnam conflict. On the Minnesota side, readers learn about the farming economy and Cash's personal history and current farm-laborer work. Cash's unofficial investigation must contend with multi-jurisdictional policing: the first murder is committed in Sheriff Wheaton's County, but because the victim was a member of the Red Lake band, federal agents must be called in and yet another jurisdictional complication arises later when the perpetrators are discovered to be Canadian.

The novel's opening is an extraordinary introduction to the region, the series, and Cash: economical, informative, effective. The RRV is brought to life with details chosen to foreground the crime fiction ahead. In *Murder on the Red River*, driving north out of Moorhead, Cash

> loved the vast expanse of farmland in either direction. Fields of wheat or oats stood waiting to be combined. Potatoes still in the ground. Hay-fields plowed under, straight black furrows from one end of a field to another, the Red River tree line a green snake heading north. The leaves giving just a hint of fall colors. She remembered someone telling her that the river was used to send furs north to Hudson Bay in Canada in the early 1800s. Once the area was opened for homesteading, the plains on either side of the river filled with Scandinavian immigrants, felling trees and marveling at the rich topsoil. Some became the richest farm-ers in America, usually the ones who hired on folks like Cash. Others struggled, barely making ends meet with the harsh winters, springtime floods and short growing season. (16–17)

Rendon's evocation is immensely satisfying to those who know the region, and as the series develops she introduces readers to more of its locations. Her investigations take her to the region's three Ojibwe reservations of Red Lake, Leech Lake, and White Earth. *Sinister Graves*, the third novel, opens with a bundled-up Cash in a fishing boat piloted by Al, presumed by Cash to be Na-tive and a Vietnam veteran. They are heading to Ada because Sheriff Whea-ton has called Cash to look at a woman's body that has floated in on the flood waters. "The spring flood covered the Valley as far to the east and west as she could see," and Cash thinks that "the prehistoric, glacial Lake Agassiz existed once again" (1).

In *Girl Gone Missing*, the second series title, Cash's first-ever trip to the Twin Cities becomes a historical, geological, geographical, agricultural, and economic tour. As the two cars head east, Cash, now a first-year student at the college in Moorhead, is not thinking about the honors she and the other students are going to be awarded; characteristically, she is wondering if the Grain Exchange that issues the daily farm market report "is an actual building" (181). Tracing their route through flat farmland, rolling hills, grazing cattle, the ridge of ancient Lake Agassiz, sandy soil with boulders emerging from the thawing soil each spring, they finally reach Minneapolis before crossing the Mississippi River into St. Paul to their destination (181–89). Cash finds the urban, private college campus of Macalester "more regal than the Moorhead State campus" and notes "well-dressed students" with fewer hippies to be seen (189). The rural contingent, all white males apart from Cash, has ideas about what to see in the Cities before their return to the RRV: an adult bookstore, the zoo, the Cathedral in St. Paul. Cash says she wants to see the Grain Exchange, not even knowing if it exists as a physical site. The college boys, who visited it with their Junior Future Farmers of America group, give her the location. She drives over on the Saturday night of their visit. She finds the Grain Exchange "beautiful" (203) and is thrilled to see from where the radio-report numbers come, linking the farmers in the fields with reality "outside of the Valley" (204).

Almost an afterthought, killing time after her visit to the Grain Exchange, she remembers the American Indian advisor on campus "saying something about the AIM [American Indian Movement] office being in downtown St. Paul in some church" (209). Following her recollection, she happens upon a post-meeting departure; noting the laughter among them and the "beat-up cars" they get into in pairs or groups of three and four, her attention is riveted by Long Braids, a man she had met in Bemidji. Over the course of the series, Cash's indifference to the nascent organization will begin to erode, but her attitude to AIM at this time is more realistic than an enthusiastic embrace of its mission would be. As Treuer notes, "the early founders of AIM—mostly Ojibwe in Minneapolis" were inspired to organize by racist conditions manifested in Minneapolis's Franklin corridor (296–97). For Cash, however, any relation to the Twin Cities is abstract. She speaks as a true midwestern provincial in discovering the "Metropolis was real" (202) while standing on the corner of 4th Street and 4th Avenue gazing upon the Grain Exchange.

Regional Crime Fiction

To address Rendon's series as regional within the genre of crime fiction, the most effective definition remains the categorization of regional crime fiction developed by Hans Bertens and Theo D'haen in *Contemporary American Crime Fiction*. Their model focuses on "authenticity" of settings that "are introduced for their own sake, to the point where they have a claim on the reader's interest that is wholly independent from the plot that they support" (66). An essential component, fully realized by Rendon's series, is that to create "a representation that will strike us as authentic, [the author] must invest emotion in the picture that she conjures up" (Bertens 68). In addition to the emotional attachment to the region displayed throughout the series, Rendon's anti-colonial themes manifest—and evoke—emotions that are supported in a different register through Rendon's author's notes in each book.

Maureen Reddy's critique of "cultural tour guide" (169) positioning in Hillerman and other white authors who write crime fiction about Native Americans[3] offers a way to see how effective, in contrast, are Rendon's regional commitments. Any tour-guide orientation appears in Rendon's crime fiction not as a patronizing approach to "the locals," but about the RRV itself, the place and the cultures it grounds, and it is never condescending. Where contextual explanations are developed within the novels, these are most often about the agricultural economy, the landscape, or weather features, an orientation suggesting something about Rendon's multiple intended readerships.

Consistent with the anti-colonial themes of her work, Rendon's "regional tourism" frequently addresses the theme of labor. Cash is connected to the land of the RRV. So are the Valley farmers and laborers whom she describes, and so too are the seasonal Mexican migrant workers (who come with families) and the Native seasonal laborers (who come alone). They know the land because they work on it. "The town folks made fun of the farmers who would stand around in the fields, tamping dirt clods down with their work shoes, chewing a strand of straw of ditch grass, scanning the horizon" (MRR 36), Cash knows. She also knows that "each of them heard the land, felt the rhythm of the seasons. That tamping of dirt clods said how dry the fields were, told them when to pray in church for rain or for god to send the clouds away" (36). Equally taciturn are the Native farm laborers who arrive in the late summer and early fall to drive grain and beet trucks: "When they did speak, they spoke Ojibwe to each other in voices barely heard" (37), but they relied extensively on "a body language so subtle it left some folks thinking the Indians could read each other's minds. Which wasn't unheard of either" (38). These communication styles are distinctive but bonded under a shared ethos of work. All those who work on the land, regardless of the racial or ethnic community to which they belong, are marked off from those who do not, like the town folks or the "smooth"-handed farmer Milt Wang, whose attire is more costume than work clothes (195). These concurrences and distinctions are among the ways Rendon's Valley illustrates how "regional crime writing presents an organic view of society" (Bertens and D'haen 75).

Extrapolating from Reddy's observations that "Hillerman's books are not written for American Indians although they are about them" and that "given the extensive anthropological descriptions in each novel, it is clear that Hillerman assumes a white audience" (170), one could say that Rendon is writing for an audience that does not know the RRV. While such an audience certainly outnumbers those who do know the region, Rendon is also mindful of the readers who will feel the accuracy of her depiction or call out any errors. Her commitment to anti-colonial themes means she does not want to alienate regional audiences while she engages national ones. Rendon also addresses audiences with differing racial and ethnic identities. Reddy argues that "conceiving of white audiences as marginal would certainly push the boundaries of the genre in a way that white-authored crime fiction about people of color currently avoids" (171). Rendon's books treat the local Scandinavian-dominated white culture from an outsider's perspective. Cash's Indigenous perspective has the effect of what Reddy describes as "placing white readers in the position of eavesdroppers, their consciousness not central but marginal" (Reddy 171). Reddy calls for "reverse discourse" as resistance to re-inscribing the racially coded conventions of the genre, and Rendon's series enacts that kind of resistance but goes beyond a binary reversal. Within the model afforded by concurrences theory, one sees that Rendon resists, and also builds, through a regional identification. "By foregrounding the space in which encounters occur," Gunlög Fur argues, "concurrent histories would need to take into account the different, at times conflicting, stories that dwell in that land. If land is the bearer of histories, it might not be restricted to ethnicities, or certain modes of thought, but might instead open up possibilities of interpretation and learning by all who cross the terrain and are willing to engage with its various layers" (54). Rendon's midwestern regional crime fiction, set in a pivotal historical period for Indigenous activism, gazes both retrospectively and potentially.

Indigenous Perspectives on Settler Colonialism

Relationship to the land, and to working the land, are of prime importance in thinking about colonial legacies. James H. Cox references Rendon's work briefly on the final page of his study on American Indian literary history, writing that the first Cash series book "looks back to the Red Power era, too, with its focus on a young White Earth woman raised in abusive foster homes but on her own as the calendar turns to 1970" (212). Rendon, notably, specifically emphasizes the land-based *economic* abuse of Cash as a Native foster child: she offers labor to be exploited in a mockery of the family structures that underpin area farming. Cash's very name underscores this theme: "Cash had been working as a farm laborer since she was eleven, when one of her foster mothers … decided she couldn't stand the sight of Cash [and] banished Cash to the fields to work with the men" (MRR 18). There, Cash adapts to the conditions of her banishment to the fields and in some ways even makes it her own:

> When the farm boys teased her about being a girl working with the men and asked why she was driving tractor instead of canning pickled beets, she would always reply, "I need the cash." … By the end of beet hauling season that first year, Renee Blackbear was forgotten and Cash was

the girl-kid farm laborer all the men knew. After a season in the fields, Cash decided there was no way she was going back to washing dishes, canning food and dusting ceramic trinkets from *the old world*. (19–20, italics in original)

As Cash learns to work with the men to create adaptations for tasks for which she is too small—such as wooden extensions so her feet can reach the pedals—she forges relationships, including her passionate bond with the land itself. Being sent to the fields is partly intended as a gender-based humiliation, but Cash prefers working on the land to the housekeeping chores allotted to girls. Her dismissal of those domestic tasks also rejects the backward-looking cultural heritage values they embody. Seeley's mid-century crime novels convey the inside view of Norwegian-American heritage in material and social realms, with townsfolk agog over the "absolutely authentic Norwegian settler" (*Whispering Cup* 23) furniture and other belongings owned by one of the murder victims. By turning these objects into mere "ceramic trinkets," Rendon adds another grace note to the hypocrisy of the settler descendants who take the land here while glorifying the place they left behind.

Cash understands the vital role of inheritance in perpetuating the injustice of the original settler land taking, an assurance of its extension generationally. Her casual relationship with married white farmer Jim Jenson blows hot and cold as she alternatively ignores or resents his complicity in the system that disenfranchises the Native population. Jim, she knows, "wasn't that many years older than her but he would inherit acres from his daddy's farm. Acres given free to his immigrant granddaddy. Probably stolen from her granddaddy. No matter how much she loved this Valley, no one was going to give her a homestead, not after they'd already stolen it from her. In that moment, she hated his whiteness" (MRR 121). By midcentury, what Odd Lovoll calls "segregated Norwegian American farming communities" (12) found their economic and ethnic power under pressure. Insofar as these powers could be kept alive in the isolated small towns of Minnesota, they did so in the face of enormous pressure away from traditional settler values and toward assimilation. These conditions reinforced the primacy of the generational landownership following the settlers' land grab, and Rendon's 1970s setting reflects the Nordic settler culture's insistence on retaining both ethnic-identified privilege and inheritance of the land itself.

Inheritance perpetuates the original land-taking of the nineteenth century. Rendon's Cash novels do not just reveal how the sustained exploitation of Native children contributes to the economic viability of these farms; they go beyond labor to look at examples of how these children—especially male children—can be disinherited again, personally. As adopted sons, both Cash's brother and her mentor Sheriff Wheaton are encouraged to work for what they believe will one day be theirs, given different names, and then cut adrift in adulthood on a pretext to preserve the property for white biological children. Inheritance is bestowed and then withdrawn, both steps enacted within the legal system. Cash's brother Mo, once Fred Blackbear, has become Paul Sivertson. A Vietnam veteran, the name on his fatigues suggests he is a member of the Scandinavian settler population, but he is doubly disconnected from his legal name. His adoptive family "told everyone in church I was their kid. *Just like one of theirs*. Shit" (79, italics in original). He worked on the farm as a member of the family, inheritance promised to him. Within a couple of weeks of his return from Vietnam, however, he is summarily ejected from the family home and told to "never come back" (79). He understands clearly that this rejection means not only a personal break, but the loss of the promised land inheritance as well. When Sheriff Wheaton learns about Cash's brother and his experiences, he shares his own tale of being the illegitimate child of a Cree woman from Canada. He too was adopted by a white family and subsequently disinherited, also after a return from military service, in his case, in Korea. Rendon's author's note says this pattern of coming-of-age disinheritance of Native youth, while difficult to quantify because of sealed adoption records, "is a common story throughout Indian country" (GGM 305). The role of inheritance in perpetuating the landgrab across the generations is shown to be not an inevitable consequence of land ownership, but yet another tool of the settlers' descendants to exploit and disenfranchise the Indigenous population again.

Conclusion

In a 2024 feature on Minnesota crime novelists published by the *Star Tribune* of Minneapolis, readers were shown the appeal of Marcie Rendon's Cash Blackbear series. Engaging and evocative of place, Rendon's series is also deeply serious, reflecting her commitments to what scholars would recognize as decolonization. Alongside a charming photo of Rendon, the feature conveys her message:

> [Rendon] does believe land can be haunted by its past, a theme emphasized by echoes of genocide in her first mystery, "Murder on the Red River." "I think there are places where the land carries memory. And there are places where that memory isn't good," said Rendon, when asked about historical trauma that lingers in lands stolen from Indigenous people.... Her detective, [Cash] Blackbear, uses those kind of inklings to solve cases, often rooted in Minnesota history. (Hewitt)

An award-winning writer in multiple genres, Rendon has always been adept at leveraging the potential of each genre to illuminate her themes. The fictional crimes provide insight into the real-world challenges faced by Native communities in the region (and beyond), and Rendon leverages the potential of crime fiction for social commentary propelled by suspenseful plots.

Concurrence theory's recognition that "people can live their lives in different temporalities and in different spaces, sometimes simultaneously" (Fur 46) can be read as an implicit call to reach across boundaries. Each book in the series includes an author's note that provides context and, in so doing, emphasizes the realism of the crimes Cash investigates. Rendon's notes sometimes convey the pure scale of the exploitation, abuse, or killing; she also cites specific examples that corroborate the validity of her fictional portrayals. For example, in the author's note to *Girl Gone Missing*, she names two Indigenous women, Tina Fontaine and Savanah Greywind, who were murdered and dumped in the Red River of the North in the 2010s, a naming also found in her contribution to *Down to the River* (190). In her standalone crime novel *Where Last They Saw Her*, Rendon's protagonist Quill belongs to a Native community, and the book shows that community participating in organized public activism, reflecting ties to the Canadian Red Dress movement and other grassroots initiatives focusing on this issue.[4] Rendon's author's note in *Girl Gone Missing* makes explicit how she is consciously using her crime fiction "to honor all missing, murdered and unwanted women" (304). She addresses readers directly to express her hope that readers will be more aware, that they will "search farther for truths once [they] have read this story" (GGM 305). This midwestern region has a settler colonial past that will continue to color its present, but Rendon uses crime fiction to hope for a more generous future: "It is my hope," she writes, "that you also see how generous Cash is in her rescue of girls who are different from her. I hope you see the resilience that inhabits us as Native people. Miigwetch" (GGM 305).

Rendon's choice of the crime-fiction genre expands her audiences and taps into the power of popular culture not only to reflect but to influence culture. In July 2024, the University of Minnesota Press published Rendon's *Anishinaabe Songs for a New Millennium*, a volume of dream-songs and poem-songs that "carries the Anishinaabe way of life forward in the world" (jacket copy). Readers of Cash are an obvious crossover market for this book, given Cash's growth in harnessing her own visions and the introduction of tribal elder Jonesey in *Sinister Graves* to guide her. Rendon's standalone crime novel *Where They Last Saw Her*, featuring a Native woman investigating the disappearance of women from the fictional Red Pine reservation in the Duluth area, was published by Bantam and given substantial marketing. This level of promotion recognizes and leverages Rendon's success and will create new readers for the Cash Blackbear series, including the fourth book, *Broken Fields* (2025). Minnesota, from the Red River Valley across the reservations and the lakes over to the port city of Duluth and the civic and commercial hub of the Twin Cities, will become familiar to a whole host of new readers through Rendon's work.

University of Minnesota Crookston

Notes

1. Oline Muus, born in 1838, immigrated to Minnesota with her husband in 1859 and spent the rest of her life in the United States. As late as 1906, however, she had neither applied for US citizenship nor adopted English as her primary language. Stenseth notes that in 1906 Muus "may have still considered herself Norwegian" (302).

2. Scholars interested in a fuller treatment of Seeley's use of Minnesota's Norwegian-American culture and folklore may consult my article "Mabel Seeley's Intermodernist Crime Fiction" (Johnsen).

3. In *Murder on the Reservation: American Indian Crime Fiction*, Ray Browne appears to endorse "an economical and comfortable form of geographical and cultural tourism, traveling to exotic societies and observing strange people and getting to know something about both the society and the people" (5) without distinguishing between Native and white authors. White authors writing Native-focused crime fiction is a matter of significance to Rendon and other Native authors. While few would say that no white author can portray Native characters, it is surprising to find crime fiction scholarship that does not make the distinction clearly, such as a 2023 article in *Clues: A Journal of Detection* by Elizabeth Abele holding aloft Craig Johnson's Longmire series.

4. In *Where They Last Saw Her*, Rendon writes, "It is a present-day, on-the-edge-of-trauma reality. Today, #mmiw and variations of that hashtag (such as #mmiwg and #mmip) signal solidarity, in order to gain attention for and stop this crisis. The red handprint, usually across the face, is another symbol utilized. Red paint, red dresses, red ribbons—red because it is believed to be the one color that spirits can see" (306).

Works Cited

Abele, Elizabeth. "From Alexie's *Indian Killer* to Johnson's Longmire Series: Expanding the Landscape of the American Indian Detective Novel." *Clues*, vol. 41, no. 2, 2023, pp. 31–42.

Bertens, Hans, and Theo D'haen. *Contemporary American Crime Fiction*. Palgrave Macmillan, 2001. Crime Files Series.

Browne, Ray B. *Murder on the Reservation: American Indian Crime Fiction*. U of Wisconsin P, 2004.

Clark, S. L. "A Sense of Property: Midwest and Money in the Novels of Mabel Seeley." *The Great Lakes Review*, vol. 6, no. 1, summer 1979, pp. 24–36.

Cox, James H. *The Political Arrays of American Indian Literary History*. U of Minnesota P, 2019.

Fur, Gunlög. "Concurrences as a Methodology for Discerning Concurrent Histories." *Concurrent Imaginaries, Postcolonial Worlds: Toward Revised Histories*, edited by Diana Brydon, Peter Forsgren, and Gunlög Fur, Brill, 2017, pp. 33–57.

Hewitt, Chris. "Land of 10,000 Maniacs: Why Minnesota Produces So Many Top Mystery Writers." *Minnesota Star Tribune*, 15 Jan. 2024, www.startribune.com/land-of-10000-maniacs-why-minnesota-produces-so-many-top-mystery-writers/600334979.

Johnsen, Rosemary Erickson. "Mabel Seeley's Intermodernist Crime Fiction." *The Space Between: Literature and Culture 1914–1945*, vol. 19, 2023, scalar.usc.edu/works/the-space-between-literature-and-culture-1914-1945/vol19_2023_johnsen.

Krauss, Cassandra. "War and Violence: Reading David Treuer's *Prudence* as Indigenous Historical Novel." *Transmotion*, vol. 7, no. 1, 2021, pp. 197–220. doi.org/10.22024/UniKent/03/tm.931.

Lovoll, Odd S. *Norwegians on the Prairie: Ethnicity and the Development of the Country Town*. Minnesota Historical Society Press, 2006.

Reddy, Maureen T. *Traces, Codes, and Clues: Reading Race in Crime Fiction*. Rutgers UP, 2003.

Rendon, Marcie R. *Anishinaabe Songs for a New Millennium*. U Minnesota P, 2024.

———. *Broken Fields*. Soho, 2025. (scheduled release March 2025)

———. *Girl Gone Missing*. 2019. Soho, 2021.

———. *Murder on the Red River*. 2017. Soho, 2021.

———. *Sinister Graves*. Soho, 2022.

———. "Tonight Wasn't Her Night to Die." *Down to the River*, edited by Tim O'Mara, Down & Out Books, 2019, pp. 183–90.

———. *Where They Last Saw Her*. Bantam, 2024.

Sackrison, Caitlin. "Space of Belonging: The History of Land Rights for Norwegian-American Women in Southern Minnesota." Presentation. Society for the Advancement of Scandinavian Study Annual Meeting, Virtual, 6–7 May, 2021.

Seeley, Mabel. *The Whispering Cup*. Grosset and Dunlap, 1940.

Stenseth, Bodil. *Muus vs. Muus: The Scandal That Shook Norwegian America*. Translated by Kari Lie Dorer and Torild Homstad, Minnesota Historical Society Press, 2024.

Treuer, David. *The Heartbeat of Wounded Knee: Native America from 1890 to the Present*. Riverhead Books, 2019.

Green People in Dingess, Roberts, and Gieni's Manifest Destiny: Flora and Fauna

Alexandria Remm

In the first volume of Chris Dingess, Matthew Roberts, and Owen Gieni's graphic novel series *Manifest Destiny,* Captain Meriwether Lewis and Second Lieutenant William Clark are haunted by a green specter and accompanied by another. The Green Man and the Green Woman, recurring figures in Western literature and folklore, appear in different forms in the first volume, *Flora and Fauna*: an evil plant-zombie entity that attacks humans and an Indigenous woman who has an ambivalent relationship with nature and the white soldiers of the expedition. The Green People's reactions to Lewis and Clark's westward progress are a direct response to an expedition meant to domesticate and conquer the land and its inhabitants. Drawing on ecocritical scholarship, I argue that the Green People in *Flora and Fauna* are a critique of actual American policies of colonial expansion. While the figures are presented in the graphic novel as evil obstacles that must be overcome by Lewis and Clark, they are also champions of both nature and Indigenous peoples displaced and traumatized by enactments of Manifest Destiny.

Manifest Destiny: Flora and Fauna highlights themes related to the ideology of the Midwest. The continuing series, which began in 2019, follows the fictionalized adventures of the real-life explorers Lewis and Clark as they map the western United States and clear it of monsters after the Louisiana Purchase of 1803, which doubled the size of the United States and included modern-day New Orleans and the land between the Mississippi River and the Rocky Mountains. The comic series begins at St. Louis when the explorers spot a vegetal arch—a clear connection to the modern-day arch in St. Louis except it is made by nature and not man—and continues westward along Lewis and Clark's historical route (Dingess, Roberts, and Gieni 5). Set in a time before the "Midwest" and the "West," the series nevertheless recognizes St. Louis as the entry point to westward expansion.

Heike Paul argues in *The Myths That Made America* that the American West is based on two concepts: agrarianism and expansionism (314). It was in the name of "agrarianism" that notable politicians like President Thomas Jefferson commissioned the Corps of Discovery Expedition (Paul 315). According to Richard Hofstadter in *The Age of Reform*, "The American mind was raised upon a sentimental attachment to rural living and upon a series of notions about rural people and rural life ... Its hero was the yeoman farmer," who was the perfect citizen (23). The agrarian farmer and the pastoral landscape he tended was a convenient ideology for the actual possession of land and the displacement of the Indigenous population. Discussing the political implications of the expedition, Paul reiterates, "the winning of the West was above all a process of taking possession" to claim the territory as American (321).

Within the first few pages of *Flora and Fauna*, the true purpose of Lewis and Clark's expedition in this fictional rendering of American expansionism is revealed: destroying all the monsters that cross their path and clearing the way for others to follow and claim the land. President Jefferson warns Lewis and Clark about the dangers ahead of them, but Lewis does not initially believe the president, remarking in the first few pages that he and his men have encountered only "birds, small game and Indians," instead of what the President insists would happen: "the Corps would be tasked with destroying monsters and clearing the way for expansion of our United States" (2–3). After the men investigate the vegetal arch at St. Louis, though, they meet their first monster: a humanoid minotaur, or "Buffalotaur," as coined by Clark (16–19, 26). The monsters of the series—including the Buffalotaur—nature, and eventually the Green People challenge American expansionism.

American expansionism was believed to be a God-given right to head west and cleanse the land of anything not American. During westward expansion, buffalo or bison were almost brought to extinction after millions were slaughtered in the High Plains region (Corstorphine 126). Instead of the settlers as the hunters, the roles are reversed in *Flora and Fauna*: the Buffalotaurs chase and hunt the white settlers. The Buffalotaurs' hostility toward the explorers is similar to the Green People's resistance to American expansionism. Although history shows that settlers believed they had a right to cleanse the area and claim the land for the United States, the idea of Manifest Destiny was not an agreed upon policy in the nineteenth century (Isenberg and Richards 14). Later, historians would credit John L. Sullivan for creating the term. Sullivan's belief that the United States had a divine right to claim the western territories as part of the nation was considered, at the time, politically extreme (Isenberg and Richards 6), but Manifest Destiny became a central reality of American policy, specifically for those living in the West who were not deemed "American." *Manifest Destiny* critiques this American policy by using ecocritical themes to depict the often-violent taming of the frontier, with the Green People as the prominent resisters in the first volume, *Flora and Fauna.*

Origins of the Green People

At the most basic, visual level, the Green Man is usually a human-vegetation hybrid, but he takes on many forms and cultural meanings in Western literature and folklore. Lady Raglan coined the term "Green Man" in 1939 as she examined the possible applications of the Green Man for Christian and pagan people in medieval Europe (50). Carved into Christian architecture like cathedrals and churches throughout Europe between the twelfth and sixteenth centuries, the Green Man was typically represented as a face with foliage surrounding it that sometimes entered the face's eyes or mouth (Keetley 2). It is unknown how the Green Man became a symbol in medieval Christian architecture, but some folklorists believe "it symbolized mythic rebirth and regeneration, and thus became linked to Christian iconography of resurrection" (Windling 9). Complicating this theory, Jeremy Harte points out that, more commonly, the Green Man in early Christian and pagan depictions was a symbol of the forest to warn people of possible dangers. The Green Man was dangerous because "a face glimpsed among the leaves might be a robber or rapist" or even a nonhuman forest fairy hungry for sex and violence (Harte 6). Whether the Green Man is considered good or bad, these depictions capture human's reactions to nature. The people of the medieval era might have been more attuned to nature and the landscape than people in the twenty-first century, but this does not mean that nature was seen as a positive force. Nature was scary and unknown. Yet, as Negus explores, medieval people merged their faith, whether Christian or pagan, with nature to represent their culture (2–7). The merging of faith with nature often created confusing and contradictory meanings that represented a hopeful message connected to resurrection and everlasting life while simultaneously being used to represent danger.

Green Man scholars Bob Curran and Gary Varner are quick to connect the Green Man to feminine figures like the Queen of the May on May Day and with Mother Nature (Mother Earth). Curran even connects the Green Man to ancient female carvings like the sheela-na-gig of Ireland and the Woman of Willendorf of Austria (30). Carvings like the Woman of Willendorf are seen as symbols celebrating and promoting female fertility in which there is a clear "reference to the sexual nature of the figure and its connections with birth and child-rearing" (Curran 30). Birth and life are connected to one of the original functions of the Green Man in Christian architecture by representing the Judeo-Christian ideas about resurrection and rebirth. The Green Woman tradition ties in with renewal and birth, even if the differences between these ideas remain biologically tied to their sex. The Green Woman narrative lends itself to the same origins as the Green Man—pagan beliefs merging into Christianity. If the Green Man began from examples like the Jack in the Green, it seems reasonable to assume that the Green Woman also began from pagan sculptures like the sheela-na-gig. Yet, the connection between these figures and the Green Woman extends beyond life-giving motifs and similar origins, because there is a connection between the Green Woman and nature. The depictions of Green Woman are also interpretations of how humans depict nature and its relationship to human beings.

Although Green People have been studied extensively by folklorists, they may be best understood in contemporary literary criticism through the recent field of ecohorror, which combines theories of the gothic/horror and ecocriticism. The Green Man and Green Woman take many forms throughout Western cultures and time periods, but there is one characteristic that remains the same—Green People fall into the literary category of the uncanny. The uncanny is a common gothic trope usually revealing itself as a humanoid figure. Sigmund Freud explores the psychological reaction to human-like creatures in his article "The Uncanny." Freud explains that the uncanny typically "arouses dread and creeping horror … it tends to coincide with whatever excited dread" (1). The uncanny encompasses the familiar or the known, which is why dolls, automatons, ghosts, and other human-like beings fall under this uncanny category—there is nothing older and more familiar than human beings to other humans (Freud 2). Ecocritical readings of the gothic uncanny explore the uneasy relationship between humans and nature, in the case of Green People, how they tap into cultural fears and reflect human's relationship with nature.

Dawn Keetley explains the vegetal uncanny in "Introduction: Six Theses on Plant Horror; or, Why Are Plants Horrifying?" from *Plant Horror* (2016). The uncanny extends beyond human-likeness, she argues, because in Western sentiment humans are "like plants" (16). Keetley explains the importance of the relationship between humans and nature by remarking that although perceived as uncanny, plants reflect our *own* nature, suggesting "alternative ways of being that challenge the inevitability of (human) being" (9). For Gary Farnell, talking plants are the primary cause of plant horror, because words express desire, a concept humans typically associate only with other humans (180). Green People's ability to speak in *Flora and Fauna* reveals that the plants have a desire and consciousness, even if the intention behind the desire is unclear. With these qualities, plants have the potential to erase the rational mind, and in extension, human society and culture. Keetley remarks on the Green Man in *Manifest Destiny: Flora and Fauna*, "This monster … thoroughly breaches the boundaries of the human body: it enters from the outside, takes over the inside, and then surges from the inside back out—colonizing where it moves" (25). Keetley sees this monster as plants claiming its human carrier, "challenging us to recognize our constitutive oneness with the vegetal" and eventually returning to the earth in death (25). Rather than seeing the Green Man as a means to humans' eventual end, however, my argument sees the Green Man as a response to the historical colonization of America. The plant becomes seen and known with the intention to enact its revenge by colonizing the colonizers. The commonality in these arguments is the use of the uncanny in portraying a vegetal-human hybrid. By using the Green Man narrative to respond to a historical event, *Flora and Fauna* reminds humans how past decisions impact the earth, the creatures living in the landscape, and the cultures lost.

The Green Man in Flora and Fauna

In *Flora and Fauna*, the Green Man avenges the natural world in the face of American western expansion by protecting nature and the surrounding landscape. This Green Man is capable of outsmarting and outmaneuvering humans to protect nature from possible trauma and American imperialism, especially as a response to Manifest Destiny and the exploitation of not only the landscape but also the Indigenous population. In that respect, *Flora and Fauna* incorporates a common trope of ecohorror. Mainstream awareness of the landscape's exploitation might have begun in the United States with Rachel Carson's *Silent Spring* (1962), which brings awareness to the ways human beings were abusing the natural world through pesticides and other harmful chemicals. As Carson explains in *Silent Spring*, specifically in the chapter "Nature Fights Back," "nature is not so easily molded and … [even] the insects are finding ways to circumvent our chemical attacks on them" (245). The creation of the United States was made possible through the exclusion and condemnation of everything not American with the intention "to tame and control the wilderness" (130). Since nature is repressed and oppressed by humans (Keetley 19), "Nature becomes an avenging force" (Smith and Hughes 11). This depiction of nature fighting back against humans' ecological threats, in fact, is *the* central trope of ecohorror.

As an uncanny representative for both human beings and nature, the Green People in *Flora and Fauna* fight back against human advancements and aggression. In one scene, the Buffalotaur creatures work with nature, or the Green

Man, to enclose Lewis and Clark's men in the epidemic-touched settlement of La Charrette. Nature, the reader finds out, has created a disease that turns humans and other animals into vegetal zombies. Closing the doors of the fort, the expedition quickly discovers the settlement seems to be abandoned: "Not a soul. Utterly deserted" (41). Without knowing how correct his gut feeling is, Lewis utters, "Maybe they all took sick. Plague or something" (42). After spotting movement through the church's window, the group enters and discovers a group of Green People, who are covered with vines, grass, roots, and a slime-like substance (Figure 1). Their eyes are green, and their skin is missing or falling off

Figure 1. Green People at the Settlement of La Charrette, panel from Dingess, Roberts, and Gieni, *Manifest Destiny, Vol. 1: Flora and Fauna,* p. 44.

their bodies, showing that their flesh has been replaced with green vegetation. They are unable to speak but chase the men out of the church before the explorers turn around and defend themselves. One of the soldiers, Sergeant Floyd, battles a Green Man who vomits green sludge on Floyd's face and torso while its vines try to enter his eyes—imagery similar to the medieval Green Man whose eyes are overrun with vines and greenery (51–53). When Clark spears the Green Man through the chest and lights him on fire, he discovers the Green People are all connected as a one living organism, like a network of moss or fungus: "They all feel the burn. As though they're of a collective conscience" (54). A collective plant-conscience plotting against humans.

Instead of being the ones who dominate nature as Manifest Destiny suggests, the explorers are overcome by the forces of nature. Not only does nature in the form of a zombie-plant fight back in this graphic novel, but it also seems to want to dominate and destroy human life. When Sergeant Floyd is injured, he mutates into a walking zombie-plant, gurgling to his former fellow soldiers, "We … Want You … All of you!!" (86; Figure 2). The use of plural pronouns here confirms the zombie-plants are connected symbiotically and can communicate as one, communal entity to protect and preserve the surrounding landscape from human aggression and colonialism. Because Sergeant Floyd was an

Figure 2. Sergeant Floyd, panel from Dingess, Roberts, and Gieni, *Manifest Destiny, Vol. 1: Flora and Fauna,* p. 86.

official member of the group of explorers completing a mission sanctioned by the President of the United States, his takeover by the green entity is an attack on the United States.

The supernatural, or liminal space, created in *Manifest Destiny: Flora and Fauna* presents the possibility that flora and fauna have a consciousness that mirrors human consciousness—a key ecocritical response to nature and how humans see themselves reflected in and as a part of nature. Farnell's argument about talking plants and their desire acknowledges the possibility of plant consciousness as it magnifies their ability not only to talk about humans but also to plot an attack against them (180). Humans are left to wonder, "What do plants want … from us?" (Farnell 181). In *Flora and Fauna*, plants want human bodies, the entity using human bodies, without the humans' consent or knowledge, as vessels to enact vengeance upon other human beings who are moving westward to conquer not only the Indigenous population but also the landscape, non-human beings, and vegetation. The green entity in *Flora and Fauna* represents a conception of consciousness that challenges both an anthrocentric understanding of consciousness and American conceptions of agrarian individualism. If midwestern and western identities are connected to the yeoman farmer taming and tending to the earth in an egalitarian society—or the idyllic symbol of American progress—then turning potential yeoman farmers into zombie-like plants represents a rejection of Manifest Destiny and American individualism. Further, nature's ability to turn humans into Green People not only stops their supposedly God-ordained progress across the West but also mirrors the United States' attempt to possess and tame the land through expansionism. In other words, nature colonizes the Lewis and Clark expedition (and other human settlements) to check their forward progress.

Like the medieval Green Man, who is sometimes represented as a benevolent entity and sometimes as a demon, the Green Man in *Flora and Fauna* is a complex figure. In fact, he is represented as *both* a savior and a demon. As Sergeant Floyd loses himself to the plant virus, for example, one of the men exclaims, "What the devil?!" when he pulls the skin from Sergeant Floyd's arm only to reveal green leaves and vines instead of red human muscles and veins (84). Floyd's former comrades kill him to stop the green entity from turning the rest of the men into plant-zombies, acting in accordance with their mission. The visual symbolism of this murder connects the incident to the crucifixion of Christ, however. In the image, which takes up an entire page, or splash page, the Green Man / Floyd is splayed on the ground as the men impale him at the wrists and ankles, as in the crucifixion (88; Figure 3). The invocation of this Christian imagery suggests the soldiers of this American expedition are simultaneously saviors and crucifiers as they purge the area of the evil plant-like zombies. Because the Green Man poses a legitimate threat to the expedition, the soldiers'

Figure 3. The Crucified Green Man / Sergeant Floyd, panel from Dingess, Roberts, and Gieni, *Manifest Destiny, Vol. 1: Flora and Fauna*, p. 88.

actions seem justified, as did the divine calling of Manifest Destiny to many nineteenth-century Americans. Yet, the image also portrays the possibility that the Green Man is a divine figure who will resurrect and be reborn, ultimately triumphing over his persecutors.

The Green Woman in Flora and Fauna

Although women are few in *Flora and Fauna*, the expedition encounters two examples of the Green Woman, one a white woman and the other an Indigenous woman. Both of these women have an ambivalent relationship with the landscape.

In the first encounter, as the expedition approaches La Charrette by boat, the men admire a naked woman standing at the top of a cliff, one man noting as they behold her, "She's beautiful" (29; Figure 4). From a distance, they cannot see many details, except for green, glowing eyes and the fact that she is naked. The men debate whether she is native to the area, but one of them notes, "She's blond, you idiot" and must therefore be a member of a European settlement or at the very least of Anglo-European descent (29). Although the men witness her plunge to the ground below, they find only a patch of moss on the ground in the shape of a human form. The novel does not confirm the woman's identity, but it seems likely she is one of the Green People from La Charrette.

On one hand, this example of the Green Woman serves as a reminder that women were part of the western story of expansion. As the cultural myths surrounding the Midwest grew to include cowboys, ranchers, and gunslingers, white women were either forgotten or seen as one of three archetypes: the helper, the schoolteacher, or the prostitute (Paul 327). The Midwest became synonymous with masculinity as the male figure serving as colonist, farmer, settler, and cultivator over a virgin land (Paul 329). Amid the male-centered expedition, this unknown female reminds readers that white women were part of American progress, even if they have faded into the background of history. On the other hand, the woman's fate is ambiguous. Does she throw herself off the cliff to avoid turning fully into a Green Woman or does she dive into the earth, becoming one

Figure 4. La Charrette Green Woman, detail from Dingess, Roberts, and Gieni, *Manifest Destiny, Vol. 1: Flora and Fauna*, Green Woman, p. 29.

with it? The woman's body becoming one with the land after her demise ties to the feminization of the landscape. As Annette Kolodny points out, the land is "essentially feminine—that is, not simply the land as mother, but the land as woman" (4). Dingess, Roberts, and Gieni at once give recognition to the pioneer woman moving westward alongside men while also remarking on the Midwest as a feminine landscape to be conquered.

Sacagawea, the other Green Woman in *Flora and Fauna*, is caught in a liminal space, both representing the Indigenous population and becoming a part of the explorers' clan and an agent of colonialism. The white men undermine her physical prowess and knowledge of the area, referring to her as a helpless child.

The explorers' desire to protect her is laughable, however, because she is more than capable of protecting herself and is arguably more qualified to lead the expedition than either Lewis or Clark. The white explorers underestimate her, though, as they do the landscape that fights back against their conquest. Clark asks, "What chance does a young, delicate girl stand" against the monsters lurking outside their camp? (Dingess, Roberts, and Gieni 64). While the explorers are wasting their time worrying about her safety, Sacagawea kills the entire band of Buffalotaur creatures—and accomplishes this feat while pregnant. The image of Sacagawea attacking an unsuspecting monster takes up a splash page of the graphic novel (64; Figure 5). This page dedicated to Sacagawea is meant to demonstrate her power and ferocity over the creatures—the same creatures who terrified, attacked, and chased the white explorers. She does not look delicate, young, or helpless, and certainly does not look like a child. Powerful muscles are seen in her arms, abdomen, and thighs while she wields a spear and carries a sword on her hip. This complicates her presence in the landscape as a liminal character moving between two different paths—one as an Indigenous person and one as someone helping the white explorers in their conquest of the land.

Sacagawea represents a form of Green Woman or Wild Woman for several reasons, the first being her connection to fertility, especially since it is discovered that she is pregnant. Varner explains that the importance of the carved Green Woman is her fertility and connection to life: "These carvings of female human-plant beings are symbolic of our link to nature in its primitive and innocent beauty and Mother Earth's life-giving force" (143). The second reason is her connection to the land and the creatures that reside in it. The Green Woman and the Wild Woman are akin to the Indigenous population who are close, and sometimes even considered one, with nature. I am using the tradition surrounding the Green Man as a philosophical idea of nature and human beings in considering Sacagawea a member of the same rich narrative. However, Sacagawea's presence in the graphic novel as an Indigenous representative lends itself to the imperialist idea that the Indigenous people were merely an insignificant part of

Figure 5. Sacagawea
Attacking a minotaur,
Dingess, Roberts, and
Gieni, *Manifest Destiny,
Vol. 1: Flora and Fauna,*
p. 64.

the landscape. Greg Garrard explains that "Indians have historically been re-duced to a mere feature in the pastoral landscape" (61). Sacagawea is caught between being human and being a part of nature. For the white explorers, she is a part of the landscape more than she is human.

As an example of a Green Woman, Sacagawea plays a vital role in demon-strating how Manifest Destiny affected the Indigenous population. Obsessed with her exoticism, Mister Jensen—one of the criminals on the expedition—hypersexualizes her. He remarks, "I'd like to have me a taste of that. Look at her hair. You know they say a squaw's cunny hair is just like the hair on top of her head? Long and straight" (Dingess, Roberts, and Gieni 80). According to Gar-rard, Indigenous women were often represented by white cultures as either "ide-alised 'noble savages' or as savages pure and simple" and, as mentioned earlier, a discernible feature of the pastoral landscape (61). Jensen's remarks about her physical appearance reveal that she is considered a savage amongst the explorers and demonstrate how she is dehumanized by them as they sexualize her appear-ance and define her as exotic. Their reaction to Sacagawea's appearance is a stark contrast to their reaction upon seeing the blond woman standing on the cliff's edge, despite the blond woman's likely willingness to destroy them and their ex-pedition. By hypersexualizing and dehumanizing Sacagawea, she is victimized along with other Indigenous populations whose culture and heritage were nega-tively impacted or destroyed during Manifest Destiny.

Just as Sergeant Floyd is a complex Green Man, Sacagawea is a complex Green Woman. Although she acts as a guide for Lewis and Clark's expedition, she also helps them in their conquest of the landscape. This ambiguity could stem from the white perspective of gender roles and gender expectations in a gender binary system. For Sacagawea, the concept of gender might not have the same meaning. Lisa Wade and Myra Marx Ferree argue, "More than one hun-dred American Indian tribes recognized or recognize people who are simulta-neously masculine and feminine" (12). Similar to humans imposing meaning onto nature, gender has different meanings depending on the human culture. The gender norms of American Indigenous populations were different from those of white Europeans'. For instance, the expectation for white women from a European background was to be a nurturing presence and mother while domes-ticating the land and not for them to defend and protect (Paul 327). Thus, the representation of Sacagawea as a warrior Others her in the minds of the white American explorers. The visual representation of her as a fairy-like creature with wings supports this Othering. On one hand, settlers could not have "tamed" the West without help from the Indigenous people. On the other hand, even though she is closer to nature than the explorers, she does not necessarily share a kinship with the supernatural creatures of the landscape, such as the Buffalotaurs.

The examples of Green People in *Flora and Fauna* are full of ambivalent and often contradictory meaning. Kolodny points out that American expansion turned the land into a feminine landscape that was attacked and brutalized by the settlers and explorers moving westward across the landscape, but the Green Man as a masculine protector is perceived as evil rather than a benevolent defender in the comic series (6). Both examples of the Green Woman in the volume are uneasily tied to the landscape. The blond-haired Green Woman perhaps takes her own life before she can succumb to a vegetal state, thus rejecting this association. Sacagawea, however, simultaneously helps the explorers make the landscape feminine by taming it and demonstrates that feminine agency is untameable, regardless of the white explorers' view of it as exotic and Other.

Conclusion

In his famous 1893 lecture "The Significance of the Frontier in American History," Frederick Jackson Turner argues that the struggle between the wilderness and civilization defines American identity. "The wilderness masters the colonists," he writes. "[A]t the frontier the environment is at first too strong for the man" (2). This is exactly the struggle depicted in *Flora and Fauna*, as the members of the fictional Lewis and Clark expedition encounter mythological and (super)natural monsters. The Green Man and Green Woman examples in the first volume of *Manifest Destiny, Flora and Fauna*, reflect on a historical event that changed the fabric of a continent and its habitants. Using the ecogothic trope of nature fighting back against humans, the volume provides an ambivalent picture of the beginning moments of the United States' expansion westward of the Mississippi River.

Central Community College, Grand Island

Works Cited

Carson, Rachel. *Silent Spring*, introduction by Linda Lear and afterword by Edward O. Wilson. Mariner Books, 2002.

Corstorphine, Kevin. "'The Blank Darkness Outside': Ambrose Pierce and the Wilderness Gothic at the End of the Frontier." *Ecogothic*, edited by Andrew Smith and William Hughes, Manchester UP, 2015, pp. 120–33.

Curran, Bob. *Walking with the Green Man: Father of the Forest, Spirit of Nature.* The Career Press, 2007.

Dingess, Chris, Matthew Roberts, and Owen Gieni. *Manifest Destiny Volume 1: Flora & Fauna.* Image Comics, 2014.

Farnell, Gary. "What Do Plants Want?" *Plant Horror: Approaches to the Monstrous Vegetal in Fiction and Film,* edited by Dawn Keetley and Angela Tenga, Palgrave McMillan, 2016, pp. 179–96. Doi: 10.1057/978-1-137-57063-5_10.

Freud, Sigmund. "The Uncanny." First published in *Imago,* Bd. V., reprinted in Sammlung, Fünfte Folge, translated by Alix Strachey, 1919, pp. 1–21.

Garrard, Greg. *Ecocriticism.* 2nd ed. Routledge, 2012.

Harte, Jeremy. *The Green Man.* Pitkin Guides: Jarrold Publishing, 2002.

Hofstadter, Richard. *The Age of Reform: From Bryan to F.D.R.* Vintage, 1955.

Isenberg, Andrew C., and Thomas Richards, Jr. "Alternative Wests." *Pacific Historical Review,* vol. 86, no. 1, Feb. 2017, pp. 4–17. *JSTOR,* www.jstor.org/stable/10.2307/26419725.

Keetley, Dawn. "Introduction: Six Theses on Plant Horror; or, Why Are Plants Horrifying?" *Plant Horror: Approaches to the Monstrous Vegetal in Fiction and Film,* edited by Dawn Keetley and Angela Tenga, Palgrave McMillan, 2016, pp. 1–30. Doi: 10.1057/978-1-137-57063-5_10.

Kolodny, Annette. *The Lay of the Land: Metaphor as Experience and History in American Life and Letters.* U of North Carolina P, 1975.

Negus, Tina. "Medieval Foliate Heads: A Photographic Study of Green Men and Green Beasts in Britain." *Folklore,* vol. 114, no. 2, Aug. 2003, pp. 247–61. Doi: 10.1080/0015587032000104248.

Paul, Heike. *The Myths That Made America: An Introduction to American Studies.* Transcript Verlag, 2014.

Raglan, Lady. "The 'Green Man' in Church Architecture." *Folklore,* vol. 50, no. 1, Mar. 1939, pp. 45–57.

Smith, Andrew and William Hughes. "Introduction: Defining the ecoGothic." *Ecogothic,* edited by Andrew Smith and William Hughes, Manchester UP, 2015, pp. 120–33.

Turner, Frederick Jackson. "The Significance of the Frontier in American History," pp. 1–9, 1893. nationalhumanitiescenter.org/pds/gilded/empire/text1/turner.pdf. 1 Sept. 2024.

Varner, Gary R. *The Mythic Forest, the Green Man and the Spirit of Nature: The Re-Emergence of the Spirit of Nature from Ancient Times into Modern Society.* Algora Publishing, 2006.

Wade, Lisa, and Myra Marx Ferree. *Gender: Ideas, Interactions, Institutions.* W. W. Norton & Company, 2015.

Windling, Terri. "Introduction: About the Green Man and Other Forest Lore." *The Green Man: Tales from the Mythic Forests,* edited by Ellen Datlow and Terri Windling with introduction by Terri Windling, Open Road Integrated Media, 2002/2020, pp. 9–12. *Hoopla,* hoopladigital.com/play/12743841.

Review Essay

Two New Books on Hemingway

Michael Schupska

Beall, John. *Hemingway's Art of Revision: The Making of the Short Fiction.* Louisiana State University Press, 2024. 310 pp.

Daiker, Donald A. *Hemingway's Earliest Heroes: Nick Adams & Jake Barnes.* Innovative Ink Publishing, 2024. 346 pp.

At this point, one might question the utility or relevance of yet another manuscript study of one of American literature's most famous—really infamous—and most studied authors. When the work of scholars like Michael Reynolds, Debra Moddelmog, and Hilary Justice exists, is another manuscript study of Ernest Hemingway's work truly necessary, and would such a text meaningfully contribute to a field that is so colossal in size that it is, as David Faris points out in his book, an "industry" unto itself? Despite the potential for redundancy and stagnation, John Beall's new book, *Hemingway's Art of Revision: The Making of the Short Fiction*, proves without question that manuscript study is still a relevant approach. Moreover, Beall, with a penchant for brief flashes of artistic flair and a keen eye for detail, offers several novel and illuminating observations that meaningfully contribute to the discourse. Similarly, Donald Daiker's latest edited collection of articles and book chapters, *Hemingway's Earliest Heroes: Nick Adams & Jake Barnes*, demonstrates the continued importance of close reading. These two new contributions to the field of Hemingway studies are welcome additions that offer a broad perspective.

As Beall expresses in his introduction, "The value of manuscript study is to trace the writer's creation of his work of art—to 'reconstruct an author's process of composition'" (2). Indeed, Beall demonstrates this value in his method of pri marily close reading early drafts and manuscripts of Hemingway's short fiction. These close readings are occasionally interspersed with references to personal letters from Hemingway and various correspondences from his direct influences, such as Gertrude Stein, Ezra Pound, and James Joyce. However, what truly distinguishes Beall's approach is a specific focus on the *additions* that Hemingway makes over the course of several drafts as opposed to what he removes or edits out. Almost as mythologized as his hyper-masculine persona, Hemingway's "Iceberg Theory" of omission has proven to dominate the discourse of Hemingway manuscript study. This is perhaps epitomized by the countless number of scholars who have contended with the cut original ending of "Big Two Hearted River," such as Debra Moddelmog's analysis in her *American Literature* article "The Unifying Consciousness of a Divided Conscience: Nick Adams as Author of *In Our Time.*" Although Beall himself addresses the cut ending in his chapter on Hemingway's revisions to "Big Two Hearted River," he contends that we can learn as much about these texts by focusing on the things Hemingway added to the manuscripts. Thus, although it is tempting to cursorily dismiss or subordinate such an approach to more theoretical methodologies, Beall's brand of textual criticism is distinct enough to warrant its inclusion in the literature, and it stands as a potential model for future textual scholarship of Hemingway's work.

Although each chapter specifically focuses on the evolution of drafts and the various additions made across them, other analytic trends are apparent, especially in the early chapters. Specifically, the first two chapters focus intently on the impact of Hemingway's earliest mentors and influences, perhaps most notably James Joyce. However, with respect to Hemingway's earliest work—the Paris *in our time* vignettes—the primary influence is undeniably Ezra Pound. Beall references a number of personal letters in his analysis, particularly one from Hemingway to Pound that strongly suggests Pound's influence. In this letter, Hemingway seems to both accept and lightly challenge editorial suggestions. The original draft of the Maera chapter from *in our time*, for example, was in first-person, and it additionally included dialogue, all of which was stripped from subsequent drafts. Perhaps on the advice of Pound, Hemingway "struck out the repetition of Maera's hyperbolic and sentimental complaints and replaced them with the third-person narrator's matter-of-fact understatements" (17).

A shift in perspective from first to third (and sometimes vice versa), in addition to adding significant lines of dialogue, would indeed become a trend in Hemingway's process, as many other stories—including "Cat in the Rain" and "Big Two Hearted River" from *In Our Time*—would change perspective over subsequent drafts. Again, Pound was a key influence on Hemingway's early revisions for "Cat." In a stylistic sense, Beall argues that the "presence of Stein and Joyce" (46) is palpably felt when observing Hemingway's revisions over multiple drafts. For instance, Hemingway revised the opening paragraph to feature a series of "concatenated repetitions" that mirror a motion commonly utilized by Joyce and Stein. However, as opposed to using repetition to imply or enhance an erotic tone (which is how Beall argues it is typically used in Stein's and Joyce's work), Hemingway uses these repetitions to convey the static and cold nature of a stagnated relationship that lacks physical affection. Similar to "Cat," "Big Two Hearted River" underwent a massive shift in perspective. Originally, the story depicted a group of men, not just Nick alone, venturing into the woods and rivers of Michigan to fish for trout. Moreover, Hemingway added a number of scenes that, in Beall's estimation, do as much to define and refine the story's themes as the famous cuts, such as the removal of the original ending of "Big Two Hearted River." In a later draft of "Now I Lay Me," Hemingway added several key details that implicitly connect it to "Big Two Hearted River." Thus, a crucial part of Hemingway's revision process in the later Nick stories was adding details that either refine perspective or implicitly connect the later Nick stories that appear in *Men Without Women* and *Winner Take Nothing* to the earlier Nick stories in *In Our Time*.

Beall appropriately concludes his study with "Fathers and Sons," yet another story that transformed significantly over time. Much has already been made of the various titles that Hemingway attempted to attach to the story in early drafts, perhaps most notably the semi-late draft titled, "Tomb of My Grandfather." However, Beall undertakes the arduous task of combing through *all* of the various drafts and manuscripts of the story, including some untitled early fragments. Like many of his other stories, Hemingway began the earliest draft of "Fathers and Sons" in first-person and then refined it over time to a close third. What is immediately clear upon a cursory glance at this early draft is that Hemingway already had all the key components; the conversation between an older Nick and his son, Nick's memories of his eagle-eyed father, his early sexual experience with a young Ojibwe woman, and the awkward conversations about sex between a young Nick and his father are all present. However, as the drafts evolved over time, Hemingway both added and removed details related to Nick's parents' marriage and shifted Nick's ire over time from his mother in early drafts to his father in the "Tomb of My Grandfather" draft.

On the subject of Nick's parents, perhaps no scholar has more scrupulously engaged with the subject than Donald Daiker. His new book, a collection of previously published book chapters and articles that focus generally on the early Hemingway stand-in characters Nick Adams and Jake Barnes, is a testament to Daiker's lasting career as a Hemingway scholar and teacher. A sharp attentiveness to small details that—once Daiker unveils their importance—prove to be key factors that alter readings of Hemingway's work is a consistent feature of his scholarship. An example of Daiker's particularly sensitive exegesis is when he demonstrates the reasonable explanation for Doctor Adams's "failure" to bring proper medical equipment for the crude cesarean he performs on an Ojibwe woman in "Indian Camp" by pointing out that the reference to St. Ignace indicates that "the Adamses are not at home near a cottage on Walloon Lake; they are on a camping and fishing trip to a remote lake in Michigan's Upper Peninsula" (3). In fact, in a number of chapters, Daiker critically engages with various scholars that, in his estimation, unfairly criticize Doctor Adams.

The book is organized into two parts, Part I focusing on Nick Adams and Part II on Jake Barnes. Although the articles in each section are related to the characters outlined in the organizational structure, some of the articles in each section veer slightly away from a singular focus on one of these two characters. For instance, the first two articles in Part I deal more directly with Nick's father than with Nick himself, and a number of articles in Part II deal more generally with *The Sun Also Rises* rather than Jake specifically. However, Daiker's style as both a writer and researcher maintains some sense of unity throughout the collection. In particular, Daiker's challenging tone when engaging in dialogue with other scholars is consistent from chapter to chapter. Another source of consistency is Daiker's attention to detail and keen eye for certain affirmative thematic qualities in some of Hemingway's fiction. For instance, his compelling argument for the inclusion of "Cross Country Snow" as one of Hemingway's best short stories is bolstered by his perceptive observation of the potential for metaphor in the mechanical operation of a funicular, due to its counterbalancing force being reflective of Nick's counterbalancing of the physical and social. According to Daiker, the "looming obligations of parenthood … enhance and perhaps even make possible the intense pleasures of the slopes and the inn" (137). In other words, the funicular car that Nick rides early in the story is perhaps a symbolic indication of the affirmative quality of the story.

As a result of Daiker's rigorous and sometimes even aggressive challenges to previous readings and analyses of Hemingway's work, scholars wishing to familiarize themselves with the field will find Daiker's book an excellent resource for quickly absorbing many of the major players and arguments in the field. In particular, I think "In Defense of Hemingway's Young Nick Adams," "In Defense of Hemingway's Dr. Adams," and "The Affirmative Conclusion of *The Sun Also Rises*" might be especially useful for scholars and students, as Daiker engages diligently with arguments from some of the field's most renowned scholars, such as Joseph Flora, Michael Reynolds, Debra Moddelmog, Mark Cirino, and Hilary Justice.

Taken together, these two new offerings to the field offer both an overview of the enduring history and promising future of Hemingway scholarship. Beall's textual scholarship and Daiker's exegesis, in tandem, offer an opportunity to acquire a significant depth of understanding of the field. This does not substitute for the plethora of intelligent, engrossing, and critically meticulous theoretical approaches that many scholars use to enrich our understanding of Hemingway's work. Indeed, ecocritical, feminist, psychoanalytical, postcolonial, and a number of other valid methodological approaches will certainly continue to make fascinating contributions to our understanding of Hemingway, and such approaches are, unfortunately, not provided here. However, Daiker and Beall might contend that an awareness of the author's composition process, biographical details, letters, and other self-writing, and close attention to detail are more than enough to offer insightful criticism. Indeed, both these texts are a testament to the effectiveness and utility of sensitive close reading backed by an intimate awareness of the history of the field.

University of Alabama

Review Essay

Floods, Fonts, and Waterways in Midwestern Poetry

Eleanor Reeds

Letcher, Kiara Nicole. *Oxblood*. Agape Editions, 2024. 112 pp.

Carson, Mary. *How to Baptize a Child in Flint, Michigan: Poems*. Persea Books, 2022. 80 pp.

Hamilton, Mark B. *Lake, River, Mountain*. Cornerstone Press, 2024. 78 pp.

———. *Upstream*. Finishing Line Press, 2024. 42 pp.

The recently published poetry featured in this review essay—Mary Carson's *How to Baptize a Child in Flint, Michigan*; Mark B. Hamilton's *Lake, River, Mountain* and *Upstream*; and Kiara Nicole Letcher's *Oxblood*—represent divergent trends in contemporary midwestern poetry as their authors learn to inhabit both barren cityscapes and fertile countryside, to draw power from as well as to doubt our geographical and other inheritances.

Kiara Nicole Letcher's first full-length collection, *Oxblood*, is the least explicitly midwestern of the examples I explore in this essay. As in her 2019 chapbook, *Scream Queen*, the "strangeness and melodrama" of Letcher's poems are inspired by horror (88): their settings are the film-set suburbs where wildness is barely kept at bay. Indeed, the speakers of these poems invite such wildness in, celebrating the emergence of what is hidden and the transfiguration of what appears unthreatening. The ocean we live so far from in the Midwest appears in *Oxblood* because it is within the woman whose voice weaves throughout the collection. Its "salt and cold" depths are "unforgiving," and the lover who is wanted with "intensity" and "desperation" retreats to avoid being drowned (48). No such fear motivates the speaker of these poems as she exclaims, "How will I get to the opulence without / wading waist deep in Oxblood?!" (47). The collection's title asks us insistently to link "all this red" (47). Cosmetic surfaces like a "deep plum stained lip" (5) show rather than conceal nature, which we are never allowed to forget is red in tooth and claw. "Period blood on silk nightgown" (68) is just one instance of Letcher's visceral and sensuous evocation of women's bodies throughout *Oxblood*.

While her publisher takes its name from the type of love Christians understand as charity, Letcher offers her readers eros in all its manifestations. There are the erotics of consumption in both its raw earthiness and contemporary commodification: the desire to "[e]at the entire fucking / pomegranate" (5) and to be drunk "like a fountain cherry cola" (6). There are the erotics of fertility, of fruitfulness in another sense: the "need to come undone" of "a mother in stunning pregnancy" (25). The pleasures of female appetite are enjoyed to rebuff guilt while gorging to excess becomes glamorous in these poems of birth and rebirth. Letcher's language becomes a sensuous feast for us to feel in our mouths. In "Cream Filled," for example, we are already feeling the rough sugar of a doughnut against our lips before we are asked to swirl our tongues around our teeth in the lines, "Lust fiend you are left / sin swollen wading waist high" (14). Words and phrases become animate beings we can see and touch in *Oxblood* as "strange X File creatures" emerge from the writer's mind, able to "scratch" and "sing … in hypnotic falsetto trill" (33).

Letcher's speaker is imperious and self-deprecating: her commands reveal her masochism as much as her sadism. She eats insults like cake in "Screwdriver" (62) and offers "a slice of unsolicited advice" in "He Left You in the Basement" (65). These poems are intensely personal lyrics that function as prayers, curses, riddles, and charms. They construct complex forms of intimacy with the addressed "you." They inhabit the intensity of a moment that is often marked—or, more aptly, bruised—by destruction or its potential. Letcher writes, "We are all just broken pieces of mountain / waiting to avalanche // I am on the lookout for thunder / perched over a high cliff waiting" (64). We are left on the precipice of a cacophonous descent, ready to be struck so that—already fragmented—we might fall with the speaker into an abyss, wreaking devastation on others as well as ourselves, obscuring all in our wake.

Most of the poems in *Oxblood* visually cluster along the left margin, but several briefer poems are centered while others experiment with reaching toward the right margin: most strikingly, in "Years of the Snake," the speaker insists we recognize the "courage" and "strength" to "strike / rather than slither … away" (41) as the lineation pulls our focus to the extreme right of the page, engaging us in the very struggle being described. Letcher usually works in free verse, opting for minimal punctuation, but occasionally she plays with the ritualistic aspects of fixed forms as in the villanelle "The Shame Language," which concludes, "I am not a fountain of temperance / I love being a woman / feminine like papaya / a dragon breathing fire" (77). How could temperance ever be a fountain? Traditional feminine virtues bely the feminine power to pour all forth.

Oxblood is a collection one can imagine placed on a modern witch's shrine next to the stack of tarot cards whose presence also makes itself known in the poems. Fittingly, the Ace of Cups—a vessel that overflows—appears in "Medicine" as the speaker struggles with racialized beauty standards (37). While some poems reveal an intense longing for reassurance amid the woes of contemporary dating, I was most struck by the depiction of frustration and fury in a long-term domestic relationship in "Lasagna," which reminded me of Taylor Swift's "tolerate it" (especially as performed in the Eras Tour). In this poem, the speaker is "burning from the inside" (58). Fire co-exists with water in the elemental vision of Letcher, whose speakers also seek transcendence: "Can I have both— // The fleshly physical and a form I cannot hold?" (4)

The final poem in *Oxblood* features the "Mother of Swords," who orders, "split me open" (81). Without negating the sexual overtones of such commands elsewhere in the collection, this bearer of weapons that can be used to cut her is a clear callback to the "[o]pen mother wound" in an earlier poem (25). The final poem of Sarah Carson's 2022 collection, *How to Baptize a Child in Flint, Michigan,* ends on a similar note:

Every day

women split

themselves

open

so that the future

can begin again. (51)

Addressing the poet's daughter, these closing lines represent the most powerful through line in *How to Baptize a Child in Flint, Michigan* as generations of maternal figures—"all the moms before … and beside" Carson's own mother and grandmothers who are recognized in the Acknowledgments (52)—persist in giving and sustaining life in the most unconducive of settings.

The collection's title—borrowed from Liv Larson Andrews—announces baldly the challenge of "living into the baptismal promise" (ix) for the residents of Flint, Michigan, with "[c]ity, city everywhere // & not a drop / to drink" (5). In a place now most famous for its toxic water supply, how can one even begin to offer a child the redemption and transformation symbolized by anointing them with liquid? While Carson confronts the endemic violence of a childhood spent in Flint as hers was, she also celebrates the many ways in which such care is very possible, including through language itself.

How to Baptize a Child in Flint, Michigan begins with a sense of dislocation and unhomeliness as "we" are not recognized by the people and objects that now populate the place in which we were raised: "now we are / the strangers" (2) who have learned they can never go home again. Flint remains, however, a deeply known place in these poems as Carson recalls childhood experiences to the soundtrack of box trucks and police interrogations. In two odes to "the City That Is Not My City," Flint looms larger as the ever-present point of comparison with the speaker's current locale. In the earlier ode, Flint is personified as a woman, relentlessly making "demands" and determined that "[n]o one leaves

/ for free" (18–19). Later, Flint becomes a mother—the speaker too has fallen pregnant and given birth as the collection unfolds—but this maternal figure is cruel and neglectful, taking without ever giving: "She'd leave the baby / in the pool // to finish a fight / in the street" (32).

Carson evokes the fear of becoming such an unfit mother, a mother who is a danger to her own child, in the directly preceding poem, which draws frightening examples from the headlines such as "MOTHER ARRAIGNED / IN DEATH OF FIVE-MONTH-OLD" (29). What is so terrifying about these sensational-ized Medea figures is that it is so easy to empathize with their "sopping wet sob-bing nights" (29) because all mothers experience them. Speaking to her young daughter, Carson wonders in vain at how she has avoided such a violent response and begs to be reassured, despite the literal and emotional proximity of "mother of / BEATEN 3-YEAR-OLD": "Promise me, love, // she is so, so different / than we" (31). This collection often includes such intensely personal wrestling with the knowledge that the poet whose work we are reading could very easily have become another casualty of poverty, crime, and the other social realities of her hometown. Carson does not shy away from the road not travelled, the place to which the poet might have gone but for the grace of God or the luck of chance.

The desire for intimacy, for shared knowledge, across generations structures many of these poems. Again addressing her daughter, Carson acknowledges her nostalgia might bemuse the younger generation and thus concludes a Buzz-feed-style "List of Things I Hope You'll Understand about Everyone I Knew in the 21st Century" with the intensity of a long-past moment in which we might dwell again as readers, "the living room curtains billowing, the phone ringing from somewhere deep inside the house" (36). Carson has a gift for colloquial and often witty titles: "Picking Up a Prescription for My Daughter at the Rite Aid That Replaced the Rite Aid Where My Mother Picked Up Prescriptions for Me" (37) is not only emblematic of the poem it names so fully but of many ele-ments in the wider collection. The chiasmus demonstrates the persistent cycle of shifting caring responsibilities across generations of women while also cap-turing how places evolve in limited and often repetitive ways.

Unsurprisingly for a collection that offers its poems as "prayers for the fullness of redemption" (ix), *How to Baptize a Child in Flint, Michigan* explores Christian principles, imagery, and narratives, especially in its depiction of familial relationships and generational obligations, including along gendered lines. The pregnant speaker contemplates her child's birth as a modern and therefore desolate nativity in which "Wise men trip an alarm / drunk on Godiva & rum" (24) and yet "you, little soul" restore our trust that "a star will / lead us home again" (26). The threat of gendered violence is cast in the terms of Eve's transgression as "what God says // about Adam's / rib bones" means that "it falls to girls // to pass the / warning" (22). Anticipating the birth of her own daughter, another girl to be warned, the speaker's language recalls her earlier description of her own mother who "held us / to her thigh as warning" (10). This mother was responsible for the speaker's religious education, but her own faith was specific and particular: "*This is my body* // is the only prayer / Momma ever believed" (11).

Conversely the speaker's brother—incarcerated for the murder of a young woman—adapts and teaches the principles of Christianity in very different ways: he offers "new commandments" on the playground as a child (7) and "swears / by the Sermon on the Mount" in prison (48). Carson's skepticism toward "Brother" and his religiosity is very pronounced by the end of the collection. Early on there is a mingled sense of concern and hope—"Brother has not covered / salvation yet" (8)—but the volta in "Brother Says in 1996, He Saw His Buddy Shoot a Girl" toward the conclusion of this collection transforms sisterly reassurance—"you only dreamed / you did" (40)—into resignation: "I saw you / shoot her" (42). This is not a story of wrongful imprisonment; this is a story about still loving a person capable of committing a terrible crime but incapable of taking responsibility for it.

In the final ode of the collection, Flint appears again as a scrappy fighter, "listening to archival tape / of our grandfathers" from the 1936 strike at General Motors (44). Imagining being woken by this figure, accused of betraying her for other places, the speaker acknowledges this history as reason to hope: "It is not /

without precedent, // after all, that we just might / save ourselves" (46). As this instance shows, Carson's poems have incredibly evocative endings, which are often less neat than in this example and thus leave more for the reader to parse. Such a suggestive style is showcased throughout the prose poem "Don't Touch," in which the reverberations of a shot rather than the shot itself are described (6). Formally, however, this poem stands out because usually Carson relies on short lines in unrhymed couplets, meaning the poems are staccato, placing weight on each word and phrase. *How to Baptize a Child in Flint, Michigan* is a collection with a clear call to action, most notably in the resources provided at the very end, but its social conscience never overwhelms the specificities of its emotional resonances nor Carson's gift with the precision and possibility of everyday language.

The third poet I will be discussing in this review, Mark B. Hamilton, moves us from the cities and suburbs, returning to a rural vision of the Midwest and its waterways along the Lewis and Clark route in both a full-length collection, *Lake, River, Mountain*, and a chapbook, *Upstream*, both published in 2024. One element that distinguishes these volumes is the former's inclusion of more autobiographical material. Hamilton seems nostalgic for past places and former friends. He traces family history across usually patrilineal generations including in a poem that concludes with the truth about a grandfather's death by suicide, "not from a heart attack / as I was told" (12). Such poems often invoke an almost mythic image of Americana as, for instance, magnolia blossoms are described "like the ladies walking" past a "wide rocking porch" (4). These personal narratives are interleaved with Hamilton's travelogues in *Lake, River, Mountain* as he describes his challenging journey along the Missouri River. The best poems in the collection tell us of his exhaustion, the effort needed to repair his boat and maintain his body, and of the conflicting landscapes he travels through as the "decay" of cities appears at intervals (45).

For instance, "City!" performs the address of its title again and again as Hamilton calls out to "your dark alleyways!" (45). These are the "spaces" he is drawn to for their "slick quiet" amid "incoherent conversations" and "traffic," evoking the poetic appeal in those aspects of urban life that we might assume to be repulsive—the homeless, the pigeons—while remaining ambivalent about how such scenes call back to him. The previous poem, "Portage at Great Falls," revels in the comfort provided in a hotel after a night in a "dusty ditch": "A bath unbends me, / restores years to my life, peels away grime, / turning aches inside out" (44). The simplicity of these sensations, enabled by modern conveniences, resonates more as we learn toward the end of his journey how few comforts Hamilton can rely on. He must "sew up … sneakers to last / another day or two" (48) and "repair the broken rudder" of his vessel (49), both having borne the brunt of the elements. However, his gratitude to the experience is always palpable in such moments of grace as when a "little brown bat" (49) alights on his feet after a day-long walk, feet that had urged him not to "hurry. Be here, do this" (48).

Frustratingly, Hamilton's version of the journey in *Lake, River, Mountain* includes dedications to "friends at Standing Rock" (33), a "tribal officer" returning his stolen rifle (28), and overheard conversations that show how "History spooks / a person" (38), but such moments feel both ahistorical and apolitical. The characters that populate the poems—from a Jamaican friend to a Sioux policeman—are described without further individuation. Tellingly, in "Renewal at New Town, Berthold Reservation," Hamilton encounters the "scowls" of the waves with much the same attitude as "The People / who are concerned for me" (19). While this is indicative of an environmental poetics that takes the inanimate world seriously, the lack of intimacy with the many people Hamilton encounters in his journey in *Lake, River, Mountain* is a missed opportunity.

There are glimpses in *Lake, River, Mountain* of Hamilton's reckoning with his "hosting ghosts" (15) along the Lewis and Clark route. He contrasts how he receives provisions via FedEx while "survival" comes in the form of "Chief Black Cat" and his "winter stories" for Lewis and Clark (8). However, it is in *Upstream* that Hamilton explicitly draws on Lewis and Clark's journals in a series of poems that describe how these early explorers went "upstream into a country that began to inhabit them" (14). While I found *Lake, River, Mountain* jarring in its eclecticism and ambivalence toward social realities, I appreciated the purity of *Upstream* and its more imagistic version of Hamilton's journey. A more deliberate and reflective tone is established and maintained through this chapbook's observations of and interactions with natural phenomena. Hamilton's use of a relatively consistent form—stanzas of three lines that are usually long, short, and then long again—matches the deeper relationship with the river that is allowed to emerge in *Upstream*.

The Hamilton that appears in *Upstream* intentionally chooses isolation, retreating from commerce and industry, and thus these poems are unpopulated, even amid deliberately brief encounters with urban settings: it is the "city" who "listens to a fast tram" as its inhabitants are blurred into a mass of indistinguishable "voices" (25). Specifically acknowledging the Indigenous scholars and teachers who inspired his eco-poetry in *Upstream*, Hamilton offers us a way of living amid non-human creatures that feels far more ethical and innovative. He is a "mallard / hiding in open water, shoulders hunched, neck stretched out" (25). He "can follow ... webbed footprints in the mud" left by geese (24). The chapbook form is far more suitable for such poetic treatment of Hamilton's experiences on the river. In *Lake, River, Mountain*, for instance, he tells us, "I'm paddling upstream on this difficult river!" and then draws out the analogy even further (8). I much prefer the unexpected metaphors in *Upstream* such as this offering to the reader: "The moon circles / around the earth's molten core; / a potato cooking in the coals" (8).

These three poets—Letcher, Carson, and Hamilton—offer distinct visions of the self, its relationship to others, and its negotiation of time and place. Their styles and subjects only occasionally overlap. However, reading their work in conversation—or confluence—as I did for this review essay enabled me to recognize a shared investment in the power of dislocation as much as location in current midwestern poetry. These writers are deeply concerned with what we receive from the places and people that raise us, inviting us all to reflect on the sources of our lives and the decisions we make in striking out toward their bourns.

I write this essay as a poet who now lives in Nebraska, less than 100 miles from the geographical center of the lower 48 states. I was raised on an island where one could never be too far from the sea, but my son will grow up in a land-locked state: his most familiar body of water will be the Platte River while mine was the North Sea. I had felt this to be a loss and thus am grateful to the poets who have helped me appreciate that the Midwest too is a place where we can be in communion with life-giving waterways.

Hastings College

MIDWESTERN ANGLES

Eric Tucker

Deeren, RS. *Enough to Lose*. Wayne State University Press, 2023. 176 pp.

Burns, Dawn. *Evangelina Everyday: A Novel in Stories*. Cornerstone Press, 2022. 150 pp.

Suhr, Kim. *Close Call: Stories*, Cornerstone Press, 2024. 210 pp.

This is obvious but bears repeating: the Midwest isn't a monolith. It's multifaceted, like a diamond or a lopsided barn or a misshapen chunk of Martian meteorite. A single perspective yields a snapshot: revealing but far from complete. To get a fuller picture, it helps to look at the Midwest from many different angles. Three new story collections do just that, taking three different storytelling approaches to illuminating the multiple planes of midwestern existence.

In *Enough to Lose*, a collection of nine interlocking stories, RS Deeren takes the reader deep into the homes, workplaces, and hangouts of an extensive cast of down-on-their-luck rural Michiganders—"Thumbodies," as Deeren calls them, after Michigan's so-called Thumb region, a peninsula of counties that juts into Lake Huron and Saginaw Bay—as they grapple with matters of love and loss, friendship and infidelity, hope and desperation.

Deeren has a keen eye for detail. You won't find any flat characters in these pages, no two-dimensional midwestern stereotypes. The author brings each Thumbody to life with honesty and empathy. Deeren employs the age-old writerly adage "show, don't tell" to impressive effect here. We are not simply *told* who these characters are. Whether mundane or momentous, the choices faced by the various residents lead to concrete actions that propel each story forward and help define their personalities. In "The Mirror," a couple must decide which of their possessions to try to save amid a sudden devastating flood that will change both of their lives forever. In the title story, a young man who earns money mowing lawns at repossessed homes contends with a demanding coworker as he stresses over his wife's desire to start a family and the agonizing decision they made many years ago. In "About the Lies," a bartender, college dropout, and former golfing prodigy wonders what might have been as she seeks temporary companionship amid the wreckage of her once-promising life. And in "Streaks of White and Color," the virtuosic final story in the collection, a tragic accident leads to a tender scene of compassion and fellowship in a scrubby clearing deep in the Michigan woods, a touching moment of human connection that, for this reader, was reminiscent of the conclusion of Raymond Carver's marvelous story "A Small, Good Thing." Deeren handles this moment with care and precision.

Deeren is impressively economical with his character descriptions, revealing much in only a few words. One character's bleary eyes feel "like burnt pie crust" (65); another overworked himself at a small tool and die shop "until he was more pain than man" (146). Through judicious use of evocative language that pulls no punches (a scene in which a character tries to move a dead deer out of the road is a gruesome standout), the author paints a stark picture of this small-town setting—at times lovely and breathtaking, at times relentlessly grim—and offers the reader an unflinching look at lives teetering on the edge. Bucky's Bridge, Kingston Tap, the Cass River, Owendale Draught—these and other landmarks reappear throughout the collection as characters move about their hardscrabble lives. Deeren displays great skill in connecting the tales. Characters who are introduced in one story drift through the background of others; events that transpired in an earlier story are commented upon in a later one. The ways in which the stories overlap never feel forced, unnecessary, or overly clever. With this technique, Deeren is able to create a sense of shared space and community, of real people dealing with real problems in real places. And, like Carver, Deeren sure knows how to end a story, finding just the right final image to leave with the reader. This is no static, lifeless portrait of small-town Michigan life. This Thumb thrums.

Also thrumming? The mind of restless midwesterner and inveterate *Downton Abbey* fan Evangelina, the protagonist of the impressive debut collection by Dawn Burns, *Evangelina Everyday*. In twenty-three short stories told in a very close third person—some less than a page in length—Burns invites the reader inside the fascinating and perpetually churning brain of Evangelina, who finds herself torn between conservative midwestern mores and her own irrepressible desires.

Burns's Evangelina is a fully three-dimensional character, filled with hopes and fears and self-doubts. She has felt dissatisfied and listless ever since her best friend Rose moved away and is frustrated with her humdrum domestic life. She is also quite funny, and her frequently humorous insights and observations, along with her more profound philosophical ponderings, make her an enjoyable and relatable companion throughout the pages of this collection. In the story "Evangelina Prays for *Downton Abbey*," she does exactly that, her nightly appeals on behalf of the various characters in the popular British drama series serving as a fanciful cover for her own suppressed needs and desires: *"God, take away Lady Edith's grief!* Evangelina prayed, for Evangelina, who still sometimes cried about Rose, knew grief when she saw it" (9). And later in the same story: "A thought Evangelina did not want sparked and threatened to flare, but she tamped it down" (9). Evangelina does a lot of tamping down of her true feelings throughout this collection (though, fortunately for us, we are privy to her innermost thoughts), until she can hold them inside no longer. Her twenty-two-year marriage to the profoundly clueless, though generally well-meaning, Russell hasn't just lost its spark; it has rendered each of them incapable of seeing the other, as well as themselves, with clarity and empathy. As the collection moves inexorably forward, Evangelina's senses—dulled since the departure of her beloved Rose—begin to sharpen as she gains confidence in herself and in her no-longer-tamped-down sexuality, leading to a passionate and narratively satisfying scene on a beach that finally awakens her to that which she needs to be truly happy ("oh, her hunger!" [25]).

Burns chronicles Evangelina's journey of self-discovery with care and compassion. Narratives that hew so closely to a single character's thoughts can sometimes feel constricting or oppressive, but that is not a problem here. Burns keeps the story moving at a brisk pace and avoids getting bogged down by unnecessary details or needlessly verbose flights of fancy; the brevity of many of the sections and the steady forward progression of the plot keep things from ever stalling out. Burns handles the collection's tonal shifts particularly well—for example, the way the author skillfully juxtaposes a humorous scene involving amorous cockroaches ("Watching cockroaches mate at 4:33 a.m. on top of her cousin Jo's bedroom dresser was not how Evangelina had planned to spend her first night" [43]) with a lush, poetic description of the interiority of a conch shell ("her fingers remembered tracing the ridges, bumps, scars, and spiraled turrets of the conch with her child's fingers until she reached the underside where everything changed" [47]). Evangelina's journey from self-doubt to self-acceptance is honest, believable, and heartfelt.

We likely could all benefit from being more honest and open with ourselves and each other. Midwesterners aren't exactly renowned for their forthrightness. From Nebraska to Indiana, from Wisconsin to Kansas, one finds no shortage of bushes to beat around. In her formally experimental collection *Close Call*, Kim Suhr has crafted a vibrant multimodal patchwork of stories that explore the difficulties that hinder human connection and the many issues that can disrupt effective communication: the misunderstandings, the missed connections, the untenable power differentials, the festering suspicions. Divided into three sections—"Signs," "The Dip," and "Eradicated"—the collection presents the reader with a medley of fraught situations that are as relatable as they are potentially combustible. In these stories, characters yearn for meaningful connections despite all the obstacles that stand in their way.

In "Jewel Tea," a young girl frets about the continued stability of her parents' marriage when a charismatic traveling salesman unexpectedly enters their lives, though she doesn't yet possess the language or life experience to express her deep-seated anxiety. In "Latent," a man whose distressing (and very, um, private) medical condition forces him into a physically vulnerable position in his doctor's office begins to doubt his wife's fidelity and the future of their relationship. In

"Pay Phone," moments of connection and disconnection abound in a series of brief yet illuminating telephone conversations. And in "Pretty People," a dissatisfied DMV worker, who is far from progressive in his notions of gender and sexuality, experiences an awakening of empathy and self-understanding when he encounters a former high school acquaintance who has undergone gender-affirming surgery.

Suhr gets amusingly playful with narrative form in the middle section, "The Dip," wherein the five connected stories—of a group of longtime friends planning a reunion while grappling with politics, religion, dominant personalities, and other forces that can either bring people together or tear them apart—take the shape of an e-mail chain, text added to a shared Google Doc, short screenplays, and even an online prayer request. With "Eradicated," the third and final section, *Close Call* concludes with the longest, most ambitious, and most thought-provoking story in the collection. Also titled "Eradicated," it takes place in a chillingly believable near-future in which a researcher seeks out sorry souls suffering from the affliction of "artism" (159)—a pathological need to create challenging works of art despite their irrelevance in a dismal world where artificial intelligence has surpassed all human capabilities: "Following the explosion of computer-generated artwork, the artists, already dwindling in numbers, were now all but gone. I wanted desperately to see them before they breathed their last, before their disease was completely eradicated, and they became a mere footnote in the DSM" (159). In this captivating final story, Suhr's empathy, attention to detail, and sense of humor converge to show us the importance of never letting the spark of creativity be extinguished in an algorithm-powered world that, much like our own, can at times feel cold and inhumane.

Doane University

Review Essay

Restoring the Upper Midwest from Landscape to Literature

Christian Knoeller

Lauck, Jon K. and Gleaves Whitney, editors. *North Country: Essays on the Upper Midwest and Regional Identity.* University Oklahoma Press, 2023. 252 pp.

Olson, Sigurd F. *A Private Wilderness: The Journals of Sigurd F. Olson.* Edited by David Backes, University Minnesota Press, 2021. 376 pp.

Gruchow, Paul. *A Paul Gruchow Reader.* Edited by Louis Martinelli, Rocket Science Press (Shipwreckt Books), 2023. 212 pp.

Rozga, Margaret. *Restoring Prairie.* Cornerstone Press, 2024. 118 pp.

This essay brings together four thematically related albeit seemingly disparate books—spanning a variety of genres—that address the ecological diversity and cultural identity of the Upper Midwest. *North Country* is a splendid new collection of essays representing a wide range of scholarly disciplines. *A Private Wilderness* presents for the first time the previously unpublished private writings of the iconic author and conservationist, Sigurd Olson. *A Paul Gruchow Reader* is a long-awaited compilation of place-based writings by this consummate yet largely overlooked literary naturalist. Finally, *Restoring Prairie* is a beautifully unified collection of new poems by Margaret Rozga, inspired by her time as artist in residence at a prairie preserve. Given such an array of materials, I seek to achieve cohesion by thematic means.

Several issues recur across these four books, including the place (and displacement) of Native Americans both historically and in our time, the cultural diversity resulting from waves of immigration and settlement, and finally the environmental degradation from extractive enterprises such as logging and mining. If there is a through-line to this multifaceted narrative—beyond a sense of regional identity—it is one of ongoing change.

North Country is a welcome and important contribution to the literature of culture and identity in the Upper Midwest. With each chapter addressing a different aspect of regional character, this multifaceted collection encompasses an impressive range of issues involving ecology, history, ethnicity, immigration, class, and gender. In aggregate, the book provides an expansive account of the social and environmental histories that have shaped the people who have called this extraordinary landscape home.

The volume opens with an engaging essay by co-editor Jon Lauck, who has contributed so much to the scholarship of midwestern history with many publications including numerous books spanning over two decades. He has also been responsible for founding and leading major organizations, above all the Midwestern History Association, charged with the ambitious aim of reinvigorating the field. For this collection, Lauck's introduction establishes the premise of the project as an exploration of just how the woodlands to the North—long associated with logging, mining, fishing and eventually tourism—have a character utterly different from croplands just to the South. That agrarian landscape has come to epitomize the region as a whole in the popular imagination.

Lauck's compelling account fittingly begins with a road trip—making his way across heavily farmed Plains states toward the North Woods. Through his eyes, we see how interlocking patterns of topography and land use shift dramatically with latitude. In fact, the transition from expansive crop fields to woodlands is abrupt as corn production drops by more than 90% in a mere matter of miles where the more northerly climate, short growing season, and severity of winter have all conspired to limit agriculture. Enroute, Lauck contemplates the geographical and ecological features as well as the cultural attributes that might help define the North Country—a landscape of large lakes and sprawling forests—as a distinct region unto itself.

To the north, conifers prevail, while deciduous trees dominate to the south. As cultural geographer Gregory Rose maintains,

Absent the stereotypical Midwestern landscape of fields of corn and soybeans stretching to the horizon, but despite its differences, this northern area is typically included within the Midwest, forming a distinctive Northern Borderland subregion that includes most of Michigan, Wisconsin and Minnesota…. [yet] the *perceptual* Midwest does not fully encompass Michigan, Wisconsin and Minnesota. The northern edge of the Midwest may exclude Minnesota altogether" (*North Country*, NC hereafter, 66–67, emphasis added).

This is the very region to be addressed in *North Country* with all its ecological variety and cultural diversity.

As Rose notes, extractive industries such as logging and mining in the "Timber Belt" attracted immigrants from countries of northern Europe such as Finland, Germany, Norway, and Sweden, resulting in "a more and greater variety of immigrants" (NC 75). For Scandinavians, in particular, a "similar environment and rigorous climate of their old and new homes drew them to the Borderland … as hardy denizens of a distinctive North," each contributing their distinctive cultural traditions to an emerging regional identity (NC 83).

Historically, however, the region had been inhabited for millennia by a succession of Indigenous nations, including the Anishinaabe and Ojibwe peoples. No account of its cultural complexity would be complete without acknowledging the interaction of European settlers with Native Americans and ultimately the displacement of many tribes. Several chapters in *North Country* chart the trajectory of that process. In "Founding Fathers and Sons: One Anishinaabe Family's Multigenerational Struggle to Resist Settler Colonialism in the Great Lakes Borderland," for example, Theodore Karamanski considers how in tandem the United States and Canada "imposed themselves on indigenous polities and for generations used policy and history to all but erase Native presence," disrupting traditional lifeways on historical homelands of the Blackfeet, Iroquois, and Wabenaki, as well as the Anishinaabe peoples including the Ojibwe (NC 16). Moreover, the imposition of a border separating the two British colonies only exacerbated the conflict.

In "Borderland to Bordered Land," Peter DeCarlo recounts how during the mid-1860s, "The fur trade society of the previous two hundred years, with its nexus in the Northwoods and Great Lakes, began to end, and the era of open warfare between Native Americans and colonial government on the Great Plains to the west began" (NC 41). Present-day debates about Native American treaty rights, particularly with regard to fishing, the subject of the closing chapter, echo this legacy of dispossession along with a corresponding counter narrative of survivance.

As historian Adam Mertz observes, beginning in the mid-1980s treaty rights emerged as a political movement among Native Americans nationally. In the case of the Upper Midwest (as well as in the Pacific Northwest), fishing arose as a particularly contentious issue. Private sportsmen as well as commercial interests argued that increased subsistence harvest by the region's Indigenous residents such as the Ojibwe could compromise tourism based on outdoor recreation. Moreover, Indian treaty rights faced a disproportionate backlash from tourist interests due to the devastating ecological consequences of vast "cutover" regions from the timber boom beginning in the 1890s, which intensified with increasingly industrial logging operations of the early twentieth century. Undaunted, in the 1970s some Ojibwe asserted the right to harvest fish beyond the boundaries of their own land based on the treaty of 1854 that had originally established reservations. Remarkably, after the Ojibwe prevailed in court, the Wisconsin legislature mandated that schools teach Native American history. As Mertz relates, "Treaty rights supporters formulated these new curricular standards and pushed for their passage in the late 1980s" (NC 221).

Any collection of essays representing such a wide array of disciplines must ultimately achieve cohesion by other means. The excellent introduction by co-editor Jon Lauck, as I've noted, goes a long way toward unifying the volume. And while every chapter can arguably stand alone, there are a number of issues that recur, regarding Native Americans, cultural diversity, and finally environmental degradation. The subregion of the Upper Midwest—dubbed *North Country*—can perhaps be seen as a microcosm of a broader national narrative.

But importantly, as this book aims to demonstrate, it is also an utterly distinct place unto itself.

A Private Wilderness, published by the University of Minnesota Press in 2021, makes the extensive private writing of Sigurd Olson available for the first time. Edited by David Backes, the volume is illustrated with a generous selection of historic black and white photographs. One can only imagine the monumental task involved in assembling, transcribing, and organizing this material from the original, fragmentary typescripts. In many respects, Backes is the ideal editor for this project. Having known Olson personally, he is perfectly positioned to provide commentary and context introducing each chronological "chapter" at successive stages of Olson's career. Moreover, he has previously authored a definitive biography as well, *A Wilderness Within: The Life of Sigurd F. Olson.*

Even in the earliest journal entries, Olson clearly aspired to achieve something extraordinary. Indeed, the inner turmoil associated with attaining such lofty goals is a recurring motif. Moreover, even at the dawn of his writing life, he grasped that originality would be essential to making a lasting contribution— one that reflected his ecstatic personal experience in the wild. These highly private journals—Olson himself at one point refers to them as "the old diary"— confide the often arduous process of coming to terms with such goals (*A Private Wilderness*, PW hereafter, 299).

While an abiding fascination with nature led Olson to consider specializing in the biological sciences, he embraced esteemed literary naturalist John Burroughs' skepticism toward what both viewed as overly analytical disciplines. By the beginning of 1932, ensconced in graduate studies that seemed to him not only a grand distraction but a troubling tradeoff, Olson continued to contemplate his future as a writer, naturalist, and teacher. Echoing Ralph Waldo Emerson's philosophies from the seminal essay "Self-Reliance," he challenged himself to articulate a purpose that could possibly fulfill his deepest aspirations. Gradually, he began to reflect on the ambitions that would guide him ever after: "What is my dream, yes what is it. *To interpret what is beautiful in nature,* to live so that I can be close to it always and bring my vision to the world" (PW 55, 5 Jan. 1933). Idealistic, certainly. Passionate? Without a doubt. Above all, the aim of bringing a profound personal appreciation of the wild into public discourse presaged his lifelong contributions as a leading conservationist.

In addition, the earliest entries from the winter of 1930 reveal a deep kinship to Henry David Thoreau, whose writing undoubtedly inspired Olson's own professional aspirations as an author as well as his engagement with the wild: "Many go through stifled by the narrowness of their daily affairs little dreaming that at their very doors for the asking is a wilderness to explore, the wilderness of their own understanding" (PW 14, 17 Jan. 1930). He acknowledged the temptation to imitate outright, declaring, "I grew up in the tradition of Thoreau and Burroughs and they I want to emulate" (PW 311, Oct. 1947). Accordingly, as critics point out, "It is thus no surprise that scholars read Olson alongside Thoreau, Emerson, Muir, Leopold and John Burroughs" to this day (Jacob Bruggeman in NC, 108).

Yet Olson also agonized over literary influence: if he were to follow the form of essays pioneered by the likes of Thoreau and Burroughs, for example, both of whom he revered, he realized his own work would inevitably be deemed derivative. Yet even as a young writer, Olson began to recognize that he had an original vision to pursue, one that might lead to a literary life celebrating untamed landscapes that sustain the wildlife he venerated.

The deep obsession with nature that would ultimately mature into a lifelong calling had in fact begun in childhood: "Animals I loved and all wildlife and it was perhaps that they gave me in them a part of the wild, which was really the shrine at which I worshipped" (PW 62, 28 Dec. 1932). The question remained just how such experiences would give serious artistic expression. After ruling out traditional essays in the manner of Emerson, as well as imaginative genres such as poetry and fiction, he realized his primary aim was to "describe everyday experiences like Thoreau, Burroughs, weaving in the *philosophy of the lover of nature*" (PW 65, 7 Jan. 1933, emphasis added)

Indeed, as early as 1930 he had already begun to articulate in these very journals the form such writing might take: "a new type of story with a touch of the spiritual in it, a deeper understanding and appreciation." *A touch of the spiritual*: consider how he described being transfixed in a mystical moment by "the gorgeous play of color on water, sky and land … was the union of myself with the plan of creation…. I feel that I was a part of the beautiful life I loved. From that moment on I was a spiritualist" (PW 20, 20 Jan. 1930). Critics often comment on this element in his writing: "Olson observed this divine ordering in nature, which for him was a wellspring of psychological and spiritual renewal" (e.g. Bruggeman in NC, 108). Such soul searching as an aspiring young writer prefigured the trajectory of his career as author and conservationist.

Having been born in Chicago, Illinois, in 1899, Olson's love of the North Country and particularly the Quetico-Superior Boundary Waters actually developed gradually, the consequence of a lifelong apprenticeship. According to Paul Gruchow, "Olson was not indigenous to this place either, but he stayed long enough once he had arrived, to notice to take account of—to discover—and so at last to learn to sing its poetry. Let us also agree that this was sufficient to have made him native" (*A Paul Gruchow Reader*, galleys 120).

Summarizing Olson's contributions as a conservationist as well as a writer cogently in his introduction to *North Country*, Jon Lauck observes the importance of place—and region—for Olson, whose "involvement in the conservation movement was guided by an environmental ethic firmly rooted in regional identity…. Olson thought that the region's historical and natural heritage was so precious that he devoted his life to protecting and writing about it…. Olson's popular appeal was made possible by cultivation of an accessible, reasonably coherent concept of the region's environmental and cultural history (NC 8–9). Moreover, a deep relationship to place was central to his interpretation of nature: "Minnesota's Northern Country and the broader region of which it is part are inextricable from Olson's environmental ethic. This link is repeatedly made explicit in Olson's writing" (Bruggeman in NC, 114).

Later in life, taking stock after stepping down from academic responsibilities as Dean of Ely Junior College, where he had taught for many years, and ascending to national prominence as an eloquent advocate for conservation, Olson reiterated the vision that had always sustained him as a writer: to communicate "the sense of naturalness, oneness with environment and animals, the harking back to aeons to living in primitive shelters, the need for renewing old earth associations, of returning to the ancient awarenesses" (PW 320, 11 Oct. 1952). At long last, his writing had achieved the very things he had always longed for.

A reverence toward nature had of course been shared by generations of American nature writers whom Gruchow admired, including Olson: "I would, finally, mark this about the literary natural historians: they are all, to the last one, celebrants of wonder.… wonder, to be astonished, to feel awe, is the beginning of a suitable humility" (*A Paul Gruchow Reader* galleys, 173). Olson squarely figured in that tradition. In fact, from the start, as these journals reveal, Olson was charting a course that would inevitably lead readers and critics to associate him with the legacy of another spiritually inclined child of Wisconsin, John Muir. Indeed, his accomplishments would ultimately ensure him a "place in that trinity of great author/conservationists—with John Muir and Aldo Leopold—to come out of the forests of the Upper Midwest" (Carey).

The consummate late-twentieth-century American literary naturalist Paul Gruchow was above all a champion of place-based ecological thinking. At last, through the generous excerpts from his major works and previously unpublished writings collected in *A Paul Gruchow Reader,* we can trace the trajectory of his prescient thinking about the most vexing ecological and moral questions we face today as climate change drives extinctions, presenting an ever greater threat to our own wellbeing as well as species diversity and ultimately the sustainability of life on Earth.

The volume has been masterfully curated by Paul's close friend and literary executor Louis Martinelli, who for many years personally stewarded the archive of unpublished writings, including an extensive set of journals kept in longhand as well as several other book manuscripts in progress, now housed at Texas Tech University in the Sowell Family Collection Archive of major American literary naturalists. Martinelli himself, Executive Director of the Paul Gruchow Foundation, confides in the introduction to this volume, "The selections I chose from Paul's five major books, as well as an essay, 'The Meaning of Natural History,' and several journal entries, demonstrate a deep consciousness of region and place" (*A Paul Gruchow Reader*, GR hereafter, 1). These previously unavailable sources appear for the first time here, along with emblematic selections from each of his best-known works: *Journal of a Prairie Year* (1985), *The Necessity of Empty Places* (1988), *Travels in Canoe Country* (1992), *Grass Roots: The Universe of Home* (1995), and *Boundary Waters: The Grace of The Wild* (1997).

Decades before such questions gained currency, Gruchow was among the first to recognize and write compellingly about how the environmental consequences of human alterations to ecosystems around the world had begun to approach a truly global scale—a legacy that is unmistakably timely today. While appreciating how biodiversity provides an essential ecological safety net, his essays also explicitly address not only *whether* we should attempt to steer natural systems toward some idealized or pre-existing state, but under what circumstances and *toward what ends*. What forms of stewardship are most warranted— and still feasible, given the extent of environmental decline?

Like his predecessors among midwestern naturalists, Gruchow was keenly aware of the extent of landscape change in the region and recognized the cumulative impact of ongoing expansion of cropland. He understood how the erasure of the grasslands and wetland ecosystems in the Upper Midwest had profound environmental consequences. He was especially concerned with the fate of remaining fragments of wetlands on the grasslands and understood that by functioning as *refugia*, such wilderness preserves comprise biological islands in time: a microcosm of the once vast tracts of grassland biome that have been plowed and planted with a handful of crops, predominantly corn. He realized that such preserves represent an ecological oasis.

While a keen observer in the field and a consummate naturalist, Gruchow was also deeply contemplative, reflecting on the ethics of our relationship to the natural world. Indeed, his best writing is often distinguished by its philosophical vision, providing a moral compass in ecologically turbulent times. In this, his legacy resembles Aldo Leopold's as a voice of conscience in the realm of conservation. He might also be likened to Sigurd Olson in his reverence for nature. In fact, he describes the central concern of many "literary natural historians: they are all, to the last one, celebrants of wonder…. To wonder, to be astonished, to feel awe, is the beginning of a suitable humility" (GR 173). Indeed, this description applies equally well to Gruchow himself as it would to Olson.

Perhaps the best way to do justice to this essential book is to quote several especially lyrical examples from Gruchow's writing. Describing the profound silence of winter in the North Woods, for instance, his inner experience of place is depicted vividly: "the landscape conveyed a strange aura of intimacy. Vastness, emptiness, austerity have the paradoxical effect of opening up the self, of rendering it vulnerable to the persuasions of the heart" (GR 127). Indeed, the northern forests of the Upper Midwest—particularly in winter—could strike him with the force of revelation: "The silence deep in the wilderness and the one at the center of the human heart are sublime and serene, and they cannot be heard except when alone, and over a broad margin of time and distance" (GR 112).

Gruchow understood how journeys were central to his approach as a literary naturalist, much as they had been for Thoreau, whom he deeply admired. In fact, he shared Thoreau's penchant for contemplating philosophical and spiritual questions grounded in close observation of the natural world. While paddling the Boundary Waters, for example, protected in large part due to the efforts of Sigurd Olson and The Wilderness Society, Gruchow wrote, "The journey is, in the American tradition, the transcendental one, from meanness toward the sublime, from sound toward silence, above all toward the silence of the soul, which is a kind of light, a luminescence, mirrored in the eye, in the sky, in the stillness of waters" (GR 114).

Gruchow clearly recognized how profoundly place shapes us, especially the *memory* of places as they once had been. Moreover, he believed memory and imagination were essential to reckoning our role in preserving and restoring environmental integrity: "the way to restore our sense of the interconnectedness of all of life is to rebuild our memories of nature by experience ... This is easiest to accomplish in the wilderness because it is a relatively pure and unadulterated representative of the memory we wish to restore" (GRG 193).

In truth, Gruchow's conception of wilderness was complex—one that anticipated debates about the place of human stewardship and management that rage to the present day. Rather than hewing to any Romantic notion of an idealized "pristine" wilderness, he grappled with the deeper ethical dilemma of what forms of stewardship are still possible given the deteriorating state of the natural world—and what purposes they might ultimately serve. He held no illusions about human stewardship, however, realizing that returning nature to any venerated ancient state was already beyond reach. This in turn precipitated a rethinking of the purpose of the preservation of a wide variety of ecosystems where processes of disruption and renewal were perpetually at work. In the context of environmental history, such surviving islands in a sea of development (such as remnants of tallgrass prairie surrounded by seemingly interminable tracts of cropland) represent an irreplaceable ecological legacy—hence the profound importance of both preservation and restoration.

Above all, Gruchow believed that the study of natural history must ultimately address its significance for humanity, complementing ecological knowledge with the emotional, ethical, and spiritual dimensions of our relationship to the rest of life on earth.

To conclude this essay, I turn to the recently published *Restoring Prairie,* a beautifully unified collection of new poems by Margaret Rozga. This work seems a fitting addition since its ecological underpinnings clearly follow in the tradition of midwestern literary naturalists such as Sigurd Olson and Paul Gruchow. Yet in several important respects, Rozga extends their vision with a lyrical rendering of ecological and cultural history based on deep personal engagement with place—one very particular place: a parcel of farmland in the process of being restored with historic prairie species. While many of these pieces are indeed "closely observed" depictions of native plant communities returning to this landscape, there is so much more. These intricate and often reflexive accounts break new ground, so to speak, by addressing the current state of environmental restoration. Moreover, the poet's emotional, philosophical and spiritual engagement with place lends tremendous depth to the telling.

While the volume is tightly unified thematically, stylistically it displays an impressive range of poetic forms, ranging from lyrical description and contemplative narrative to much shorter forms including a few striking haiku. Beyond revealing the poet's range in terms of craft, such variety also serves to modulate the pace, as if walking a trail through changing terrain and vegetation.

A brief foreword establishes an overall historical backdrop: the arrival of European settlers displacing Indigenous peoples, followed by a legacy of clearing, plowing, and planting that dramatically altered the rich ecosystems of the region. Rozga depicts the toll on Native American communities with what seems understated outrage: "Removal. Some people survived. Some managed to return, though their land was not returned. Much was lost. Culture. Prairie. Many old scars remain. Some newer are inflicted" (*Restoring Prairie*, RP hereafter, xx).

Attempts in our time to restore species diversity to denuded landscapes have actually been underway on this parcel, we learn, for half a century. Rozga herself witnesses and participates in this process, one that at times turns out to be surprisingly straightforward: "On the unfarmed old railroad bed, look carefully. Find enduring prairie grass and wildflower seeds. Gather them. Plant them. Each fall more seeds. The prairie the settlers broke begins slowly to take root again" (RP xx).

Reseeding, whether naturally occurring or through our intervention, also provides an ideal metaphor for the role writing might play in advocating ecological integrity.

> beyond the present grief
> I believe under foot like fallen mulberries, drive
> words take root here near the barn, there near
> the wood-fired kiln built into the hill, or

in the woods, ripe, and waiting to be pulled up

from the damp soil. (RP from "Mulberries" 14)

Contemplating the pendulum of destruction and renewal, she juxtaposes poems of hope with those that lament the extent of centuries of development, often leaving landscapes that are a mere shadow of historic natural bounty. Like Gruchow or Thoreau, she poignantly expresses the loss of an ancient ecological order as *personal* longing: "I want the wellness of then, the health / of then, its ripeness, the careless / assumption of forever of then" ("English Sparrow," RP 9). Could we but imagine the magnitude of such loss that all of us, as readers, implicitly share in the face of increasing extinctions and declining species biodiversity.

Rozga describes the collective effort to come to terms with such staggering landscape change. She recounts modern-day gatherings of fellow writers and artists, for instance, who join her near Waterville, Wisconsin, to share visual and literary creations inspired by this prairie preserve. Yet many of her poems also credit those who explored this place long before, including nineteenth-century immigrant Thure Kumlien, the Swedish scientist whose pioneering biological studies are credited as the earliest attempt to systematically identify plant species of the region. However, the Linnaean binomial nomenclature for classification of species alone is hardly the be-all and end-all of our layered relationship to nature, but rather just a beginning, as the poet notes: "Names offer one way to know / what you see, what you hear." And, on a more philosophical level, "Knowing is always smaller / than the abundance to be known" ("Mid-summer," RP 37).

Again and again, Rozga and her compatriots—artists and writers of many kinds—return to these prairie restoration acres for the inspiration that close attention to a dynamic landscape can provide. Personally, she strives to *internalize* the place, as well as reflecting on her own perception and interpretation of what has been witnessed on rambles there, longing to become a part of this place physically and spiritually. And, like Robert Frost famously beseeched in "The Pasture," invites us along:

Its roots and my roots, yours, too
touch, intertwine, somewhere
unmapped, under where we stand.

I carry the image, the imprint of its bark
as if it were a line of poetry, as if
it were a poem I committed to heart. ("Imprint of Bark," RP 40)

While the primary theme of this volume is how the ongoing threat of whole-sale landscape change can be mitigated by active restoration in rare places like this one, other forms of grief are intertwined, including the deeply personal loss of loved ones, as well as global woes such as relentless warfare and the pandemic raging as these poems were being conceived. In fact, Rozga succeeds in weaving all these troubling issues into the collection. Remarkably, she does so with an understatement and discretion that adds moral complexity while greatly deepening the emotional valence of the collection as a whole.

In the end, each of these reckonings is at once an act of conscience and a journey of the heart more than ever calling for the courage to hope. In aggregate, the book can be read as a hymn and prayer for healing.

Purdue University

Works Cited

Carey, Richard Adams. "'A Private Wilderness' Review: Seeking the Path." *The Wall Street Journal,* 13 Aug. 2021, www.wsj.com/articles/a-private-wilderness-review-seeking-the-path-sigurd-olson-environmentalist-11628865398.

Writings of Paul Gruchow

Gruchow, Paul, *Boundary Waters: The Grace of the Wild.* Milkweed, 1997.

———. *Grass Roots: The Universe of Home.* Milkweed, 1995.

———. *Journal of a Prairie Year.* Milkweed, 2009.

———. *Letters to a Young Madman: A Memoir.* Levins Publishing, 2012.

———. "The Meaning of Natural History." *Prairie Roots: Call of the Wild*, by Paul Gruchow et al., Ice Cube Press, 2001.

———. *The Necessity of Empty Places*. 1988. Milkweed, 1999.

———. Unpublished journals, 1987–2003. Paul Gruchow Papers, Texas Tech U, Sowell Family Collection Archive, Collection R46.1.

———. Unpublished journals, 1987–2003. Paul Gruchow Foundation, paulgruchow.org/journalofpaulgruchow.html.

Annual Bibliography of
Midwestern Literature, 2022

Robert Beasecker, Editor
Grand Valley State University

This bibliography includes primary and secondary sources of midwestern literary genres published, for the most part, during 2022. Criteria for inclusion of authors are birth or residence within the twelve-state area that defines the Midwest. Fiction and poetry using midwestern locales are included irrespective of their authors' ties with this region. Primary sources are listed alphabetically by author, including (if applicable) designations of locale within square brackets at the end of each citation. However, because of space constraints, primary source materials are limited to separately published works; those appearing in literary journals and magazines are generally not included. Secondary sources, usually journal articles, books, or doctoral dissertations, are listed by subject; critical editions of midwestern authors will be found here as well. The third section lists *Library of America* editions of midwestern authors issued in 2022.

Not included in this bibliography are the following types of material: works only published in electronic format; reprints or reissues of earlier works, except for some new or revised editions; baccalaureate or masters theses; entries in reference books; separate contents of collected essays or *Festschriften*; audio or video recordings; electronic databases; and internet websites, which have the tendency to be unstable or ephemeral.

Abbreviations used in the citations denoting genre and publication types are as follows:

A	Anthology	jrnl	Journalism
bibl	Bibliography	juv	Juvenile fiction
biog	Biography	lang	Language; linguistics
corr	Correspondence	M	Memoir

crit	Criticism	N	Novel
D	Drama	P	Poetry
gen	General studies	pub	Publishing; printing
hist	History	rev	Review essay
I	Interview(s)	S	Short fiction

Citations for novels, poetry, short stories, memoirs, and other types of literature about the Midwest, as well as those written by midwestern authors, are continually sought by the editor for inclusion in this annual bibliography. Please send them to Robert Beasecker, Director of Special Collections, Grand Valley State University Libraries, 1 Campus Drive, Allendale, Michigan 49401.

Primary Sources

Abani, Chris. *Smoking the Bible* (P). Port Townsend, Wash.: Copper Canyon Press, 2022. [Midwest]

Adamov, Bob. *Sunset Blues* (N). Wooster, Ohio: Packard Island Publishing, 2022. [Put-in-Bay, Ohio]

———. *White Spider Night* (N). Wooster, Ohio: Packard Island Publishing, 2022. [Put-in-Bay, Ohio]

Adams, Elle M. *Engaging Emma* (N). American Fork, Utah: Covenant Communications, 2022. [Mo.]

Adams, George Rollie. *Look unto the Land* (N). Pittsford, N.Y.: Barn Loft Press, 2022. [Ind.]

Adams, John Wendell. *Ruthless* (N). Skokie, Ill.: AMS Strategic Solutions, 2022. [Chicago, Ill.]

Agen, Jerusha. *Covert Danger* (N). Solon, Ohio: SDG Words, 2022. [Minn.]

Aguirre, Ann. *Boss Witch*. Naperville, Ill.: Sourcebooks Casablanca, 2022. [Midwest]

Ahmed, Samira. *Hollow Fires* (juv). NY: Little, Brown, 2022. [Chicago, Ill.]

Ahrens, Tim. *The Grand Game* (N). Austin, Tex.: Atmosphere Press, 2022. [Wis.]

Albert, Melissa. *Our Crooked Hearts* (N). NY: Flatiron Books, 2022. [Chicago, Ill.]

Alikhan, Salima. *Ollie Escapes the Great Chicago Fire* (juv). North Mankato, Minn.: Stone Arch Books, 2022. [Chicago, Ill.]

Allan, Barbara. *Antiques Liquidation* (N). Edinburgh: Severn House, 2022. [Iowa]

Allocco, Len. *Lily & Josie Have a Plan* (juv). Bloomington, Ind.: Xlibris, 2022. [Neb.]

Andersen, Hans Holst. *Along the Margins* (N). Eugene, Or.: Labbwerk Publishing, 2022. [S.D.]

Andersen, Jay. *The Flayed Man* (N). Aitkin, Minn.: River Place Press, 2022. [Minn.]

Anderson, Michael. *Zoey Lyndon's Misadventures at Camp* (juv). Seminole, Fla.: JOA Press, 2022. [Mo.]

Anderson, Paul M. *Lucas, Age 31* (N). S.l.: Wordpool Press, 2022. [Mt. Pleasant, Mich.]

Andersson, Ingrid. *Jordemoder* (P). Duluth, Minn.: Holy Cow! Press, 2022.

Andrews, Patrick. *Wichita Payback* (N). Las Vegas, Nev.: Rough Edges Press, 2022. [Wichita, Kan.]

Angela, Mary. *Mining for Murder* (N). NY: Lyrical Underground, 2022. [S.D.]

Anne, L.B. *Secret of Shadow and Light* (juv). Fla.: JOA Press, 2022. [Mich.]

Apps, Jerold W. *A Summer of Peas and Pickles* (N). Milwaukee, Wis.: Three Towers Press, 2022. [Wis.]

Arendt, Victoria. *Champlain Street* (N). Sarasota, Fla.: Elusive Orao, 2022. [Toledo, Ohio]

Ashkanani, Tariq. *Follow Me to the Edge* (N). Seattle: Thomas & Mercker, 2022. [Neb.]

Austin, Winter. *Hush, My Darling* (N). S.l.: Tule Publishing, 2022. [Iowa]

Bahr, Dane. *The Houseboat* (N). Berkeley, Calif.: Counterpoint, 2022. [Iowa]

Baker, David. *Whale Fall* (P). NY: W.W. Norton, 2022.

Baker, Marvin. *Crypt of Horror* (N). Carpio, N.D.: Heritage Sons Publishing, 2022. [Midwest]

Balzo, Sandra. *French Roast* (N). Edinburgh: Severn House, 2022. [Wis.]

Barile, Paul. *The Legend of Aguila Azul* (juv). Chicago: Lexigraphic Press, 2022. [Chicago, Ill.]

Barker, Ellen. *East of Troost* (N). Berkeley, Calif.: She Writes Press, 2022. [Kansas City, Mo.]

Barker, J.D. *see* Patterson, James

Barnes, Steven *see* Due, Tananarive

Baron, Melissa. *Twice in a Lifetime* (N). S.l.: Alcove Press, 2022. [Mo.]

Barr, Lois Baer. *Tracks: Poems on the "L"* (P). Georgetown, Ky.: Finishing Line Press, 2022. [Chicago, Ill.]

Barron, Rena. *Maya and the Lord of Shadows* (juv). Boston: Clarion Books, 2022. [Chicago, Ill.]

Bartels, Erin. *The Girl Who Could Breathe under Water* (N). Grand Rapids, Mich.: Revell, 2022. [Mich.]

Bartosch, Kim. *Ask the Girl* (N). Norwalk, Conn.: Woodhall Press, 2022. [Parkville, Mo.]

Baxter, Charles. *Wonderlands: Essays on the Life of Literature* (A). Minneapolis: Graywolf Press, 2022.

Bayless, Sally. *Antiques, Artifacts & Alibis* (N). Rolla, Mo.: Kimberlin Belle Publishing, 2022. [Mo.]

Beartrack-Algeo, Alfreda. *The Land Grab* (juv). Summertown, Tenn.: 7th Generation, 2022. [S.D.]

Beck, Hazel. *Small Town, Big Magic* (N). NY: Graydon House Books, 2022. [Mo.]

Beckett, Connie L. *Murder at the Tindari* (N). S.l.: Next Chapter, 2022. [Kansas City, Mo.]

Beckley, Gary W. *Oh! Susannah* (N). Meadville, Pa.: Fulton Books, 2022. [Ohio]

Beckstrand, Jennifer. *His Amish Sweetheart* (N). NY: Zebra Books, 2022. [Wis.]

Beil, Michael D. *Wreck at Ada's Reef* (juv). NY: Pixel+Ink, 2022. [Lake Erie; Ohio]

Bell, Gregg. *The Perfect Lawyer* (N). Itasca, Ill.: Thriveco, 2022. [Chicago, Ill.]

Bellinger, DeMisty D. *New to Liberty* (N). Los Angeles: Unnamed Press, 2022. [Kan.]

Benning, Patti. *Murder in Michigan* (N). S.l.: Summer Prescott Books Publishing, 2022. [Mich.]

———. *Warned in Wisconsin* (N). S.l.: Summer Prescott Books Publishing, 2022. [Wis.]

Benson, Raymond. *The Mad, Mad Murders of Marigold Way* (N). NY: Beaufort Books, 2022. [Ill.]

Berg, Sue. *Driftless Deceit* (N). Mineral Point, Wis.: Little Creek Press, 2022. [La Crosse, Wis.]

Besing, Megan. *The Rancher's Want Ad Mix-Up* (N). Toronto: Love Inspired, 2022. [Mo.]

Bester, Damone. *Mendel* (juv). Stamford, Conn.: Story Plant, 2022. [Chicago, Ill.]

Beyfuss, Brooke. *After We Were Stolen* (N). Naperville, Ill.: Sourcebooks Landmark, 2022. [Kan.]

Bidania, V.T. *Astrid and Apollo and the Awesome Dance Audition* (juv). North Mankato, Minn.: Picture Window Books, 2022. [Minn.]

———. *Astrid & Apollo and the Family Fun Fair Day* (juv). North Mankato, Minn.: Picture Window Books, 2022. [Minn.]

———. *Astrid and Apollo and the Ice Fishing Adventure* (juv). North Mankato, Minn.: Picture Window Books, 2022. [Minn.]

———. *Astrid & Apollo and the Super Staycation* (juv). North Mankato, Minn.: Picture Window Books, 2022. [Minn.]

Biggs, Kathy. *The Luck* (N). Aberystwyth: Honno Welsh Women's Press, 2022. [Midwest]

Bird, James. *The Second Chance of Benjamin Waterfalls* (juv). NY: Feiwel and Friends, 2022. [Minn.]

Bird, Laura Anne. *Crossing the Pressure Line* (juv). Waukesha, Wis: Orange Hat Publishing, 2022. [Wis.]

Birk, Cynthia. *Finding Lilacs* (N). S.l.: Picnic Basket Press, 2022. [Mackinac Island, Mich.]

Bishop, Bill. *West River* (N). Eugene, Or.: Resource Publications, 2022. [Dak.]

Blade, Scott. *Kill Promise* (N). S.l.: Black Lion Media, 2022. [N.D.]

Blake, Olivie. *Alone with You in the Ether* (N). NY: Tor Books, 2022. [Chicago, Ill.]

Blakely, Jason Franklin. *Collecting Ghosts* (P). Akron, Ohio: Poetry Is Life Publishing, 2022. [Ohio]

Blaustein, Sue. *The Beer Line* (P). Milwaukee, Wis.: The Bindery, 2022.

Block, Ed. *Moments Strange* (P). American Fork, Utah: Kelsay Books, 2022. [Wis.]

Blumberg, Chandra. *Digging up Love* (N). Seattle: Montlake, 2022. [Chicago, Ill.]

———. *Stirring up Love* (N). Seattle: Montlake, 2022. [Ill.]

Boldt, Jeffrey D. *Blue Lake* (N). Austin, Tex.: River Grow Books, 2022. [Wis.]

Booth, Claire. *Dangerous Consequences* (N). Edinburgh: Severn House, 2022. [Branson, Mo.]

Boren, Karen Lee. *Secret Waltz* (N). Minneapolis: Flexible Press, 2022. [Milwaukee, Wis.]

Borin, Fran. *Orion O'Brien and the Ghost of Samuel Grayhawk* (juv). Traverse City, Mich.: Mission Point Press, 2022. [Kan.]

Boston, Amelia. *Where She Was Going* (N). Eugene, Or.: Resource Publications, 2022. [Grand Rapids, Mich.]

Brandt, Juliana. *Monsters in the Mist* (juv). Naperville, Ill.: Sourcebooks Young Readers, 2022. [Minn.]

Branum, Renée. *Defenestrate* (N). NY: Bloomsbury Publishing, 2022. [Midwest]

Brayden, Melissa. *The Last Lavender Sister* (N). Valley Falls, N.Y.: Bold Strokes Books, 2022. [Kan.]

Brenner, Judith F. *The Moments between Dreams* (N). Austin, Tex.: Greenleaf, 2022. [Chicago, Ill.]

Bretzlauf, Mary Beth *see* Dotson, Jennifer

Brinkman, William. *The Rift* (N). S.l.: Anti-Psychic Kitty Press, 2022. [Bolingbrook, Ill.]

Broaddus, Maurice. *Unfadeable* (juv). NY: Katherine Tegen Books, 2022. [Indianapolis, Ind.]

Bromke, Elizabeth. *A Homestead Holiday* (N). White Mountains, Ariz.: Publishing in the Pines, 2022. [S.D.]

———. *A Prairie Creek Christmas* (N). White Mountains, Ariz.: Publishing in the Pines, 2022. [S.D.]

Bronski, Sally Nelson. *Running Uphill: A Minnesota Theatre Memoir* (M). Edina, Minn.: Afton Press, 2022. [Minn.]

Brown, Kathy L. *The Big Cinch* (N). San Francisco: Montag Press, 2022. [St. Louis, Mo.]

Brown, Spencer K.M. *Hold Fast* (N). Menominee Falls, Wis.: Wiseblood Books, 2022. [Minn.]

Brown, William Randy. *Twelve O'Clock Haiku* (P). Johnston, Iowa: Middle West Press, 2022. [Iowa]

Bruce, Camilla. *All the Blood We Share* (N). NY: Berkley Books, 2022. [Kan.]

Brunstetter, Wanda E. *The Apple Creek Announcement* (N). Uhrichsville, Ohio: Barbour Publishing, 2022. [Ohio]

———. *The Sugarcreek Surprise* (N). Uhrichsville, Ohio: Barbour Publishing, 2022. [Ohio]

Brunsvold, Sara. *The Extraordinary Deaths of Mrs. Kip* (N). Grand Rapids, Mich.: Revell, 2022. [Kansas City, Mo.]

Bryan, Blair. *When Wren Came Out* (N). S.l.: Teal Butterfly Press, 2022. [Minn.]

Bryce, Denny S. *In the Face of the Sun* (N). NY: Kensington Books, 2022. [Chicago, Ill.]

Buckhanon, Kalisha. *Running to Fall* (N). Tampa, Fla.: AALBC Aspire, 2022. [Chicago, Ill.]

Bull, Barbara E. *Come by Here* (N). Shelby, Mich.: Cherry Point Publishing, 2022. [Mich.]

Burns, Dawn. *Evangelina Everyday* (N). Stevens Point, Wis.: Cornerstone Press, 2022. [Ind.]

Burns, Valerie. *Two Parts Sugar, One Part Murder* (N). NY: Kensington Books, 2022. [Mich.]

Burton, Jeffrey B. *The Lost* (N). NY: Minotaur Books, 2022. [Glencoe, Ill.]

Burton, Sherry A. *Port Hope* (N). S.l.: Dorry Press, 2022. [Port Hope, Mich.]

Byers, Ron. *To Our Lady of Lost Delights* (P). Viroqua, Wis.: Ramshackle Press, 2022.

Cain, Kathryn. *Simon Hunter* (N). S.l.: Upon the Moment Publishing, 2022. [Ind.]

Cain, Steven. *War at Home* (N). S.l.: Upon the Moment Publishing, 2022. [Chicago, Ill.]

Camalliere, Pat. *The Miracle at Assisi Hill* (N). Lemont, Ill.: CAMPAT Publications, 2022. [Ill.]

Campanella, Nick. *Order from Chaos* (N). Vero Beach, Fla.: La Maison Publishing, 2022. [Minn.]

Campbell, Tom Harley. *Blue Book* (N). Trumansburg, N.Y.: Cayuga Street Press, 2022. [Dayton, Ohio]

Caña, Natalie. *A Proposal They Can't Refuse* (N). Toronto: Mira Books, 2022. [Chicago, Ill.]

Carlson, Rachel. *Dump Road* (N). Monee, Ill.: Spotted Dreams Press, 2021. [Iowa]

Carson, Sarah. *How to Baptize a Child in Flint, Michigan* (P). NY: Persea Books, 2022. [Flint, Mich.]

Carter, A.F. *The Hostage* (N). NY: Mysterious Press, 2022. [Midwest]

Casey, Amy E. *The Sturgeon's Heart* (N). Chicago: Gibson House Press, 2022. [Duluth, Minn.]

Cass, Laurie. *The Crime That Binds* (N). NY: Berkley Prime Crime, 2022. [Mich.]

Cassidy, Carla. *Closing in on the Cowboy* (N). Toronto: Harlequin, 2022. [Kan.]

———. *Gunsmoke in the Grassland* (N). Toronto: Harlequin, 2022. [Kan.]

———. *Revenge on the Ranch* (N). Toronto: Harlequin, 2022. [Kan.]

Castillo, Linda. *The Hidden One* (N). NY: Minotaur Books, 2022. [Ohio]

Cesare, Adam. *Frendo Lives* (juv). NY: HarperTeen, 2022. [Mo.]

Chalker, Dawn. *Bear Me in Mind* (N). Traverse City, Mich.: Hepatica Books, 2022. [Mich.]

Chambers, Christopher. *Kind of Blue* (S). Stevens Point, Wis.: Cornerstone Press, 2022. [Midwest]

Chandler, Eric. *Kekekabic* (P). Georgetown, Ky.: Finishing Line Press, 2022. [Minn.; Wis.]

Chang, Lan Samantha. *The Family Chao* (N). NY: W.W. Norton, 2022. [Wis.]

Chaon, Dan. *Sleepwalk*. NY: Henry Holt, 2022.

Chapin, Malissa. *Hope for Christmas* (N). Oshkosh, Wis.: Ivory Keys Press, 2022. [Wis.]

———. *Murder Goes Solo* (N). Oshkosh, Wis.: Ivory Keys Press, 2022. [Wis.]

———. *The Road Home* (N). Oshkosh, Wis.: Ivory Keys Press, 2022. [Wis.]

Chapman, Robin S. *Panic Season* (P). Huntington Beach, Calif.: Tebot Bach, 2022.

Chapman, Vannetta. *An Amish Proposal for Christmas* (N). Toronto: Love Inspired, 2022. [Ind.]

Charara, Hayan. *These Trees, Those Leaves, This Flower, That Fruit* (P). Minneapolis: Milkweed Editions, 2022.

Childs, Lisa. *Hotshot Heroes under Threat* (N). Toronto: Harlequin, 2022. [Mich.]

Christensen, Mark. *A Quick Reveal* (P). Bemidji, Minn.: Birch Tree Publishing, 2022. [Minn.]

Cintrón, Esperanza. *Boulders* (P). Ithaca, N.Y.: Chestnut Review Chapbooks, 2022. [Detroit, Mich.]

Clark, Suzie. *Enigma* (N). Valley Falls, N.Y.: Bold Strokes Books, 2022. [Barberton, Ohio]

Clausen, Kristin. *Waiting for the Glacier* (N). S.l.: Woodthrush Press, 2022. [Madison, Wis.]

Close, Jennifer. *Marrying the Ketchups* (N). NY: Alfred A. Knopf, 2022. [Chicago, Ill.]

Cloud, Debra Jo. *Safe at Home* (juv). Pittsburgh: Dorrance Publishing Co., 2022. [Ill.]

Coble, Colleen. *Edge of Dusk* (N). Nashville, Tenn.: Thomas Nelson, 2022. [Mich.]

Cochran, Peg. *Berry the Evidence* (N). S.l.: Beyond the Page Publishing, 2022. [Mich.]

Coco, Nancy. *A Midsummer Night's Fudge* (N). NY: Kensington Books, 2022. [Mackinac Island, Mich.]

Colby, Scott. *Vengeance Squad* (N). Kansas City, Mo.: Outland Entertainment, 2022. [Detroit, Mich.]

Coleman, Trenton. *Still No Time for Clocks* (S). S.l.: DBA Tipton Publishing Co., 2022. [Ohio]

Collette, Abby. *A Killer Sundae* (N). NY: Berkley Prime Crime, 2022. [Ohio]

Collin, Tyson. *Homecoming Heist* (N). Austin, Tex.: Atmosphere Press, 2022. [Mo.]

Collins, Max Allan. *The Big Bundle* (N). NY: Hard Case Crime, 2022. [Kansas City, Mo.]

Conger, Trace. *The Shadow Broker* (N). S.l.: Black Mill Books, 2022. [Cincinnati, Ohio]

Connell, John A. *Upon a Bloodstained Land* (N). S.l.: Nailhead Publishing, 2022. [Chicago, Ill.]

Conrad, Emily. *To Believe in You* (N). Oshkosh, Wis.: Hope Anchor, 2022. [Wis.]

Conradt, Ronald. *One Way Ticket* (N). Bloomington, Ind.: Xlibris, 2022. [Mich.]

Cook, Christian. *Growing in the Grey* (N). Nashville, Tenn.: Idun, 2022. [Chicago, Ill.]

Cooney, Jeanne. *It's Murder, Dontcha Know?* (N). St. Cloud, Minn.: North Star Press, 2022. [Minn.]

Cooper, James P. *Listening for Low Tide* (P). Leavenworth, Kan.: Choeofpleirn Press, 2022. [Kan.]

Cooper, Shantiana and Markida Thomas. *Trapped in the Arms of a Dope Boy* (N). Alpharetta, Ga.: Cole Hart Signature, 2022. [Chicago, Ill.]

Cooper, Sharon C. *Love under Contract* (N). London: One More Chapter, 2022. [Cincinnati, Ohio]

Couch, Robbie. *Blaine for the Win* (N). NY: Simon & Schuster, 2022. [Chicago, Ill.]

Coulson, Art. *Fishing on Thin Ice* (juv). North Mankato, Minn.: Stone Arch Books, 2022. [Minn.]

Coyne, Connor. *The Darkest Road* (N). Flint, Mich.: Gothic Funk Press, 2021. [Mich.]

———. *The Spring Storm* (N). Flint, Mich.: Gothic Funk Press, 2022. [Mich.]

Crary, Justin Hart. *Archangel* (N). S.l.: Lionhart Publications, 2022. [Neb.]

Crispin, Jessa. *My Three Dads: Patriarchy on the Great Plains* (M). Chicago: U Chicago P, 2022. [Kan.]

Crummer, Josh. *We Are the Raiders* (P). Columbia, S.C.: Alien Budda Press, 2022. [Zilwaukee, Mich.]

Cullen, Orv. *No Gentle Rain* (N). S.l.: Sunshine Publishing Company, 2022. [Milwaukee, Wis.]

Dahmen, Sara. *Outcast 1883* (N). S.l.: Promontory Press, 2022. [Dak.]

Dallman, Ann. *Cady and the Bear Necklace* (juv). Ann Arbor, Mich.: Modern History Press, 2022. [Mich.]

———. *Cady and the Birchbark Box* (juv). Ann Arbor, Mich.: Modern History Press, 2022. [Mich.]

Daniels, Vee. *Graceton* (N). Charleston, S.C.: Palmetto Publishing, 2022. [N.D.]

Danvers, Holly. *Long Overdue at the Lakeside Library* (N). NY: Crooked Lane, 2022. [Wis.]

Dargan, Cherie. *The Gift* (N). Cody, Wyo.: WordCrafts Press, 2022. [Iowa]

Darosa, Luana. *Falling for Her Off-Limits Boss* (N). Toronto: Harlequin, 2022. [Chicago, Ill.]

Davidson, Clifford. *At the Edge of Memory and Time* (P). Kalamazoo, Mich.: Logres, 2022.

Davidson, MaryJanice. *Mad for a Mate* (N). Naperville, Ill.: Sourcebooks Casablanca, 2022. [Minn.]

Davies, Deb. *White Nights* (N). Livonia, Mich.: BHC Press, 2022. [Mich.]

Davis, Brooke Lauren. *After Dark with Roxie Clark* (juv). NY: Bloomsbury YA, 2022. [Ind.]

Davis, Olena Kalytiak. *Late Summer Ode* (P). Port Townsend, Wash.: Copper Canyon Press, 2022.

Dawson, Kay P. *A Lawman's Reward* (N). Las Vegas, Nev.: CKN Christian Publishing, 2022. [Abilene, Kan.]

Day, Maddie. *Batter off Dead*. NY: Kensington Books, 2022. [Ind.]

De Cadenet, Gia. *Getting His Game Back* (N). NY: Dell, 2022. [Detroit, Mich.]

Deaver, Jeffrey. *Hunting Time* (N). NY: G.P. Putnam's Sons, 2022. [Midwest]

DeWylde, Saranna. *It Happened One Midnight* (N). NY: Zebra Books, 2022. [Mo.]

Dicken, Angie. *Once upon a Farmhouse* (N). Toronto: Love Inspired, 2022. [Iowa]

Dickey, Elissa Grossell. *Iris in the Dark* (N). Seattle: Lake Union Publishing, 2022. [S.D.]

Dieker, Nicole. *Ode to Murder* (N). Sandy, Or.: Shortwave Publishing, 2022. [Iowa]

DiGangi, Diana. *Last Chance Chicago* (N). Ann Arbor, Mich.: Bywater Books, 2022. [Chicago, Ill.]

Digweed, Frank. *Silent Survival* (N). Red Bank, N.J.: Newman Springs Publishing, 2022. [Dak.]

Dixon, Catharine Bernadette. *What Happens in Nebraska* (P). Nacogdoches, Tex.: Stephen F. Austin State U P, 2022. [Neb.]

Dobrinska, Leah. *Death Checked Out* (N). Olney, Md.: Level Best Books, 2022. [Wis.]

Dodd, Quentin. *The Man-Goat of Camp Cornelius* (juv). Crawfordsville, Ind.: Snake Year Press, 2022. [Ind.]

Doench, Meredith. *Whereabouts Unknown* (N). Valley Falls, N.Y.: Bold Strokes Books, 2022. [Dayton, Ohio]

Doller, Trish. *The Suite Spot* (N). NY: St. Martin's Griffin, 2022. [Kelleys Island, Ohio]

Dominique, J. *In Thug Love with a Chi-Town Millionaire* (N). Alpharetta, Ga.: Cole Hart Signature, 2022. [Chicago, Ill.]

———. *In Thug Love with a Chi-Town Millionaire 2* (N). Alpharetta, Ga.: Cole Hart Signature, 2022. [Chicago, Ill.]

———. *In Thug Love with a Chi-Town Millionaire 3* (N). Alpharetta, Ga.: Cole Hart Signature, 2022. [Chicago, Ill.]

Dorris, David. *The West Side Kids in a Pocket Full of Wishes* (juv). Bloomington, Ind.: AuthorHouse, 2022. [Burlington, Iowa; Davenport, Iowa]

———. *The West Side Kids in the Space Aliens Are Coming* (juv). Bloomington, Ind.: AuthorHouse, 2022. [Davenport, Iowa]

Dotson, Jennifer and Mary Beth Bretzlauf, eds. *Odes* (P). Highland Park, Ill.: Highland Park Poetry, 2022.

Douglas, William R. *The Death and Resurrection of Baseball* (juv). McHenry, Ill.: Woodbridge Publications, 2022. [Ill.; Iowa]

Downing, Erin Soderberg. *Controlled Burn* (juv). NY: Scholastic Press, 2022. [Minn.]

Drexler, Jan. *The Case of the Artist's Mistake* (N). Keystone, S.D.: Swift Wings Press, 2022. [S.D.]

———. *The Sign of the Calico Quartz* (N). Keystone, S.D.: Swift Wings Press, 2022. [S.D.]

Driscoll, Jack. *Twenty Stories* (S). Wainscott, N.Y.: Pushcart Press, 2022. [Mich.]

Driscoll, Sara. *Still Waters* (N). NY: Kensington Books, 2022. [Minn.]

Dubas, Ron. *Wildflowers beyond the Road* (N). Kearney, Neb.: Morris Publishing, 2022. [Neb.]

DuCharme, Judy. *Addy of the Door Islands* (N). Greenville, S.C.: Ambassador International, 2022. [Wis.]

Due, Tananarive and Steven Barnes. *The Keeper* (N). NY: Abrams ComicArts, 2022. [Detroit, Mich.]

Dunbar, Carol. *The Net beneath Us* (N). NY: Forge Books, 2022. [Wis.]

Dundee, Wayne D. *Massacre Canyon* (N). Las Vegas, Nev.: Wolfpack Publishing, 2022. [Kan.; Neb.]

Dunn, Stephane. *Snitchers* (juv). NY: Cinco Puntos Press, 2022. [Ind.]

Eastep, Amanda Cleary. *Mystery in Crooked Creek Woods* (juv). Chicago: Moody Publishers, 2022. [Ill.]

Eding, Stephanie. *The Unplanned Life of Josie Hale* (N). Naperville, Ill.: Sourcebooks Casablanca, 2022. [Ill.]

Edmonds, David Allen. *Unexpected Love* (N). Medina, Ohio: Snowbelt Publishing, 2022. [Ohio]

Eichmann, Mim. *Whatever Happened to Cathy Martin* (N). Centennial, Colo.: Living Springs, 2022. [Ind.]

Eley, Larry T. and M.T. Eley. *Mifflin Drift* (N). St. Louis, Mo.: Reedy Press, 2022. [Ohio]

Ellis, David. *Look Closer* (N). NY: G.P. Putnam's Sons, 2022. [Chicago, Ill.]

Ellis, Gina. *Fire-Hair Woman* (N). Firestone, Colo.: Prairie Spirit, 2022. [Neb.]

Ellis, K.M. *Jack and the Magical Portal* (juv). Altona, Man.: FriesenPress, 2022. [Mo.]

Enger, John. *Radium* (N). Fargo: North Dakota State U P, 2022. [Minn.]

Erickson, Alex. *Death by Spiced Chai* (N). NY: Kensington Books, 2022. [Ohio]

Erickson, Thomas J. *Cutting the Dusk in Half* (P). Middleton, Wis.: Bent Paddle Press, 2022.

Eschmann, Reese. *Etta Invincible* (juv). NY: Aladdin Books, 2022. [Chicago, Ill.]

Eskens, Allen. *Forsaken Country* (N). NY: Mulholland Books, 2022. [Minn.]

Estleman, Loren D. *Monkey in the Middle* (N). NY: Forge, 2022. [Detroit, Mich.]

———. *Paperback Jack* (N). NY: Forge, 2022.

Etlinger, Sarah A. *The Weather Gods* (P). Newburg, Or.: Fernwood Press, 2022.

Evans, Donald G. and Robin Metz, eds. *Wherever I'm At: An Anthology of Chicago Poetry* (P). Elmwood Park, Ill.: Chicago Literary Hall of Fame, 2022.

Everett, Sarah. *How to Live without You* (juv). Boston: Clarion Books, 2022. [Ohio]

Fader, Molly. *The Sunshine Girls* (N). Toronto: Graydon House, 2022. [Iowa]

Fairey, Ellen. *Support Group for Men* (D). NY: Dramatists Play Service, 2022. [Chicago, Ill.]

Fast, Katherine. *The Drinking Gourd* (N). Olney, Md.: Level Best Books, 2022. [Oberlin, Ohio]

Feehan, Christine. *Shadow Fire* (N). NY: Jove Books, 2022. [Chicago, Ill.]

Ferrell, Miralee. *Plus One at an Amish Wedding* (N). White Salmon, Wash.: Mountain Brook Ink, 2022. [Ohio]

Fetzer, Martina. *Fun Times in a Dystopic Hellscape* (N). S.l.: Befuddling Books, 2022. [Ind.]

Flanagan, Erin. *Blackout* (N). Seattle: Thomas & Mercer, 2022. [Dayton, Ohio]

Flower, Amanda. *Peanut Butter Panic* (N). NY: Kensington Books, 2022. [Ohio]

———. *Put Out to Pasture* (N). Naperville, Ill.: Poisoned Pen Press, 2022. [Mich.]

Flower, Paul. *The Great American Boogaloo* (N). Richmond upon Thames: Farrago, 2022. [Mich.]

Flowers, Ashley. *All Good People Here* (N). NY: Bantam Books, 2022. [Ind.]

Fluke, Joanne. *Caramel Pecan Roll Murder* (N). NY: Kensington Books, 2022. [Minn.]

Foley, Aaron. *Boys Come First* (N). Cleveland, Ohio: Belt Publishing, 2022. [Detroit, Mich.]

Fordham, Rachel. *Where the Road Bends* (N). Grand Rapids, Mich.: Revell, 2022. [Iowa]

Foster, Lori. *The Honeymoon Cottage* (N). NY: HQN Books, 2022. [Ind.]

Foster, Sam. *Beardstown* (N). Redondo Beach, Calif.: Agave Americana Books, 2022. [Ill.]

———. *A Panther Crosses Over* (N). Redondo Beach, Calif.: Agave Americana Books, 2022. [Ill.]

Fox, Tim. *A Place to Grow You* (juv). Ripon, Wis.: Journeys Publications, 2022. [Wis.]

Frankenstein, Casanova. *How to Make a Monster* (N). Seattle: Fantagraphics Books, 2022. [Chicago, Ill.]

Fredrickson, Jack. *Kill Her Twice* (N). Edinburgh: Severn House, 2022. [Chicago, Ill.]

Freeman, Brian. *The Ursulina* (N). Ashland, Or.: Blackstone Publishing, 2022. [Duluth, Minn.]

———. *The Zero Night* (N). Ashland, Or.: Blackstone Publishing, 2022. [Duluth, Minn.]

Freeman, Cal. *Poolside at the Dearborn Inn* (P). Tucson, Ariz.: R&R Press, 2022. [Mich.]

Friday, T. *The Ultimate Hustle* (N). Farmingdale, N.Y.: Urban Books, 2022. [Detroit, Mich.]

Frye, Andy. *Ninety Days in the 90s* (N). Austin, Tex.: Atmosphere Press, 2022. [Chicago, Ill.]

Fuerst, Carl. *The Falling Crystal Palace* (N). S.l.: Planet Bizarro Press, 2022. [Ind.]

Fuller, Kathleen. *Love in Plain Sight* (N). Grand Rapids, Mich.: Zondervan, 2022. [Ohio]

Furlong, Dayle. *Lake Effect* (S). Toronto: Cormorant Books, 2022. [Great Lakes]

Gahl, Kathryn. *Messengers of the Gods* (P). Stevens Point, Wis.: Cornerstone Press, 2022.

———. *The Yellow Toothbrush* (P). Green Bay, Wis.: Two Shrews Press, 2022.

Gallagher, Leigh N. *Who You Might Be* (N). NY: Holt, 2022. [Mich.]

Galligan, John. *Bad Day Breaking* (N). NY: Atria Books, 2022. [Wis.]

Gelman, Laurie. *Smells Like Tween Spirit* (N). NY: Henry Holt, 2022. [Kan.]

Geltner, Jonathan. *Absolute Music* (N). Seattle: Slant Books, 2022. [Cincinnati, Ohio]

Gengler, Mark. *Marshfield 1919* (N). Gleneden Beach, Or.: Soul Fire Press, 2022. [Marshfield, Wis.]

Geye, Peter. *The Ski Jumpers* (N). Minneapolis: U Minnesota P, 2022. [Minn.]

Gibson, Rachel. *Drop Dead Gorgeous* (N). NY: Gallery Books, 2022. [Grosse Pointe, Mich.]

Giddings, Megan. *The Women Could Fly* (N). NY: Amistad Books, 2022. [Midwest]

Gietl, Kelsey. *For a Noble Purpose* (N). St. Charles, Mo.: Purple Mask Publishing, 2022. [Mo.]

Gilbert, Julie. *Maddy and the Monstrous Storm* (juv). North Mankato, Minn.: Stone Arch Books, 2022. [Dak.]

Gilgen, J.S. *The Cop, the Paramedic, and the Barista* (N). Meadville, Pa.: Christian Faith Publishing, 2022. [Ind.]

Gilsdorf, Janet R. *Fever* (N). NY: Beaufort Books, 2022. [Mich.]

Giorgio, Kathie. *Olivia in Five, Seven, Five* (P). Georgetown, Ky.: Finishing Line Press, 2022. [Wis.]

Goble, Steve. *Wayward Son* (N). Sarasota, Fla.: Oceanview Publishing, 2022. [Ohio]

Godfrey, Bradeigh. *Imposter*. Ashland, Or.: Blackstone Publishing, 2022. [Chicago, Ill.]

Gonzales, Chuck. *Carlos Gomez Freestyles: Heavy on the Style* (juv). NY: Reycraft Books, 2022. [S.D.]

Goodman, Juliana. *The Black Girls Left Standing* (juv). NY: Feiwel and Friends, 2022. [Chicago, Ill.]

Gordon, Lydia. *The Fundamentals* (N). Chicago: Wells Street Press, 2022. [Ill.]

Gorman, John F. *Death before Life* (N). S.l.: GMS Publishing, 2022. [Chicago, Ill.]

Gould, Leslie. *Threads of Hope* (N). Minneapolis: Bethany House, 2022. [Nappanee, Ind.]

Grandinetti, Danielle. *As Silent as the Night* (N). S.l.: Hearth Spot Press, 2022. [Wis.]

———. *A Strike to the Heart* (N). Birmingham, Ala.: Iron Stream Fiction, 2022. [Wis.]

Granger, Mimi. *Murder of a Mail-Order Bride* (N). NY: Berkley Prime Crime, 2022. [Ohio]

Grant, Pippa. *The One Who Loves You* (N). Seattle: Montlake, 2022. [Wis.]

———. *Rich in Your Love* (N). Seattle: Montlake, 2022. [Wis.]

Grate, Anthony D. *see* Rapino, Anthony J.

Graves, Michael D. *Shadows and Sorrows* (N). Emporia, Kan.: Meadowlark, 2022. [Wichita, Kan.]

Graves, T. Patrick. *Let Us Not Talk Falsely Now* (N). Bloomington, Ind.: Xlibris, 2022. [Iowa]

Gray, P.J. *Coal Spell* (juv). Costa Mesa, Calif.: Saddleback Educational Publishing, 2022. [Ohio]

Gray, Shelley Shepard. *Christmas at the Amish Market* (N). Studio City, Calif.: Hallmark, 2022. [Ohio]

———. *Edgewater Road* (N). Ashland, Or.: Blackstone Publishing, 2022. [Ohio]

———. *Happily Ever Amish* (N). NY: Kensington Books, 2022. [Ohio]

Green, Jocelyn. *Drawn by the Current* (N). Minneapolis: Bethany House, 2022. [Chicago, Ill]

Green, Stacy. *Her Frozen Heart* (N). London: Bookouture, 2022. [Stillwater, Minn.]

———. *The Trapped Ones* (N). London: Bookouture, 2022. [Stillwater, Minn.]

Greer, Heather. *Cake That!* (N). Morrilton, Ark.: Scrivenings Press, 2021. [St. Louis, Mo.]

Griffith, Cary J. *Cougar Claw* (N). Cambridge, Minn.: Adventure Publications, 2022. [Minn.]

———. *Wolf Kill* (N). Cambridge, Minn.: Adventure Publications, 2021. [Minn.]

Griggs, Winnie. *Her Amish Springtime Miracle* (N). NY: Forever, 2022. [Ohio]

Gruenberg, Linda. *Blazes & Brimstone* (N). Falmouth, Mich.: Kenda Press, 2022. [Holland, Mich.]

Gundy, Bud. *Inherit the Lightning* (N). Valley Falls, N.Y.: Bold Strokes Books, 2022. [Cleveland, Ohio]

Gunter-Seymour, Kari, ed. *I Thought I Heard a Cardinal Sing: Ohio's Appalachian Voices* (P). Russell, Ky.: Sheila-Na-Gig Editions, 2022. [Ohio]

Gunty, Tess. *The Rabbit Hutch* (N). NY: Alfred A. Knopf, 2022. [Ind.]

Haddix, Margaret Peterson. *The Secret Letters* (juv). NY: HarperCollins, 2022. [Ohio]

Hagen, Carla. *Muskeg* (N). Minneapolis: Calumet Editions, 2022. [Minn.]

Hagen, Kira. *Strangeling* (N). S.l.: Whispering Candle, 2022. [Minn.]

Hahn, Erin. *Built to Last* (N). NY: St. Martin's Griffin, 2022. [Mich.]

Hamm, Justin. *Drinking Guinness with the Dead* (P). Kansas City, Mo.: Spartan Press, 2022. [Midwest]

Hanania, Denisa Nickell. *The Traveling Cabin* (juv). Indianapolis: Stories That Captivate, 2022. [Ind.]

Hance, Marjorie Mathison. *The Man Three Cottages Down* (N). Plymouth, Minn.: North Lakes Press, 2022. [Minn.]

Hanford, Patrick. *Fabricated Lies* (N). Lubbock, Tex.: Savoy House Publishing, 2022. [Chicago, Ill.]

Hanna, Danielle Lincoln. *Mailboat V: The End of Summer* (N). Missoula, Mont.: Hearth & Homicide Press, 2022. [Lake Geneva, Wis.]

Hannah, Darci. *Murder at the Blueberry Festival* (N). NY: Kensington Books, 2022. [Mich.]

Hannon, Irene. *Body of Evidence* (N). Grand Rapids, Mich.: Revell, 2022. [Mo.]
———. *Labyrinth of Lies* (N). Grand Rapids, Mich.: Revell, 2021. [Mo.]

Hardy, Mina. *We Knew All Along* (N). NY: Crooked Lane Books, 2022. [Ohio]

Harris, Kai. *What the Fireflies Knew* (N). NY: Tiny Reparations Books, 2022. [Mich.]

Harrison, Kim. *Trouble with the Cursed* (N). NY: Ace Books, 2022. [Cincinnati, Ohio]

Hasselstrom, Linda. *Walking: The Changes* (P), Hermosa, S.D.: Lame Johnny Press, 2022. [S.D.]

Hastings, Katherine. *Rule Number One* (N). S.l.: Flyte Publishing, 2022. [Wis.]

Hautala, Beth. *Miracle Season* (juv). NY: Viking Books, 2022. [Wis.]

Havig, Chautona. *Twice Sold Tales* (N). Ridgecrest, Calif.: Havilah Press, 2022. [Red Wing, Minn.]

Hawke, Christopher. *The Chamber* (N). Farmington, Me.: Encircle, 2022. [Traverse City, Mich.]

Hawley, Noah. *Anthem* (N). Grand Central Publishing, 2022. [Ill.]

Haynes, Berneta L. and Lornett B. Vestal. *Aya and the Alphas* (N). Atlanta, Ga.: Snake Doctor Press, 2022. [Chicago, Ill.; Ind.]

Hazelwood, Ann Watkins. *Christmas Surprises at the Door* (N). Lafayette, Calif.: C&T Publishing, 2022. [Wis.]
———. *Quilted Cherries* (N). Lafayette, Calif.: C&T Publishing, 2022. [Wis.]

Hechtman, Betty. *Making It Write* (N). Edinburgh: Severn House, 2022. [Ill.]

Hein, Michelle Webster *see* Webster-Hein, Michelle

Heinsen, Victoria King. *Robbie F. Woods, Entrepreneur* (N). Conneaut Lake, Pa.: Page Publishing, 2022. [Ohio]

Hellewell, Amber Lynn. *Summer's Call* (juv). Ann Arbor, Mich.: Sleeping Bear Press, 2022. [Mich.]

Hellman, Matthew. *The Biting Cold* (N). Charleston, S.C.: Beacon, 2022. [Copper Harbor, Mich.]

Hellmann, Libby Fischer. *DoubleBlind* (N). Chicago: Red Herrings Press, 2022. [Chicago, Ill.]

Hemmert, Andrew. *Blessing the Exoskeleton* (P). Pittsburgh: U Pittsburgh P, 2022. [Mich.]

Henderson, Craig. *Welcome to the Game* (N). NY: Atlantic Monthly Press, 2022. [Detroit, Mich.]

Hill, Gregory W. *Sister Liberty* (N). S.l.: Daisy Dog Press, 2022. [Ind.]

Hitchcock, Kelly I. *Community Klepto* (N). Berkeley, Calif.: She Writes Press, 2020. [Kansas City, Kan.]

Hockman, Angie. *Dream On* (N). NY: Gallery Books, 2022. [Cleveland, Ohio]

Hogan, Chuck. *Gangland* (N). NY: Grand Central Publishing, 2022. [Chicago, Ill.]

Hogue, Dawn. *Summit Road* (N). Sheboygan, Wis.: Water's Edge Press, 2022. [Wis.]

Hoover, Greg. *The Pain Killer* (N). Castroville, Tex.: Black Rose Writing, 2022. [Chicago, Ill.]

House, Alexandria. *Goal* (N). Ark.: Pink Cashmere Publishing, 2022. [St. Louis, Mo.]

Housewright, David. *Something Wicked* (N). NY: Minotaur Books, 2022. [Minn.]

Houston, Victoria. *Wolf Hollow* (N). NY: Crooked Lane Books, 2022. [Wis.]

Hovey, Dean L. *Fatal Business* (N). Calgary, Alta.: BWL Publishing, 2022. [Minn.]

———. *Whistling Artist* (N). Calgary, Alta.: BWL Publishing, 2022. [Two Harbors, Minn.]

———. *Whistling Bake Off* (N). Calgary, Alta.: BWL Publishing, 2022. [Two Harbors, Minn.]

Howland, Amanda R. *Beasts and Creature* (N). Lakewood, Ohio: Erie Oak Moon, 2022. [Cleveland, Ohio]

Hubbard, Charlotte. *Love Blooms in Morning Star* (N). NY: Zebra Books, 2022. [Mo.]

Huge, Robert W. *Dying Breath* (N). Meadville, Pa.: Christian Faith Publishing, 2022. [Minneapolis, Minn.]

Husom, Christine. *Cold Way to Go* (N). Buffalo, Minn.: wRight Press, 2022. [Minn.]

Iloh, Candice. *Break This House* (juv). NY: Dutton, 2022. [Mich.]

Irvin, Kelly. *The Warmth of Sunshine* (N). Grand Rapids, Mich.: Zondervan, 2022. [Kan.]

Ivy, Alexandra. *Unstable* (N). NY: Zebra Books, 2022. [Wis.]

Jackson, C.J. *Hunting Wildflowers* (N). Milford, Ohio: Chilidog Press, 2022. [Loveland, Ohio]

Jackson, Danielle. *The Accidental Pinup* (N). NY: Jove Books, 2022. [Chicago, Ill.]

Jackson, James M. *Granite Oath* (N). Amasa, Mich.: Wolf's Echo Press, 2022. [Mich.]

Jacobs, Simon. *String Follow* (N). NY: MCD x FSG Originals, 2022. [Adena, Ohio]

Jacobson, Kathy J. *A Change of Heart* (N). Austin, Tex.: Atmosphere Press, 2022. [Wis.]

Janko, James. *What We Don't Talk About* (N). Madison: U Wisconsin P, 2022. [Ill.]

Janz, Jonathan. *Marla* (N). Concord, Mass.: Earthling Publications, 2022. [Ind.]

Jebber, Molly. *Magdelena's Choice* (N). NY: Zebra Books, 2022. [Ohio]

Jeffers, Jean. *Lulu's Plight* (N). Cincinnati: Omega One Press, 2022. [Cincinnati, Ohio]

Jennings, Regina. *Engaging Deception* (N). Minneapolis: Bethany House, 2022. [Joplin, Mo.]

Johanson, Lynn-Steven. *Corrupted Souls* (N). Olney, Md.: Level Best Books, 2022. [Chicago, Ill.]

Johns, Patricia. *A Deputy in Amish Country* (N). Toronto: Harlequin Heartwarming, 2022. [Ohio]

Johnson, Anna Rose. *The Star That Always Stays* (juv). NY: Holiday House, 2022. [Boyne City, Mich.]

Johnson, Janice Kay. *What Is Hidden* (N). Toronto: Harlequin Intrigue, 2022. [Mo.]

Johnson, Katharine. *Sylvie's Silence* (juv). Cloquet, Minn.: Silver Fox Books, 2002. [Minn.]

Johnson, Kristin. *Fearless* (juv). Monee, Ill.: KFJ Books, 2022. [Minn.]

Johnson, Mark S. *Though the Earth Gives Way* (N). Baltimore, Md.: Bancroft Books, 2022. [Mich.]

Johnson, Wayne. *The Red Canoe* (N). Aberdeen, N.J.: Agora Books, 2022. [Minn.]

Johnson-Bartee, Bonnie. *Cord Blood* (P). Neb.: Sandhills Press, 2022. [Neb.]

Johnstone, J.A. *see* Johnstone, William W.

Johnstone, William W. and J.A. Johnstone. *Black Hills Blood Hunt* (N). NY: Pinnacle Books, 2022. [Deadwood, S.D.]

———. *Hard Road to Vengeance* (N). NY: Pinnacle Books, 2022. [Dak.]

Jones, Charles Forrest. *The Illusion of Simple* (N). Iowa City: U Iowa P, 2022. [Kan.]

Jones, Michael. *Dangerous Curves Ahead* (N). Bloomington, Ind.: AuthorHouse, 2022. [Cleveland, Ohio]

Jones, Saeed. *Alive at the End of the World* (P). Minneapolis: Coffee House Press, 2022.

Jones, Zachariah. *Genesis* (N). Stillwater, Minn.: Water Sign Books, 2022. [St. Paul, Minn.]

Jorgensen, Dan. *Rainbow Rock* (N). Naples, Fla.: Speaking Volumes, 2022. [S.D.]

Jude, Caroline. *The Elemental Lies* (N). Minnetonka, Minn.: Sigma's Bookshelf, 2022. [Duluth, Minn.]

Kaminski, Jake. *Beneath the Polish Moon* (N). Bloomington, Ind.: Archway Publishing, 2022. [Milwaukee, Wis.]

Kane, Carolyn. *The Piper in the Woods* (juv). S.l.: New Dublin Books, 2022. [Wis.]

Kapcala, Jason. *Hungry Town* (N). Morgantown: West Virginia U P, 2022. [Lodi, Ohio]

Kapelke-Dale, Rachel. *The Ingenue* (N). NY: St. Martin's Press, 2022. [Milwaukee, Wis.]

Kava, Alex. *Fallen Creed* (N). Omaha, Neb.: Prairie Wind Publishing, 2022. [Neb.]

Kay, Arlene. *Murder at First Blush* (N). Olney, Md.: Level Best Books, 2022. [Mich.]

Kay, Libby. *Falling Home* (N). Murrells Inlet, S.C.: Inkspell Publishing, 2022. [Ohio]

Keillor, Garrison (N). *Boom Town* (N). Blaine, Minn.: Prairie Home Productions, 2022. [Minn.]

Kelly, Jake. *Blowing Minds* (N). Cleveland, Ohio: Stone Church Press, 2022. [Cleveland, Ohio]

Kelly, Sofie. *Whiskers and Lies* (N). NY: Berkley Prime Crime, 2022. [Minn.]

Kennedy, Deborah E. *Billie Starr's Book of Sorries* (N). NY: Flatiron Books, 2022. [Ind.]

Kennedy, Sharon M. *View from the SideRoad* (S). Ann Arbor, Mich.: Modern History Press, 2022. [Mich.]

Kenney, J.C. *Record Store Reckoning* (N). Olney, Md.: Level Best Books, 2022. [Ind.]

Kensington, Kayla. *Finding Her Family's Love* (N). Georgetown, Tenn.: Mt Zion Ridge Press, 2022. [Ill.]

Kerr, Judy M. *Silent Service* (N). Portland, Or.: Lauch Point Press, 2022. [Minn.]

Khan, Sabina. *Meet Me in Mumbai* (juv). NY: Push, 2022. [Bloomington, Ill.]

Kildegaard, Athena. *Prairie Midden* (P). Red Wing, Minn.: Tinderbox Editions, 2022. [Midwest]

King Rio. *The Brick Man 3* (N). Stockbridge, Ga.: Lock Down Publications, 2022. [Chicago, Ill.]

———. *The Brick Man 4* (N). Stockbridge, Ga.: Lock Down Publications, 2022. [Chicago, Ill.]

———. *The Brick Man 5* (N). Stockbridge, Ga.: Lock Down Publications, 2022. [Chicago, Ill.]

Kingsbury, Karen. *The Baxters* (N). NY: Atria Books, 2022. [Bloomington, Ind.]

Kjeldsen, Jim. *Anarchy in Ohio* (N). NY: Austin Macauley Publishers, 2022. [Ohio]

Knittel, Janna. *Real Work* (P). Minneapolis: Nodin Press, 2022. [Minn.]

Knoedler, Michael. *Bridgeton* (N). Mineral Point, Wis.: Little Creek Press, 2022. [Wis.]

Knox, Kipling. *Under the Moon in Illinois* (S). Ill.: Prairie State Press, 2022. [Ill.]

Koepp, David. *Aurora* (N). NY: Harper, 2022. [Aurora, Ill.]

Kolbe, Steven J. *Rogue the Drum* (N). Adams Basin, N.Y.: Wild Rose Press, 2022. [Chicago, Ill.]

Komarnyckyj, Andrew. *Revenge of Joe Wild* (juv). Solana Beach, Calif.: Santa Monica Press, 2022. [Ill.]

Kooser, Ted and Connie Wanek. *Marshmallow Clouds* (P). Somerville, Mass.: Candlewick Press, 2022.

Kousoulas, Bill and Jacqueline Kousoulas. *Bridging the Tragedy: Silver Linings in the Mysterious Ohio River Valley* (N). Chicago: Bird Mountain Books, 2022. [Ohio]

Kraus, Daniel. *The Ghost That Ate Us* (N). Bowie, Md.: Raw Dog Screaming Press, 2022. [Iowa]

Krueger, William Kent. *Fox Creek* (N). NY: Atria Books, 2022. [Minn.]

Kulper, Kendall. *Murder for the Modern Girl* (juv). NY: Holiday House, 2022. [Chicago, Ill.]

LaDelle, Ebony. *Love Radio* (juv). NY: Simon & Schuster BFYR, 2022. [Detroit, Mich.]

Lageschulte, Melanie. *The Route That Takes You Home* (N). S.l.: Fremont Creek Press, 2022. [Iowa]

Laighean, Sean. *The Ghosts of Gaylord* (N). Meadville, Pa.: Fulton Books, 2022. [Gaylord, Mich.]

Laird, Thomas. *Child of the Night* (N). Castroville, Tex.: Black Rose Writing, 2022. [Chicago, Ill.]

Landes, Martha Kemm. *Framed Fur Murder* (N). S.l.: Elemar Publishing, 2022. [Brookings, S.D.]

Landry, Jess, ed. *That Which Cannot Be Undone: An Ohio Horror Anthology* (S). S.l.: Cracked Skull Press, 2022. [Ohio]

Landvik, Lorna. *Last Circle of Love* (N). Seattle: Lake Union Publishing, 2022. [Minn.]

Landwehr, Jim. *At the Lake* (M). Stevens Point, Wis.: Cornerstone Press, 2022. [Wis.]

Lane, Ellison. *From Now until September* (N). S.l.: Scout + Jem Books, 2022. [Wis.]

Lange, Erin Jade. *Mere Mortals* (juv). NY: Harper Teen, 2022. [Iowa]

Langer, Adam. *Cyclorama* (N). NY: Bloomsbury Publishing, 2022. [Evanston, Ill.]

Langford, William T. *Detroit: Workers, Teachers, Lovers* (P). Georgetown, Ky.: Finishing Line Press, 2022. [Detroit, Mich.]

Langtry, Leslie. *Mayor for Murder* (N). Los Gatos, Calif.: Gemma Halliday Publishing, 2022. [Iowa]

———. *Memories Are Murder* (N). Los Gatos, Calif.: Gemma Halliday Publishing, 2022. [Iowa]

———. *Munchies and Murder* (N). Los Gatos, Calif.: Gemma Halliday Publishing, 2022. [Iowa]

Lantz, Mary. *A Plain and Perfect Love* (N). S.l.: Vidorra House, 2022. [Berlin, Ohio]

Lastufka, Alan. *Face the Night* (N). S.l.: Shortwave Media, 2022. [Ohio]

Lavender, Shay. *Canceled* (N). S.l.: Mahogany Pen Publishing, 2022. [Mich.]

Lawrence, Susan R. *Flight of the Red-Winged Blackbird* (N). Morrilton, Ark.: Scrivenings Press, 2022. [Iowa]

Lawson, Mike. *Redemption* (N). NY: Atlantic Monthly Press, 2022. [Ill.]

Lazzara, Misha. *Manmade Constellations* (N). Ashland, Or.: Blackstone Publishing, 2022. [Minn.]

Le, Jade Moon. *Invisible Orphans* (N). Los Angeles: Rare Bird, 2022. [Ind.]

Leali, Michael. *The Civil War of Amos Abernathy* (juv). NY: HarperCollins, 2022. [Ill.]

Leasman, Nancy Packard. *Moving On* (N). Long Prairie, Minn.: Leatherwood Publishing, 2022. [Minn.]

———. *Mrs. Elfin and the Crow* (N). Long Prairie, Minn.: Leatherwood Publishing, 2022. [Minn.]

———. *Paddled* (N). Long Prairie, Minn.: Leatherwood Publishing, 2022. [Minn.]

Lee, Marie Myung-Ok. *The Evening Hero* (N). NY: Simon & Schuster, 2022. [Minn.]

Lentz, Richard D. *Accidental Journey* (N). Minneapolis: Calumet Editions, 2022. [Minn.]

Lenz, Londyn. *Locked in Love with the Illest* (N). S.l.: Miss Candice Presents, 2022. [Detroit, Mich.]

Levin, Adam. *Mount Chicago* (N). NY: Doubleday, 2022. [Chicago, Ill.]

Lewis, Joseph. *Blaze In, Blaze Out* (N). Castroville, Tex.: Black Rose Writing, 2022. [Chicago, Ill.; Wis.]

Liasson, Miranda. *The Sweetheart Deal* (N). Shrewsbury, Pa.: Entangled Publishing, 2022. [Ind.]

———. *The Sweetheart Fix* (N). Shrewsbury, Pa.: Entangled Publishing, 2022. [Ind.]

Liautaud, Leslie. *Black Bear Lake* (N). Amarillo, Tex.: Blue Handle Publishing, 2022. [Wis.]

Lillard, Amy. *The Amish Matchmaker* (N). NY: Zebra Books, 2022. [Mo.]

———. *Dairy, Dairy, Quite Contrary* (N). NY: Kensington Books, 2022. [Kan.]

———. *Marry Me, Millie* (N). NY: Zebra Books, 2022. [Mo.]

Linde, Kenneth. *Let Go* (N). McHenry, Ill.: Waldwick Partners, 2022. [Madison, Wis.]

Lintemuth, Janet and John Opskar. *Autumn Nightmare* (N). Thermopolis, Wyo.: Powder River Publishing, 2022. [Chicago, Ill.]

Litton, Melvin. *Banks of the River* (N). Hertford, N.C.: Gordian Knot Books, 2022. [Kan.]

———. *King Harvest* (N). Hertford, N.C.: Gordian Knot Books, 2022. [Kan.]

Liu, Anni. *Border Vista* (P). NY: Persea Books, 2022.

Lochner, Courtney. *The French House* (N). Minneapolis: Calumet Editions, 2022. [Madison, Wis.]

Lopez, Angelina M. *After Hours on Milagro Street* (N). Toronto: Carina Press, 2022. [Kan.]

Lore, Danny and Greg Pak. *Stranger Things: Erica the Great* (juv). Milwaukie, Or.: Dark Horse Books, 2022. [Ind.]

Lourey, Jess. *Monday Is Murder* (N). S.l.: Toadhouse Books, 2022. [Battle Lake, Minn.]

————. *The Quarry Girls* (N). Seattle: Thomas & Mercer, 2022. [Minn.]

Love, Goddess. *Lil Project Chick from the Chi* (N). Alpharetta, Ga.: Cole Hart Signature, 2022. [Chicago, Ill.]

Lovegreen, Kevin. *The Best Day Ever!* (juv). Eagan, Minn.: Lucky Luke, 2022. [Minn.]

Lucille, Sherry. *Falling* (N). Madison, Wis.: Inspiring Destiny Press, 2022. [Chicago, Ill.]

Luczak, Raymond. *Chlorophyll* (P). Ann Arbor, Mich.: Modern History Press, 2022. [Mich.]

Lukins, Robert. *Loveland* (N). Crows Nest, N.S.W.: Allen & Unwin, 2022. [Neb.]

Lund, Natalie. *The Wolves Are Watching* (juv). NY: Viking Books, 2022. [Ill.]

Lund, R.T. *Who Are You?* (N). Mineral Creek, Wis.: Little Creek Press, 2022. [Minneapolis, Minn.]

Lutterman, Brian. *Northfall* (N). St. Paul, Minn.: Oak Ridge Press, 2022. [Minn.]

Lyders, Richard A. *Traces from My Inner Journey* (P). Peacham, Vt.: Perpetua Press, 2022. [N.D.]

McBain, Tim *see* Vargus, L.T.

McCarthy, Cormac. *Stella Maris*. NY: Alfred A. Knopf, 2022. [Wis.]

McCarthy, Cory. *Man o' War* (juv). NY: Dutton, 2022. [Ohio]

McCarthy, Kevin. *The Wintering Place* (N). NY: W.W. Norton, 2022. [Dak.]

McClane, Mattie. *Wen Wilson* (N). Kure Beach, N.C.: Myrtle Hedge Press, 2022. [Mo.]

McClay, Jocelyn. *Her Unlikely Amish Protector* (N). Toronto: Love Inspired, 2022. [Ohio]

McDonald, Michael, et al. *Indiana Fall* (N). Linden, Mich.: Raventhorne Books, 2022. [Ind.]

McGinnis, Mindy. *The Last Laugh* (juv). NY: Katherine Tegen Books, 2022. [Ohio]

McGinnis, Penny Frost. *Home Where She Belongs* (N). Georgetown, Tenn.: Mt. Zion Ridge Press, 2022. [Ohio]

McGonegal, Richard F. *Ghoul Duty* (N). Warrensburg, Mo.: Cave Hollow Press, 2022. [Mo.]

McGuire, Shawn. *Wayward Secrets* (N). S.l.: Brown Bag Books, 2022. [Wis.]

McIntire, Jonie. *Semidomesticated* (P). Russell, Ky.: Sheila-Na-Gig Editions, 2022.

McKee, Kittredge. *Prairie* (N). Red Bank, N.J.: Newman Springs Publishing, 2022. [Neb.]

McKenzie, Pepi. *Street Life: Freedom* (N). Port Angeles, Wash.: Cadmus Publishing, 2022. [Minneapolis, Minn.]

McKinney, Kate. *When to Hold On* (N). Barneveld, Wis.: Spiral North Books, 2022. [Wis.]

MacLaren, Sharlene. *Her Guarded Heart* (N). New Kensington, Pa.: Whitaker House, 2022. [Ohio]

McNamara, Frances. *Death in a Time of Spanish Flu* (N). Chicago: Rudiyat Press, 2022. [Chicago, Ill.]

McNees, Kelly O'Connor. *The Myth of Surrender* (N). NY: Pegasus Books, 2022. [Ill.]

Manansala, Mia P. *Blackmail and Bibingka* (N). NY: Berkley Prime Crime, 2022. [Ill.]

———. *Homicide and Halo-Halo* (N). NY: Berkley Prime Crime, 2022. [Ill.]

Mann, Michael. *Heat 2* (N). London: HarperCollins, 2022. [Chicago, Ill.]

March, Nev. *Peril at the Exposition* (N). NY: Minotaur Books, 2022. [Chicago, Ill.]

Markert, Jenny. *Waterlines* (N). Crystal Bay, Minn.: Elder Eye Press, 2022. [Minn.]

Marks, John. *Rail against Injustice* (N). Castroville, Tex.: Black Rose Writing, 2022. [Mich.]

Marrocco, Christina. *Addio, Love Monster* (N). S.l.: Ovunque Siamo Press, 2022. [Chicago, Ill.]

Martin, Lee. *The Glassmaker's Wife* (N). Ann Arbor, Mich.: Dzanc Books, 2022. [Ill.]

Martin, Terri. *High on the Vine* (N). L'Anse, Mich.: Gnarly Woods Publications, 2022. [Mich.]

Martone, Michael. *Plain Air: Sketches from Winesburg, Indiana* (S). Reno, Nev.: Baobab Press, 2022. [Ind.]

Mast, Kathryn. *Cornmeal Samaritan* (juv). Harrisonburg, Va.: Christian Light Publications, 2022. [Ohio]

Mathews, Sarah Thankam. *All This Could Be Different* (N). NY: Viking Books, 2022. [Milwaukee, Wis.]

Maus, Ruth. *Puzzled* (P). Emporia, Kan.: Meadowlark Press, 2022. [Kan.]

Maxfield, Brenda. *The Recent Widower* (N). S.l.: Tica House Publishing, 2022. [Ind.]

Mayfield, Steven. *Delphic Oracle U.S.A.* (N). Raleigh, N.C.: Regal House Publishing, 2022. [Neb.]

Mehl, Nancy. *When Angels Whisper* (N). Danbury, Conn.: Guideposts, 2022. [Ohio]

Meissner, William. *Summer of Rain, Summer of Fire* (N). Nacogdoches, Tex.: Stephen F. Austin State U P, 2022. [Wis.]

Menes, Orlando Ricardo, ed. *The Open Light: Poets from Notre Dame, 1991–2008* (A). Notre Dame, Ind.: U Notre Dame P, 2022.

Meno, Joe. *Book of Extraordinary Tragedies* (N). Brooklyn, N.Y.: Akashic Books, 2022. [Chicago, Ill.]

Merriam, Michael. *Last Car to Annwn Station* (N). Minneapolis: Queen of Swords Press, 2022. [Minneapolis, Minn.]

Mesa, Desideria. *Bindle Punk Bruja* (N). NY: Harper Voyager, 2022. [Kansas City, Mo.]

Metz, Robin *see* Evans, Donald G.

Meyer, Gabrielle. *The Soldier's Baby Promise* (N). Toronto: Love Inspired, 2022. [Minn.]

Meyer, Karen. *Secrets in the Sky Nest* (juv). Glendale, Ariz.: Sable Creek Press, 2022. [Salem, Ohio]

Miksa, Matt. *Don't Get Close* (N). NY: Crooked Lane Books, 2022. [Chicago]

Miles, Olivia. *A Chance on Me* (N). S.l.: Rosewood Press, 2022. [Mich.]

———. *A New Beginning* (N). S.l.: Rosewood Press, 2022. [Mich.]

———. *Summer of Us* (N). S.l.: Rosewood Press, 2022. [Mich.]

Miley, Mary. *Deadly Spirits* (N). Edinburgh: Severn House, 2022. [Chicago, Ill.]

Miller, Cate. *From Wags to Riches* (juv). Waukesha, Wis.: Orange Hat Publishing, 2022. [Wis]

Miller, Hannah. *The Roadside Stand* (N). S.l.: Tica House Publishing, 2022. [Ohio]

Miller, Julie. *Decoding the Truth* (N). Toronto: Harlequin Intrigue, 2022. [Kansas City, Mo.]

———. *K-9 Patrol* (N). Toronto: Harlequin Intrigue, 2021. [Kansas City, Mo.]

Miller, Latisha. *Chaos in da Chi* (N). Madison, Wis.: New Book Authors Publishing, 2022. [Chicago, Ill.]

Millett, Larry. *Rafferty's Last Case* (N). Minneapolis: U Minnesota P, 2022. [St. Paul, Minn.]

Miłowicki, Aleksander. *Boj* (N). Gdynia: Novae Res, 2022. [Chicago, Ill.]

Mindel, Jenna. *A Secret Christmas Family* (N). Toronto: Love Inspired, 2022. [Mich.]

Moehling, Joshua. *And There He Kept Her* (N). Scottsdale, Ariz.: Poisoned Pen Press, 2022. [Minn.]

Moffett, Sandy. *The Ghost of Craven Snuggs* (N). North Liberty, Iowa: Ice Cube Press, 2022. [Iowa]

Moncrieff, J.H. *Dragonfly Summer* (N). London: Flame Tree Press, 2022. [Minn.]

Montag, Kassandra. *Those Who Return* (N). London: Quercus, 2022. [Neb.]

Montgomery, Jess. *The Echoes* (N). NY: Minotaur Books, 2022. [Ohio]

Montgomery, K.L. *Little Shop of Murder* (N). Georgetown, Del.: Mountains Wanted Publishing, 2022. [Ind.]

Moore, Charles E. *Call Me Sam* (N). Parker, Colo.: Outskirts Press, 2022. [Kan.]

Moore, Hilton Everett. *North of Nelson* (S). Covington, Mich.: Silver Mountain Press, 2022. [Mich.]

Moore, Joseph L. *The Call of Jeremiah McGill* (juv). Tampa, Fla.: Gatekeeper Press, 2022. [Mo.]

Morris, Bob. *Secret Service Journals* (N). Columbus, Ind.: PathBinder Publishing, 2022. [Detroit, Mich.]

Morrissey, Hannah. *The Widowmaker* (N). NY: Minotaur Books, 2022. [Wis.]

Mosley, Faith. *Sky Court* (N). Portland, Or.: Circuit Breaker Books, 2022. [Ill.]

Mulhern, Julie. *Evil Woman* (N). S.l.: J&M Press, 2022. [Kansas City, Mo.]

———. *Watching the Detectives* (N). S.l.: J&M Press, 2022. [Kansas City, Mo.]

Mullen, Chris. *Rowdy: Dead or Alive* (juv). Las Vegas, Nev.: Wise Wolf Books, 2022. [Kan.]

Mullins, Kimberly. *Haunted Christmas* (N). Houston, Tex.: JKJ Books, 2022 [Chicago, Ill.]

———. *Unexpected Outcome* (N). Houston, Tex.: JKJ Books, 2022. [Chicago, Ill.]

Munroe, Fatima. *Weak for a Coldhearted Goon* (N). Atlanta, Ga.: Monreaux Publications, 2022. [Milwaukee, Wis.]

Muntz, Kyle. *The Pain Eater* (N). Troy, N.Y.: Clash Books, 2022. [Mich.]

Murphy, Jennifer. *Scarlet in Blue* (N). NY: Dutton, 2022. [South Haven, Mich.]

Murphy, Lee Ann S. *Scrooge and Marlee* (N). Pensacola, Fla.: World Castle Publishing, 2022. [Mo.]

———. *Where Dreams Come True* (N). Pensacola, Fla.: World Castle Publishing, 2022. [Mo.]

Musch, Naomi. *Season of My Enemy* (N). Uhrichsville, Ohio: Barbour Publishing, 2022. [Wis.]

Myers, Andrea. *Behind the Wire* (N). S.l.: Good Morning Publishing, 2022. [Neb.]

Myers, M. Ruth. *A Dame Worth Killing* (N). S.l.: Tuesday House, 2022. [Dayton, Ohio]

Myers, Tom *see* Teodo, Paul

Myers, William L., Jr. *Backstory* (N). Sarasota, Fla.: Oceanview Publishing, 2022. [Kan.]

Myles, Anne. *What Woman That Was* (P). Cedar Falls, Iowa: Final Thursday Press, 2022.

Navickas, Julie. *I Love You Today* (N). Murrells Inlet, S.C.: Inkspell Publishing, 2022. [Chicago, Ill.]

Neelly, Rock. *Salt Fork Stations* (N). Goshen, Ky.: Hydra Publications, 2022. [Wichita, Kan.]

Neill, Chloe. *Devouring Darkness* (N). NY: Berkley Books, 2022. [Chicago, Ill.]

Nichols, Oleta M. *When the Little Wings are Stronger* (N). Columbia, Mo.: AKA Publishing, 2022. [Mo.]

Nickles, Carol. *Thumb Fire Desire* (N). Adams Basin, N.Y.: Wild Rose Press, 2022. [Mich.]

Nickless, Barbara. *Dark of Night* (N). Seattle: Thomas & Mercer, 2022. [Chicago, Ill.]

Niesner, Mershon. *The Bootmaker's Wife* (N). Marco Island, Fla.: The Bell Group, 2022. [Neb.]

Noblin, Annie England. *Christmas in Blue Dog Valley* (N). NY: Avon, 2022. [Wis.]

Norlander, Linda. *Death of a Snow Ghost* (N). Olney, Md.: Level Best Books, 2022. [Minn.]

Novak, Kathleen. *Steel* (N). Minneapolis: Black Cat Text, 2022. [Chicago, Ill.]

Novak,. Richard. *A Pathologist's Journey* (N). Rockford, Ill.: SW Publishing, 2022. [Rockford, Ill.]

Novic, Sara. *True Biz* (N). NY: Random House, 2022. [Ohio]

Nye, Naomi Shihab. *The Turtle of Michigan* (juv). NY: Greenwillow Books, 2022. [Ann Arbor, Mich.]

Oates, Joyce Carol. *Babysitter* (N). NY: Alfred A. Knopf, 2022. [Detroit, Mich.]

Obuobi, Shirlene. *On Rotation* (N). NY: Avon Books, 2022. [Chicago, Ill.]

Oclon, Kim. *The War on All Fronts* (N). Deerfield, Ill.: Trism Books, 2022. [Madison, Wis.]

Ohlert, Kelly. *To Get to the Other Side* (N). S.l.: Alcove Press, 2022. [Chicago, Ill.]

Olson, Michèle. *Being Wendy* (N). Green Bay, Wis.: Lake Girl Publishing, 2022. [Mackinac Island, Mich.]

Olson, Richard A. *A Man of Stihl* (N). Pittsburgh: Dorrance Publishing Co., 2022. [Peoria, Ill.]

Olzmann, Matthew. *Constellation Route* (P). Farmington, Me.: Alice James Books, 2022.

Ondrus, Suzanne. *Death of an Unvirtuous Woman* (P). Georgetown, Ky.: Finishing Line Press, 2022. [Ohio]

Opskar, John *see* Lintemuth, Janet

Orner, Peter. *Still No Word from You: Notes in the Margin* (S). NY: Catapult, 2022.

Owens, John. *One Winter Up North* (juv). Minneapolis: U Minnesota P, 2022. [Minn.]

Oxford, Alana. *Scotsman in the Stacks* (N). S.l.: 8N Publishing, 2022. [Mich.]

Packa, Sheila. *Surface Displacements* (P). Duluth, Minn.: Wildwood River Press, 2022. [Minn.]

Pagel, Caryl. *Free Clean Fill Dirt* (P). Akron, Ohio: U Akron P, 2022. [Midwest]

Painter, Lynn. *The Do-Over* (juv). NY: Simon & Schuster, 2022. [Omaha, Neb.]

Pak, Greg *see* Lore, Danny

Palmer, Charly. *The Legend of Gravity* (juv). NY: Farrar, Straus and Giroux, 2022. Milwaukee, Wis.]

Pancholy, Maulik. *Nikhil out Loud* (juv). NY: Balzer + Bray, 2022. [Ohio]

Paretsky, Sara. *Overboard* (N). NY: William Morrow, 2022. [Chicago, Ill.]

Parker, Eliot. *A Final Call* (N). Terra Alta, W.V.: Publisher Page, 2022. [Cleveland, Ohio]

Patterson, James. *Escape* (N). NY: Little, Brown, 2022. [Chicago, Ill.]

——— and J.D. Barker. *Death of the Black Widow* (N). NY: Grand Central Publishing, 2022. [Detroit, Mich.]

Payne, Melissa. *A Light in the Forest* (N). Seattle: Lake Union Publishing, 2022. [Ohio]

Pearce, Robyn R. *They Said I Couldn't Do It* (N). Pukekohe, N.Z.: GettingAGrip Publishing, 2022. [Ohio]

Peck, Jay. *Vision of Death* (N). S.l.: Raven Tale Publishing, 2022. [St. Joseph, Mo.]

Peele, Amy S. *Hold* (N). Berkeley, Calif.: She Writes Press, 2022. [Chicago, Ill.]

Pellicano, Anthony. *The Neighborhood* (N). Phoenix, Ariz.: Phoenix Books, 2022. [Chicago, Ill.]

Pennington, Lindsey. *Risking Her Heart* (N). S.l.: 12-153-44 Publishing, 2022. [Minn.]

Perkins, R.S. *Tensile Town* (N). S.l.: Innovo Publishing, 2022. [Ohio]

Peter, Gary Eldon. *The Complicated Calculus (and Cows) of Carl Paulsen* (juv). Raleigh, N.C.: Regal House Publishing, 2022. [Minn.]

Peterson, R.L. *Leave the Night to God* (N). Raleigh, N.C.: Regal House Publishing, 2022. [Midwest]

Petrie, Nick. *The Runaway* (N). NY: G.P. Putnam's Sons, 2022. [Neb.]

Pfaff, Dan. *No Land of Mine* (N). Hill Point, Wis.: Grapevine Publishing, 2022. [Midwest]

Phillips, Carl. *My Trade Is Mystery: Seven Meditations from a Life in Writing* (M). New Haven, Conn.: Yale U P, 2022.

———. *Then the War and Selected Poems, 2007–2020* (P). NY: Farrar, Straus and Giroux, 2022.

Phillips, Susan Elizabeth. *When Stars Collide* (N). NY: William Morrow, 2021. [Chicago, Ill.]

Philo, Jolene. *See Jane Run!* (N). Polk City, Iowa: Midwestern Books, 2022. [S.D.]

———. *See Jane Sing!* (N). Polk City, Iowa: Midwestern Books, 2022. [S.D.]

Pinckney, Darryl. *Come Back in September: A Literary Education on West Sixty-Seventh Street, Manhattan* (M). NY: Farrar, Straus and Giroux, 2022.

Pinkus, Harry. *Human Collateral* (N). N.C.: BQB Publishing, 2022. [Chicago, Ill.]

Pittman, Allison. *Laura's Shadow* (N). Uhrichsville, Ohio: Barbour Publishing, 2022. [Minneapolis, Minn.; De Smet, S.D.]

Platt, Cynthia. *Postcards from Summer* (juv). NY: Simon & Schuster BFYR, 2022. [Mackinac Island, Mich.]

Polito, Frank Anthony. *Renovated to Death* (N). NY: Kensington Books, 2022. [Mich.]

Polk, C.L. *Even Though I Knew the End* (N). NY: Tom Doherty Associates, 2022. [Chicago, Ill.]

Popovich, C.A. *The Kiss* (N). Valley Falls, N.Y.: Bold Strokes Books, 2022. [Mich.]

Porter, Summer. *A Mouse Tail on Mackinac Island* (juv). Ann Arbor, Mich.: Modern History Press, 2022. [Mackinac Island, Mich.]

Posthumus, David C. *The Legend of the Dogman* (N). Bountiful, Utah: Timber Ghost Press, 2022. [Mich.]

Potos, Andrea. *Her Joy Becomes* (P). Newburg, Or.: Fernwood Press, 2022.

Potter, Jim. *Deputy Jennings Meets the Amish* (N). Hutchinson, Kan.: Sandhenge, 2022. [Kan.]

Price, Sylvia. *The Beekeeper's Calendar* (N). S.l.: Penn and Ink Writing, 2022. [Ind.]

———. *The Herbalist's Remedy* (N). S.l.: Penn and Ink Writing, 2022. [Ind.]

———. *The Origins of Cardinal Hill* (N). S.l.: Penn and Ink Writing, 2022. [Ind.]

———. *The Soapmaker's Recipe* (N). S.l.: Penn and Ink Writing, 2022. [Ind.]

Quigley, Mindy. *Six Feet Deep Dish* (N). NY: St. Martin's Paperbacks, 2022. [Wis.]

Rabe, Jean. *The Dead of Autumn* (N). Ill.: Boone Press, 2022. [Ind.]

Rabin, David. *In Danger of Judgment* (N). Castroville, Tex.: Black Rose Writing, 2022. [Chicago, Ill.]

Rabushka, Jerrold. *Truckin' to Please* (N). New Orleans: Queer Mojo, 2022. [St. Louis, Mo.]

Randolph, Anne. *This Is What Life Does* (P). American Fork, Utah: Kelsay Books, 2022.

Randolph, Ladette. *Private Way* (N). Lincoln: U Nebraska P, 2022. [Lincoln, Neb.]

Rapino, Anthony J. and Anthony D. Grate. *Tommy and the Order of Cosmic Champions* (juv). Austin, Tex.: Greenleaf Book Group, 2022. [Ohio]

Rea, Kerry. *Lucy on the Wild Side* (N). NY: Berkley Books, 2022. [Columbus, Ohio]

Rebot, Allen. *Rise of Ancients* (N). Austin, Tex.: Atmosphere Press, 2022. [Chicago, Ill.]

Reed, Dwayne. *Simon B. Rhymin' Takes a Stand* (juv). NY: Little, Brown, 2022. [Chicago, Ill.]

Rehm, Daniel. *Let Flowers Be Flowers* (N). North Branch, Minn.: Rudbeckia, 2022. [Minn.; Wis.]

Rein, Arthur Kevin. *Rolling in the Deep* (N). Morrison, Colo.: Open Books, 2022. [Wis.]

Rendon, Marcie R. *Sinister Graves* (N). NY: Soho Crime, 2022. [Minn.]

Reynolds, Eric T. *The Legend of Mulberry School* (N). Kansas City: Hadley Rille Books, 2022. [Kan.]

Reynolds, Rose. *Husband (Not) Wanted* (N). Beavercreek, Ohio: Dusty Rose Publishing, 2022. [Dak.]

Rhodes, David. *Painting beyond Walls* (N). Minneapolis: Milkweed Editions, 2022. [Wis.]

Richey, Sheri. *Cat in Cahoots* (N). Tallahassee, Fla.: Cagelink Publishing, 2022. [Ohio]

Ricketts, Patricia. *Speed of Dark* (N). Berkeley, Calif.: She Writes Press, 2022. [Chicago, Ill.]

Riker, Leigh. *The Runaway Rancher* (N). Toronto: Harlequin Heartwarming, 2022. [Kan.]

Rindo, Ronald J. *Breathing Lake Superior* (N). St. Louis, Mo.: Brick Mantel Books, 2022. [Wis.]

Rivers, Krystina. *Something between Us* (N). Valley Falls, N.Y.: Bold Strokes Books, 2022. [Chicago, Ill.]

Robins, Eden. *When Franny Stands Up* (N). Naperville, Ill.: Sourcebooks Landmark, 2022. [Chicago, Ill.]

Rodgers, Regina. *The Gamble on Love* (N). S.l.: Forget Me Not Romances, 2022. [Mo.]

Rodó, Candy. *Baker and Taylor in the Hunt for the Missing Ring* (juv). Ashland, Ohio: Paw Prints Publishing, 2022. [Chicago, Ill.]

Roesch, Benjamin. *Blowin' My Mind Like a Summer Breeze* (juv). Winnipeg: Deep Hearts YA, 2022. [Midwest]

Rogal, Margaret. *Field Notes* (P). Fargo: North Dakota State U P, 2022. [N.D.]

Rolfes, Luke. *Impossible Naked Life* (S). Austin, Tex.: Kallisto Gaia Press, 2022. [Midwest]

Ronan, Kelsey. *Chevy in the Hole* (N). NY Henry Holt, 2022. [Flint, Mich.]

Rooney, Kathleen. *Where Are the Snows* (P). Huntsville: Texas Review Press, 2022.

Rose, Caroline Starr. *Miraculous* (juv). NY: G.P. Putnam's Sons, 2022. [Ohio]

Rosengren, Gayle. *MacKenzie's Last Run* (juv). Milwaukee, Wis.: Three Towers Press, 2022. [Madison, Wis.]

Ross, William Mitchell. *The Spellbinding Tale of Fiona Brown* (N). Bloomington, Ind.: Xlibris, 2022. [Monroe, Wis.]

Rought, K.M. *see* Ryan, L.T.

Russell, Aurora. *Semper Fitz* (N). United Kingdon: Totally Bound Publishing, 2022. [Minn.]

Rutkoski, Marie. *Real Easy* (N). NY: Henry Holt, 2022. [Ill.]

Ryan, Annelise. *A Death in Door County* (N). NY: Berkley Books, 2022. [Wis.]

Ryan, L.T. *Concealed in Shadow*. Monee, Ill.: Liquid Mind Media, 2022. [Chicago, Ill.]

——— and K.M. Rought. *The Last Stop* (N). Monee, Ill.: Liquid Mind Media, 2022. [Ill.]

Rylander, Chris. *The Hurricanes of Weakerville* (juv). NY: Walden Pond Press, 2022. [Iowa]

Salsbury, Brett. *Surrender Dorothy* (P). Fargo: North Dakota State U P, 2022.

Sanders, Scott Jameson. *Driving through Shaker Heights* (N). Conneaut Lake, Pa.: Page Publishing, 2022. [Shaker Heights, Ohio]

Sanders, Scott Russell. *Small Marvels* (S). Bloomington: Indiana U P, 2022.

Sandford, John. *Righteous Prey* (N). NY: G.P. Putnam's Sons, 2022. [Minn.]

Sass, Adam. *The 99 Boyfriends of Micah Summers* (juv). NY: Viking Press, 2022. [Chicago, Ill.]

Sawyer, Kim Vogel. *Still My Forever* (N). Colorado Springs, Colo.: WaterBrook, 2022. [Kan.]

Sayles, John. *Yellow Earth* (N). Chicago: Haymarket Books, 2022. [N.D.]

Scanlon, Liz Garton. *Lolo's Light* (juv). San Francisco: Chronicle Books, 2022. [Chicago, Ill.]

Schaafsma, David, Roxanne Pilat, and Lauren DeJulio Bell, eds. *Growing Up Chicago* (S). Evanston, Ill.: Northwestern U P, 2022. [Chicago, Ill.]

Schaffhausen, Joanna. *Long Gone* (N). NY: Minotaur Books, 2022. [Chicago, Ill.]

Schiffer, Kiersten. *Fast Forward My Heart* (N). S.l.: Sweet Light Press, 2022. [Ind.]

———. *Rewind My Love* (N). S.l.: Sweet Light Press, 2022. [Ind.]

Schiller-Hartnett, Tanya. *The Purge* (N). London: Austin Macauley Publishers, 2022. [Neb.]

Schneider, Diane Cohen. *Andrea Hoffman Goes All In* (N). Berkeley, Calif.: She Writes Press, 2022. [Chicago, Ill.]

Schoonmaker, Frances. *Sid Johnson and the Phantom Slave Stealer* (juv). Havertown, Pa.: Auctus Publishers, 2022. [Ill.]

Schroeder, James. *The Devil You Know* (N). S.l.: Weathered Knight Publishing, 2022. [Chicago, Ill.]

Schwartz, Ben G. *The Way It Went* (N). Berkeley, Calif.: El Leon Literary Arts, 2022. [Mo.]

Scott, Jeremy. *When the Corn Is Waist High* (N). Nashville, Tenn.: Keylight Books, 2022. [Ind.]

Scott, Laura. *Explosive Truth* (N). Readscape Publishing, 2022. [Milwaukee, Wis.]

———. *Protection Detail* (N). S.l.: Readscape Publishing, 2022. [Milwaukee, Wis.]

———. *Tailing Trouble* (N). NY: Crooked Lane Books, 2022. [Wis.]

Scott, Mark E. *Drunk Log* (N). Naples, Fla.: Speaking Volumes, 2022. [Cincinnati, Ohio]

Searle, Newell. *Copy Desk Murders* (N). Minneapolis: Calumet Editions, 2022. [Minn.]

Seedorf, Julie. *Weed Lake* (N). Minn.: Granny Edith Books, 2022. [Minn.]

Seifert, Mary. *Maverick, Movies & Murder* (N). Angel Fire, N.M.: Secret Staircase Books, 2022. [Minn.]

———. *Rescues, Rogues & Renegades* (N). Angel Fire, N.M.: Secret Staircase Books, 2022. [Minn.]

———. *Santa, Snowflakes, & Strychnine* (N). Angel Fire, N.M.: Secret Staircase Books, 2022. [Minn.]

———. *Tinsel, Trials, & Traitors* (N). Angel Fire, N.M.: Secret Staircase Books, 2022. [Minn.]

Sell, Chad. *Doodleville: Art Attacks!* (juv). NY: Alfred A. Knopf, 2022. [Chicago, Ill.]

Sellers, Julie A. *Ann of Sunflower Lane* (juv). Emporia, Kan.: Meadowlark Press, 2022. [Kan.]

Sensel, Joni. *A Curse on the Wind* (juv). Adams Basin, N.Y.: Wild Rose Press, 2022. [Ohio]

Senter, Joshua. *Still the Night Call* (N). S.l.: Roubidoux Press, 2022. [Mo.]

Sereno, Annie. *Blame It on the Brontës* (N). NY: Forever, 2022. [Ill.]

Shaiken, Mark A. *Automatic Stay* (N). Denver, Colo.: 1609 Press, 2022. [Kansas City, Mo.]

Sharer, Judy. *Love-Challenged Life* (N). Adams Basin, N.Y.: Wild Rose Press, 2022. [Kan.]

Sharp, Diamond. *Super Sad Black Girl* (P). Chicago: Haymarket Books, 2022. [Chicago, Ill.]

Shea, Brian. *Hunting the Mirror Man* (N). Leesburg, Va.: Severn River Publishing, 2022. [Iowa]

Shepard, Tagan. *Two Knights Tango* (N). Tallahassee: Bella Books, 2022. [Chicago, Ill.]

Shiloah, Shira. *Grave Intervention* (N). Memphis, Tenn.: Salty Air Publishing, 2022. [Naperville, Ill.]

Shipman, Viola. *The Edge of Summer* (N). Toronto: Graydon House, 2022. [Mich.]

———. *A Wish for Winter* (N). Toronto: Graydon House, 2022. [Mich.]

Shore, Nathan. *The Blue Flame* (N). Tucson, Ariz.: Barque Point Press, 2022. [Mich.]

Sidwell, Cole. *I Hate Rabbits* (N). S.l.: Bell Cow Publishing, 2022. [Mo.]

Sigafus, Kim. *Whisper to the Sky* (juv). S.l.: 7th Generation, 2022. [Minneapolis, Minn.]

Silver, Kimber. *Broken Rhodes* (N). S.l.: Silver Plains Publications, 2022. [Kan.]

Sinclair, Elke. *Eagles Cove* (N). Bloomington, Ind.: AuthorHouse, 2022. [Brainerd, Minn.]

Skalka, Patricia. *Death Casts a Shadow* (N). Madison: U Wisconsin P, 2022. [Wis.]

Sloan, Lynn. *Midstream* (N). Burlington, Vt.: Fomite, 2022. [Chicago, Ill.]

Smelter, Lisa. *Sarah's Garden* (N). Columbus, Ohio: Gatekeeper Press, 2022. [Minn.]

———. *Susan's Return* (N). Columbus, Ohio: Gatekeeper Press, 2022. [Minn.]

Smiley, Jane. *A Dangerous Business* (N). NY: Alfred A. Knopf, 2022.

Smith, Anthony Neil. *Slower Bear* (N). S.l.: Fahrenheit Thirteen, 2022. [Neb.]

Smith, Cynthia Leitich. *Indian Shoes* (juv). NY: Heartdrum, 2022. [Chicago, Ill.]

Smith, Jamie Lyn. *Township* (S). Stevens Point, Wis.: Cornerstone Press, 2022. [Ohio]

Smith, Laurie Stroup. *Pockets of Peace* (N). Ladson, S.C.: Vinspire Publishing, 2022. [Ohio]

Smith, Ryan Elliott. *Fly Over This: Stories from the New Midwest* (S). Chicago: Tortoise Books, 2022. [Midwest]

Smith, S.L. *Dead Reckoning* (N). St. Paul, Minn.: Sightline Press, 2022. [St. Paul, Minn.]

Smoker, M.L. *Thunderous* (juv). Los Angeles: Curiosity Books, 2022. [S.D.]

Snelling, Lauraine. *A Time to Bloom* (N). Minneapolis: Bethany House, 2022. [Neb.]

Snelson, Richard O. *Long Ride for Justice* (N). Rogers, Ark.: Solander Press, 2022. [Mo.]

Solberg, Barb. *What We Leave Behind* (N). Trenton, Ga.: BookLocker, 2022. [N.D.]

Sontheimer, Barbara. *Victor's Blessing* (N). Austin, Tex.: Atmosphere Press, 2022. [Ste. Genevieve, Mo.]

Soukup, Frederick. *Blood up North* (N). Australia: Vine Leaves Press, 2022. [Minn.]

Spear, Terry. *While the Wolf's Away* (N). Naperville, Ill.: Sourcebooks Casablanca, 2022. [Minn.]

Spredemann, Jennifer. *The Newcomer* (N). Ind.: Blessed Publishing, 2022. [Ind.]

Stahl, Dick. *My Cancer Chronicle* (P). Rock Island, Ill.: Midwest Writing Center Press, 2022. [Iowa]

Stamper, Phil. *Small Town Pride* (juv). NY: HarperCollins, 2022. [Ohio]

Steadman, Robert A. *I Killed Sam* (N). Traverse City, Mich.: Mission Point Press, 2022. [Flint, Mich.]

Stelljes, Roger. *Missing Angel* (N). London: Bookouture, 2022. [Minn.]

Stevens, Patrick. *Panning Gold* (P). Oakland, Calif.: Finns Way Books, 2022. [Minn.]

Stone, Kyla. *The Dark We Seek* (N). Atlanta, Ga.: Paper Moon Press, 2022. [Mich.]

———. *The Light We Lost* (N). Atlanta, Ga.: Paper Moon Press, 2022. [Mich.]

Stone, Victoria Helen. *At the Quiet Edge* (N). Seattle: Lake Union Publishing, 2022. [Kan.]

Stoudt, Jamie. *Donna Carlasccio* (N). St. Paul, Minn.: Beaver's Pond Press, 2022. [Stillwater, Minn.]

Stryk, Lydia. *The Teachers' Room* (N). Ann Arbor, Mich.: Bywater Books, 2022. [Ill.]

Summie, Caitlin H. *Geographies of the Heart* (N). Burlington, Vt.: Fomite, 2022. [Minneapolis, Minn.]

Sutphen, Joyce. *This Long Winter* (P). Pittsburgh: Carnegie Mellon U P, 2022.

Sutter, Bart. *So Surprised to Find You Here* (P). Minneapolis: Nodin Press, 2022. [Minn.]

Swan, Erin. *Walk the Vanished Earth* (N). NY: Viking Books, 2022. [Kan.]

Swanson, Terry. *Grasshoppers in My Bed* (juv). St. Paul, Minn.: Ramsey County Historical Society, 2022. [Minn.]

Sweazy, Larry D. *The Broken Bow* (N). NY: Pinnacle Books, 2022. [Dak.]

Sweeney, Sandra. *Morning Train North* (N). Green Bay, Wis.: TitleTown Publishing, 2022. [Wis.]

Sykes, Dorian. *A New Generation* (N). Farmingdale, N.Y.: Urban Books, 2022. [Detroit, Mich.]

Taylor, Dennis E. *Roadkill* (N). NY: Ethan Ellenberg Literary Agency, 2022. [Ohio]

Taylor, K.C. *Sincerely Yours, Mrs. Taylor-Walsh* (P). Indianapolis: Sapati Ingera Publishing, 2022. [Ind.]

Teodo, Paul and Tom Myers. *South of Cermak: Chicago Stories* (S). S.l.: Literate Ape Press, 2022. [Chicago, Ill.]

Thomas, Markida *see* Cooper, Shantiana

Thompson, Kasha. *Holding Back the Years* (N). Lincoln, Calif.: Webster Avenue, 2022. [Mich.]

Tian, Xixi. *This Place Is Still Beautiful* (juv). NY: Balzer + Bray, 2022. [Midwest]

Tibbs, Carlos E. *Myles to Go: Beginnings* (N). Parker, Colo.: Outskirts Press, 2022. [Chicago, Ill.]

Timko, Esther L. *Essie's Poetry* (P). Meadville, Pa.: Fulton Books, 2022. [Ill.]

Todd, Susan Amond. *Life's Fortune* (N). Charlotte, N.C.: Warren Publishing, 2022. [Wis.]

Torres, Vanessa L. *The Turning Pointe* (juv). NY: Alfred A. Knopf, 2022. [Minneapolis, Minn.]

Toten, Teresa. *Eight Days* (juv). Toronto: Scholastic Canada, 2022. [Chicago, Ill.]

Tran, Paul. *All the Flowers Kneeling* (P). NY: Penguin, 2022.

Trelstad, Nick. *A Threshold We Carry* (P). American Fork, Utah: Kelsay Books, 2022. [Minn.]

Turonek, E. Raye. *Rural Route 8* (N). Farmingdale, N.Y.: Urban Books, 2022. [Clarkston, Mich.]

———. *Unrequited Love* (N). Farmingdale, N.Y.: Urban Books, 2022. [Clarkston, Mich.]

Turow, Scott. *Suspect* (N). NY: Grand Central Publishing, 2022. [Ill.]

Tuttle, Susan L. *Out of the Blue* (N). Birmingham, Ala.: Iron Stream Fiction, 2022. [Mich.]

Tynion, James. *The Nice House on the Lake* (N). Burbank, Calif.: DC Comics, 2022. [Wis.]

Undlin, Lindsey. *Stolen* (N). Nashville, Tenn.: Idun, 2022. [N.D.]

Urban, Linda. *Talk Santa to Me* (juv). NY: Atheneum, 2022. [Ind.]

Van Fleet, Heather. *The Liars Beneath* (juv). Las Vegas, Nev.: Wise Wolf Books, 2022. [Iowa]

Vance-Tompkins, Sarah. *Wishing for Mr. Right* (N). S.l.: Tule Publishing, 2022. [Mich.]

Vanderah, Glendy. *The Oceanography of the Moon* (N). Seattle: Lake Union Publishing, 2022. [Wis.]

Vanderhorst, A.J. *Dark Sky's Ashes* (N). S.l.: Lion & Co. Press, 2022. (Kansas City, Mo.]

VanDerSys, Robyn. *Black Hills Fall* (N). Linden, Mich.: Raventhorne Books, 2022. [S.D.]

———. *One Hundred Miles* (N). Linden, Mich.: Raventhorne Books, 2022. [S.D.]

Varga, James. *Tombs of Little Egypt* (N). Eugene, Or.: Resource Publications, 2022. [Ill.]

Vargus, L.T. and Tim McBain. *Couple Killer* (N). S.l.: Smarmy Press, 2022. [Mich.]

Vaughan, Robert. *A Rambling Man* (N). Las Vegas, Nev.: Wolfpack Publishing, 2022. [Mo.]

Vaughn, Gareth. *Ishcrin Affair* (N). S.l.: JMS Books, 2022. [Wis.]

Vestal, Lornett B. *see* Haynes, Berneta L.

Viets, Elaine. *Late for His Own Funeral* (N). Edinburgh: Severn House, 2022. [Mo.]

Villhard, Doug. *Company of Women* (N). S.l.: Mabel Publishing, 2022. [St. Louis, Mo.]

Vizenor, Gerald. Literary Favors: Native Heart Stories of Survivance (M). *MidAmerica*, 49 (2022), 95–100.

Von Schrader, Eric. *A Universe Disrupted* (N). Carpinteria, Calif.: ABSOM Books, 2022. [St. Louis, Mo.]

Wacek, Michele Pariza. *Loch Ness Murder* (N). Prescott, Ariz.: Love-Based Publishing, 2022. [Wis.]

————. *Murder Next Door* (N). Prescott, Ariz.: Love-Based Publishing, 2022. [Wis.]

————. *The Murder of Sleepy Hollow* (N). Prescott, Ariz.: Love-Based Publishing, 2022. [Wis.]

Waggoner, Tim. *We Will Rise* (N). London: Flame Tree Press, 2022. [Ohio]

Walker, Thomas. *Cosmic Background Radiation* (juv). Polk City, Iowa: Midwestern Books, 2022. [S.D.]

Wanek, Connie *see* Kooser, Ted

Warren, Mark. *The Westering Trail Travesties* (S). Waterville, Me.: Five Star, 2022. [Kan; Neb.]

Weaver, James. *Last Chance Road* (N). Las Vegas, Nev.: Wolfpack Publishing, 2022. [Mo.]

Weber, Frank F. *Black and Blue* (N). Pierz, Minn.: Moon Finder, 2022. [Minneapolis, Minn.]

Webster-Hein, Michelle. *Out of Esau* (N). Berkeley, Calif.: Counterpoint Press, 2022. [Mich.]

Welckle, Kenneth Bruce. *Lost Love* (N). Pittsburgh: Dorrance Publishing Co., 2022. [Mankato, Minn.]

Wentling, Mark G. *Kansas Kaleidoscope* (N). Lubbock, Tex.: Wild Lark Books, 2022. [Kan.]

West, Adrian Nathan. *My Father's Diet* (N). Sheffield: And Other Stories, 2022. [Midwest]

West, Kathleen. *Home or Away* (N). NY: Berkley Books, 2022. [Minn.]

Westreich, Melvyn. *According to Their Deeds* (N). Oak Park, Mich.: Laurel Publishing, 2022. [Minn.]

Whicker, Mike. *Evansville's Finest Hour* (N). S.l.: Walküre, 2022. [Evansville, Ind.]

Whitacer, Bruce E. *The Elk in the Glade* (P). Forest Hills, N.Y.: Crown Rock Media, 2022. [Neb.]

Whitaker, Tori. *Matter of Happiness* (N). Seattle: Lake Union Publishing, 2022. [Detroit, Mich.]

White, Roseanna M. *Shadowed Loyalty* (N). Cumberland, Md.: Chrism Press, 2022. [Chicago, Ill.]

Wieland, Chris. *The Crabtree Monsters* (juv). Pasadena, Calif.: Smart Aleck Press, 2022. [Mich.]

Wilford, Kathleen. *Cabby Potts: Duchess of Dirt* (juv). Wood-Ridge, N.J.: Blue Bronco, 2022. [Kan.]

Willis, Jason Lee. *Tales of the Blue Earth* (S). Mapleton, Minn.: Lura Publications, 2022. [Minn.]

Wimmer, Mary B. *The Art of the Break* (N). Madison: U Wisconsin P, 2022. [Wis.]

Winfrey, Kerry. *Just Another Love Song* (N). NY: Jove Books, 2022. [Ohio]

Winston, Sherri. *Catastrophe* (juv). NY: HarperChapters, 2022. [Mich.]

———. *New Pup on the Block* (juv). NY: HarperChapters, 2022. [Mich.]

———. *The Runaway Robot* (juv). NY: HarperChapters, 2022. [Mich.]

Winter, W.A. *My Name Is Joe LaVoie* (N). Hoboken: Seventh Street Books, 2022. [Minneapolis, Minn.]

Wiseman, Beth. *The Bookseller's Promise* (N). Grand Rapids, Mich.: Zondervan, 2022. [Ind.]

———. *The Story of Love* (N). Grand Rapids, Mich.: Zondervan, 2022. [Ind.]

Wolfe, Toya. *Last Summer on State Street* (N). NY: William Morrow, 2022. [Chicago, Ill.]

Wolff, T.G. *Razing Stakes* (N). Lutz, Fla.: Down & Out Books, 2022. [Cleveland, Ohio]

Women of Words, comp. *Minnesota Stories* (S). Burnsville, Minn.: Kirk House Publishers, 2022. [Minn.]

Wright, Jaime Jo. *The Premonition at Withers Farm* (N). Minneapolis: Bethany House, 2022. [Mich.]

———. *The Souls of Lost Lake* (N). Minneapolis: Bethany House, 2022. [Wis.]

Wright, Pamela Desmond. *Finding Her Amish Home* (N). Toronto: Love Inspired, 2022. [Wis.]

Wyckoff, Vincent. *Refuge from the Sea* (N). St. Cloud, Minn.: North Star Press, 2022. [Minn.]

Yee, Lisa. *Maizy Chen's Last Chance* (juv). NY: Random House, 2022. [Minn.]

Young, Catherine. *Geosmin* (P). Sheboygan, Wis.: Water's Edge Press, 2022.

Young, Erin. *The Fields* (N). NY: Flatiron Books, 2022. [Iowa]

Zacharias, Pete. *The Man Burned by Winter* (N). Seattle: Thomas & Mercer, 2022. [Minn.]

Zellar, Brad. *Till the Wheels Fall Off* (N). Minneapolis: Coffee House Press, 2022. [Minn.]

Zhao, Katie. *The Lies We Tell* (juv). NY: Bloomsbury Publishing, 2022. [Mich.]

———. *Winnie Zeng Unleashes a Legend* (juv). NY: Random House, 2022. [Mich.]

Zink, William. *North Hill* (N). S.l.: Sugar Loaf Press, 2022. [Akron, Ohio]

Zrull, Lindsay S. *Goth Girl, Queen of the Universe* (juv). Mendota Heights, Minn.: North Star Editions, 2022. [Detroit, Mich.]

Secondary Sources

General

Afflerbach, Ian. On the Literary History of Selling Out: Craft, Identity, and Commercial Recognition (crit). *PMLA*, 137 (Mar. 2022), 230–45. [Iowa Writers' Workshop]

Bair, Jesse Roy. Fantastic Realism in Unrealistic Midwestern Fiction: A Review Essay (rev). *MidAmerica*, 49 (2022), 128–35.

Baxter, Charles. *Wonderlands: Essays on the Life of Literature* (crit). Minneapolis: Graywolf Press, 2022.

Beasecker, Robert, ed. Annual Bibliography of Midwestern Literature, 2020 (bibl). *MidAmerica*, 49 (2022), 136–90.

Becker, Molly. Talking American in the Midwest: Linguistic Diversity and Authenticity in the Twentieth-Century United States (crit; lang). *Journal of American Studies*, 56 (Feb. 2022), 65–86.

Das, Joanna Dee and Jay Buchanan. The Branson Hillbilly: Commingling Power and Marginalization on the "Heartland" Stage (crit). *Theatre History Studies*, 41 (2022), 88–106. [Mo.]

Delgadillo, Theresa, et al., eds. *Building Sustainable Worlds: Latinx Placemaking in the Midwest* (gen). Urbana: U Illinois P, 2022.

Duncan, Daniel. Merger Reversal in St. Louis: Implementation and Implications (lang). *Journal of English Linguistics*, 50 (Mar. 2022), 72–105. [St. Louis, Mo.]

————. "Missouree Was Always Out of Step with Missourah": Sociolinguistic Variants as Moral Toponyms (crit; lang). *Names: A Journal of Onomastics*, 70 (3) 2022, 24–38. [Mo.]

Faigin, Erin. "There Are No Cultural Islands Like Ceshinsky's": Ceshinsky's Community Bookstore and Intellectual Space in Chicago, 1922–1966 (gen). *Middle West Review*, 8 (Spr. 2022), 15–30. [Chicago, Ill.]

Halvorson, Britt E. and Joshua O. Reno. *Imagining the Heartland: White Supremacy and the American Midwest* (crit). Oakland: U California P, 2022.

Kirzane, Jessica. *Eyzehu M'koman Shel Zevakhim?* [What is the Site of the Ritual Sacrifice?]: Yiddish Writers Encounter the Chicago Meatpacking Industry (crit). *Middle West Review*, 8 (Spr. 2022), 31–44. [Chicago, Ill.]

Lauck, Jon K. Midwestern Studies Meets Critical Race Theory: Notes on *Imagining the Heartland* (rev). *Middle West Review*, 9 (Fall 2022), 126–65.

Miller, Monica Carol. *Dear Regina: Flannery O'Connor's Letters from Iowa* (corr; crit). Athens: U Georgia P, 2022. [Iowa Writers' Workshop]

Monaco, Pamela. It's the Journey: Three Novels of Self-Discovery: A Review Essay (rev). *MidAmerica*, 49 (2022), 121–27.

Morgart, James. *The Haunted States of America: Gothic Regionalism in Post-War American Fiction* (crit). Cardiff: U Wales P, 2022.

Rozga, Margaret. Abroad, in the Field, and Close to Home: Three Midwestern Poets: A Review Essay (rev). *MidAmerica*, 49 (2022), 108–14.

Sears, Jeff. One Hundred Years of Chicagoland: A Review Essay (rev). *MidAmerica*, 49 (2022), 103–07.

Watts, Edward. Recovery, Trauma, and Memory in Three Recent Small-Town Midwestern Novels: A Review Essay (rev). *MidAmerica*, 49 (2022), 115–20.

Wilhite, Keith. *Contested Terrain: Suburban Fiction and U.S. Regionalism, 1945–2020* (crit). Iowa City: U Iowa P, 2022.

Addams, Jane (1860–1935)

Steiner, Michael C. "The Internationalism That Is So Peculiarly American": Jane Addams, Grace Abbott, and the Promise of the Cosmopolitan Neighborhood, 1907–1917 (crit). *MidAmerica*, 49 (2022), 22–36.

Algren, Nelson (1909–1981)

Bales, Richard F. *The Short Writings of Nelson Algren: A Study of His Stories, Essays, Articles, Reviews, Poems and Other Literature* (crit). Jefferson, N.C.: McFarland & Co., 2022.

Lewin, James A. A Bard on the Wild Side (crit). *MidAmerica*, 49 (2022), 81–91.

Anderson, Sherwood (1876–1941)

McCracken, David. Sherwood Anderson's Grotesques in Thomas Boyd's *Points of Honor* (crit). *ANQ*, 35 (Mar. 2022), 82–88.

Yongju, Yuan. An Analysis of *Winesburg, Ohio* from the Perspective of Fromm's Alienation Theory (crit). *IRA-International Journal of Education & Multidisciplinary Studies*, 18 (4) 2022, 53–58.

Audubon, John James (1785–1851)

Clavreul, Denis. *In the Footsteps of Audubon* (biog). Princeton, N.J.: Princeton U P, 2022.

Austin, Mary Hunter (1868–1934)

Oxler, Elizabeth. Casting a Wider Net: Women's Regional Writing 1890–1950 (crit). Ph.D. Dissertation, U Louisiana Lafayette, 2022.

Baker, Ray Stannard (1870–1946)

Neu, Charles E. *The Wilson Circle: President Woodrow Wilson and His Advisers* (biog). Baltimore: Johns Hopkins U P, 2022.

Bang, Mary Jo (b. 1946)

Prada, Paula Currás. Objects Can Be Unintentionally Beautiful: Feminist Ekphrasis and Object-Orientation in the Poetry of Mary Jo Bang and Bernadette Mayer (crit). *Atlantis: Revista de la Asociación Española de Estudios Anglo-Norteamericanos*, 44 (1) 2022, 92–112.

Baum, L. Frank (1856–1919)

Dudziak, Mary L. Somewhere "over the Horizon" (crit) *American Quarterly*, 74 (Sept. 2022), 552–55.

McGowan, David. "I'll Get You, Tom and Jerry. And That Little Dog, Too!": Adaptation, Transmedia, and Franchise Management in the *Tom and Jerry* and *Wizard of Oz* Crossovers (crit). *Adaptation: The Journal of Literature and Screen Studies*, 15 (Aug. 2022), 149–70.

Bellamann, Henry (1882–1945)

Pinna, Lenny, ed. *A Face from Uranus: Correspondence between Tedd Burr and Henry Bellamann, 1943–1945* (corr; crit). Johnstown, Pa.: Ecclesia Arts, 2022.

Berryman, John (1914–1972)

Logan, William. Africa (crit). *Raritan: A Quarterly Review*, 42 (Sum. 2022), 16–35.

Mills, Nathaniel. John Berryman's Blackface Jokes: The Insights of Literary Failure (crit). *Journal of Modern Literature*, 45 (Sum. 2022), 58–76.

Bierce, Ambrose (1842–1914?)

Chittenden, Kelly. EcoGothic Anxiety in Ambrose Bierce's "The Eyes of the Panther" and Lauren Groff's "The Midnight Zone" (crit). *Studies in the American Short Story*, 3 (1–2) 2022, 93–111.

Myers, Robert. Ambrose Bierce's Ecophobic War against Nature (crit). *ISLE: Interdisciplinary Studies in Literature and Environment*, 29 (Sum. 2022), 406–23.

Walsh, Richard. Eventuality in Fiction: Contingency, Complexity and Narrative (crit). *Narrative*, 30 (Oct. 2022), 287–303.

Bloch, Robert (1917–1994)

Hand, Richard J. "Awed Listening": H.P. Lovecraft in Classic and Contemporary Audio Horror (crit). *Horror Studies*, 13 (1) 2022, 97–115.

Bly, Robert (1926–2021)

Pichaske, David R. A Poet of the Midwest: Robert Bly, 1926–2021. *Middle West Review*, 8 (Spr. 2022), 128–34.

Boyd, Thomas A. (1898–1935)

McCracken, David. Sherwood Anderson's Grotesques in Thomas Boyd's *Points of Honor* (crit). *ANQ*, 35 (Mar. 2022), 82–88.

Bradbury, Ray (1920–2012)

Aronoff, Eric. Martian Modernism: Modernist Anthropology, Science Fiction, and the Idea of Culture in Ray Bradbury's "—And the Moon Be Still as Bright" (crit). *Modernism/Modernity*, 16 (May 2022), unpaginated.

Öztürk, Fatih. *Self and Subjectivity in the Twentieth Century Dystopian Fiction* (crit). Newcastle upon Tyne: Cambridge Scholars Publishing, 2022.

Brooks, Gwendolyn (1917–2000)

Abdul-Ghani, Casarae Lavada. *Start a Riot! Civil Unrest in Black Arts Movement Drama, Fiction, and Poetry* (crit). Jackson: U P Mississippi, 2022.

Allan, Samantha. Memory at Work: Domestic Archives in Documentary Poetry by Women of Color (crit). Ph.D. Dissertation, U Texas Austin, 2022.

Anderson, David D. A Letter to Gwendolyn Brooks (corr). *Midwestern Miscellany*, 50 (Spr. 2022), 49–53.

Beall, John. Teaching Gwendolyn Brooks's Poetry and Lorraine Hansberry's *A Raisin in the Sun* (crit). *Midwestern Miscellany*, 50 (Spr. 2022), 12–19.

Fogarty, William. *The Politics of Speech in Later Twentieth-Century Poetry: Local Tongues in Heaney, Brooks, Harrison, and Clifton* (crit). London: Palgrave Macmillan, 2022.

Harper, Mary Catherine. Gwendolyn Brooks: Her Art/Culture Alliance (crit). *Midwestern Miscellany*, 50 (Spr. 2022), 20–36.

Minock, Mary. Let Us Hear from Satin-Legs: A New Take on the (Un)Hero of "The Sundays of Satin-Legs Smith" (crit). *Midwestern Miscellany*, 50 (Spr. 2022), 37–47.

Morin, Edward. "Lurk Late": A Reader's Response to "We Real Cool" (crit). *Midwestern Miscellany*, 50 (Spr. 2022), 8–11.

Osbrink, Keeley. Gwendolyn Brooks: A Primary and Secondary Source Bibliography (bibl). *Midwestern Miscellany*, 50 (Spr. 2022), 65–67.

Park, Seoyoung. Between Tradition and the Avant-Garde: On the Intersection of Literary Self-Consciousness and Innovative Impulse in Postwar American Poetry (crit). Ph.D. Dissertation, U Arizona Tucson, 2022.

———. Counter-Hegemonic Hegemonic Writing: Heroic Epic Tradition and the Postwar Black Female Subjectivity in Gwendolyn Brooks' "The Anniad" (crit). *Women's Studies*, 51 (Oct.–Nov. 2022), 744–62.

Sorensen, Jennifer. The Politics of the Page: Recontextualizing Willa Cather, Zora Neale Hurston, Gwendolyn Brooks, and Una Marson (crit). *Textual Cultures*, 15 (Fall 2022), 56–88.

Williams, Justin R. From Langston Hughes to Black Studies: Higher Education through the Lens of Black Poets (crit). Ph.D. Dissertation, U Memphis, 2022.

Brown, Frank London (1927–1962)

Rudds, Crystal S. On Perspective and Value: Black Urbanism, Black Interiors, and Public Housing Fiction (crit). *American Literature*, 94 (Sept. 2022), 527–49.

Burroughs, Margaret Taylor (1915–2010)

Hardy, Debra Anne. "More Beautiful and Better": Dr. Margaret Burroughs and the Pedagogy of Bronzeville (crit). Ph.D. Dissertation, Ohio State U, 2022.

Burroughs, William S. (1914–1997)

Alessandro, Brian and Tom Cardamone, eds. *Fever Spores: The Queer Reclamation of William S. Burroughs* (crit). New Orleans: Rebel Satori Press, 2022.

Calonne, David Stephen. *The Beats in Mexico* (crit). New Brunswick, N.J.: Rutgers U P, 2022.

Gontarski, S.E., ed. *Burroughs Unbound: William S. Burroughs and the Performance of Writing* (crit). NY: Bloomsbury Academic, 2022.

Lloyd, Declan. *Authors and Art Movements of the Twentieth Century: Painterly Poetics* (crit). NY: Routledge, 2022.

Stopel, Bartosz. Rubbing Out Forever or Cutting Up? Dialectics of the Mystical and the Subversive Attitude to Language in William Burroughs' *The Nova Trilogy* (crit). *Critique*, 63 (1) 2022, 57–66.

Campbell, Bonnie Jo (b. 1962)

Atlas, Marilyn Judith. Lazarus Rising in Bonnie Jo Campbell's *American Salvage*: Mirrors, Doubles, and Becoming a Hero in "Boar Taint" (crit). *MidAmerica*, 49 (2022), 64–80.

Castillo, Ana (b. 1953)

Ahn, Hakyoung. Female Martyrdom as Hybrid Resistance in Ana Castillo's *So Far from God* (crit). *South Central Review*, 39 (Spr. 2022), 1–19.

Solomon, Meagan. Homointimate Friendship and Queer Possibility in Ana Castillo's *The Mixquiahuala Letters* (crit). *Chicana/Latina Studies*, 21 (Spr. 2022), 30–57.

Cather, Willa (1873–1947)

Kahan, Benjamin. Willa Cather's Voyeuristic Realism (crit). *ELH: English Literary History*, 89 (Sum. 2022), 463–87.

Kim, Heidi and Rachel Warner. Inspiration, Memory, and Migration from *My Ántonia* to *Minari* (crit). *Modernism/Modernity*, 6 (Apr. 2022), unpaginated.

Kimmet, Sarah. Economic Ecosystems and Postcapitalist Futures in *The Professor's House* (crit). *Novel: A Forum on Fiction*, 55 (Aug. 2022), 263–82.

Larsen, Haley A. Mother Eve and Making Meaning on the Mesa: Feminist Silences in Willa Cather's *The Professor's House* (crit). *Feminist Modernist Studies*, 5 (1) 2022, 21–35.

McCullough, Aaron. Sheaths, Molds, and Shards: The Formation of an Anthropological Aesthetics in Willa Cather's *The Song of the Lark* (crit). *Journal of Modern Literature*, 45 (Spr. 2022), 121–39.

Oxler, Elizabeth. Casting a Wider Net: Women's Regional Writing 1890–1950 (crit). Ph.D. Dissertation, U Louisiana Lafayette, 2022.

Powell, David McKay. *Cather and Opera* (crit). Baton Rouge: Louisiana State U P, 2022.

Sorensen, Jennifer. The Politics of the Page: Recontextualizing Willa Cather, Zora Neale Hurston, Gwendolyn Brooks, and Una Marson (crit). *Textual Cultures*, 15 (Fall 2022), 56–88.

Chesnutt, Charles W. (1858–1932)

Halpern, Faye. Charles Chesnutt, Rhetorical Passing, and the Flesh-and-Blood Author: A Case for Considering Authorial Intention (crit). *Narrative*, 30 (Jan. 2022), 47–66.

Hopkins, Izabela. "Taken for White": Passing in Charles W. Chesnutt's Short Stories (crit). *Mississippi Quarterly*, 75 (Jan. 2022), 37–59.

Chopin, Kate (1850–1904)

Frye, Katie Berry. The Frame Story in Kate Chopin's "A Lady of Bayou St. John" and "La Belle Zoraide" (crit). *Studies in the American Short Story*, 3 (1–2) 2022, 54–74.

Hu, Aihua. The Art of Repetition in "The Story of an Hour" (crit). *ANQ*, 35 (Oct.–Dec. 2022), 458–63.

———. "The Story of an Hour": Mrs. Mallard's Ethically Tragic Song (crit). *ANQ*, 35 (Apr.–June 2022), 141–47.

Ostman, Heather, ed. *The New View from Cane River: Critical Essays on Kate Chopin's* At Fault (crit). Baton Rouge: Louisiana State U P, 2022.

Oxler, Elizabeth. Casting a Wider Net: Women's Regional Writing 1890–1950 (crit). Ph.D. Dissertation, U Louisiana Lafayette, 2022.

Shen, Dan. Naturalistic Covert Progression behind Complicated Plot: Chopin's "A Pair of Silk Stockings" (crit). *Journal of Narrative Theory*, 52 (Win. 2022), 1–24.

Cisneros, Sandra (b. 1954)

Jarrin, Felicia. Ending the Cycle of Abuse: Intimate Partner Violence, Gender Roles, and Sisterhood in "Woman Hollering Creek" and "Sabrina & Corina" (crit). *Sigma Tau Delta Review*, 19 (2022), 206–13.

Korneliusa, Kristina. The Search for Identity in "Never Marry a Mexican" by Sandra Cisneros (crit). *Ostrava Journal of English Philology*, 14 (2) 2022, 35–45.

Clemens, Samuel L. (1835–1910)

Bentley, Nancy. Amy Kaplan on Realism and the Imperatives of Empire (crit). *American Literary Realism*, 54 (Spr. 2022), 234–37.

Brenner, Gerry. Through Another Looking Glass: The Complex Satires of Twain's "A Fable" (crit). *Studies in the American Short Story*, 3 (1–2) 2022, 112–20.

Bronson-Bartlett, Blake. The California and Hawaii Notebooks: Pencils, Pocket Notebooks, and the Messiness of Mark Twain (crit). *Mark Twain Annual*, 20 (2022), 70–87.

Cao, Qilin. Translating Mark Twain: The Construction of America in 1950s China (crit). *Orbis Litterarum*, 77 (Oct. 2022), 333–46.

Caron, James E. Mark Twain's Rival Washoe Correspondents: William Wright and J. Ross Browne (crit). *Mark Twain Annual*, 20 (2022), 22–37.

Collins, Michael J. *No. 44, The Mysterious Stranger*: Mark Twain's Critique of Progressive Era Meritocracy (crit). *Textual Practice*, 36 (Oct. 2022), 1665–88.

Conway, Christopher. The American West and the Redemption of Huckleberry Finn in Phong Nguyen's *The Adventures of Joe Harper* and Robert Coover's *Huck Out West* (crit). *Mark Twain Annual*, 20 (2022), 115–29.

Driscoll, Kerry. Mark Twain's Masculinist Fantasy of the West (crit). *Mark Twain Annual*, 20 (2022), 100–14.

Eddings, Dennis W. "Poe, Twain, and Limburger Cheese" Revisited (crit). *Edgar Allan Poe Review*, 23 (Fall 2022), 163–70.

Eutsey, Dwayne. "Thick as Thieves": Mark Twain and the West's Spiritual Frontiers (crit). *Mark Twain Annual*, 20 (2022), 38–52.

Faverón Patriau, Gustavo. El Twain de Borges: Alusiones, elisiones y desilusiones de la historia en un manuscrito de 1949 (crit). *Variaciones Borges,* 54 (2022), 81–100.

Fredericks, Sarah Elizabeth. Mark Twain's Western Rhetoric of Insults (crit). *Mark Twain Annual*, 20 (2022), 143–57.

Goldstein, Philip. *The Theory and Practice of Reception Study: Reading Race and Gender in Twain, Faulkner, Ellison, and Morrison* (crit). NY: Routledge, 2022.

Greenhill, Jennifer A. Mark Twain's Undictionarial Italian: The Politics and Visual Humor of Mistranslating Newspaper Scraps (crit). *Word & Image*, 38 (July–Sept. 2022), 165–89.

Gribben, Alan. *Mark Twain's Literary Resources, Volume 2: Twain's Collection, Owned and Borrowed* (bibl; crit). Athens: U Georgia P, 2022.

Hebard, Andrew. Political Corruption and Mark Twain's West (crit). *Mark Twain Annual*, 20 (2022), 174–89.

Holbrook, Myrial Adel. "The Most Unique and Spicy Volume in Existence": A Picaresque Reappraisal of Mark Twain's *Innocents Abroad* (crit). *Comparative Literature Studies*, 59 (2) 2022, 402–18.

———. The *Terra Comica* between Mark Twain and Sherman Alexie (crit). *Mark Twain Annual*, 20 (2022), 130–42.

Hsiao, Alison. Haunting Black Feminist Geographies in *Pudd'nhead Wilson* (crit). *Arizona Quarterly*, 78 (Spr. 2022), 81–103.

Jing, Yu. What Was Huck Running away From? Rebellion, Canonicity, and the Chinese Translation of *The Adventures of Huckleberry Finn* (crit). *International Research in Children's Literature*, 15 (Feb. 2022), 53–65.

Kaplan, Amy. Realism and Power in Mark Twain's *A Connecticut Yankee in King Arthur's Court* (crit). *American Literary Realism*, 54 (Spr. 2022), 193–233.

Leonard, James Wharton. Mark Twain's Ambivalent Encounter with the Western Landscape (crit). *Mark Twain Annual*, 20 (2022), 190–200.

Melton, Jeffrey. Nature and Mobility in Mark Twain's *Roughing It* (crit). *Mark Twain Annual*, 20 (2022), 201–13.

Michelson, Bruce. *Roughing It* as Restless Art (crit). *Mark Twain Annual*, 20 (2022), 1–8.

Reesman, Jeanne Campbell. The Mountain Meadows Massacre, as Told by Mark Twain and Jack London (crit). *Mark Twain Annual*, 20 (2022), 9–21.

Robinson, Michelle. The Indispensable (and Strangely Disposable) Corpse in Early Parodies of Detective Fiction (crit). *Genre: Forms of Discourse and Culture*, 55 (Dec. 2022), 179–203.

Scharnhorst, Gary. *The Life of Mark Twain, Volume 3: The Final Years, 1891–1910* (biog; crit). Columbia: U Missouri P, 2022.

———. Samuel Clemens on Capital Punishment: A Recovered Note (crit). *American Literary Realism*, 54 (Spr. 2022), 277–78.

——— and Leslie Diane Myrick. A Note on Mark Twain and Chinese Missions (crit). *American Literary Realism*, 54 (Spr. 2022), 275–76.

Seybold, Matt. Amy Kaplan and the McDonaldization of Mark Twain (crit). *American Literary Realism*, 54 (Spr. 2022), 189–92.

———. The Mail-Bag Bed of Empire: *Roughing It* and the Gossamer Network (crit). *Mark Twain Annual*, 20 (2022), 88–99.

Thompson, Todd Nathan. "Why We Should Annex": Reprints and Repercussions of Twain's *New York Tribune* Letters on Hawai'i (crit). *Mark Twain Annual*, 20 (2022), 53–69.

Young, Alex Trimble. "The Vigorous New Vernacular": Settler Colonialism and the Politics of Irony in *Roughing It* (crit). *Mark Twain Annual*, 20 (2022), 158–73.

Cook, George Cram (1873–1924)

Noe, Marcia. *Three Midwestern Playwrights: How Floyd Dell, George Cram Cook, and Susan Glaspell Transformed American Theatre* (crit). Bloomington: Indiana U P, 2022.

Coover, Robert (b. 1932)

Conway, Christopher. The American West and the Redemption of Huckleberry Finn in Phong Nguyen's *The Adventures of Joe Harper* and Robert Coover's *Huck Out West* (crit). *Mark Twain Annual*, 20 (2022), 115–29.

Gruić Grmuša, Lovorka. Postmodern Film and Fiction Intermediating: Texture, Spectacle, Theatricality, and Violence in Robert Coover's Texts (crit). *Journal of American Studies of Turkey*, 57 (Spr. 2022), 5–26.

Sylvestre, Fernanda Aquino. O Maravilhoso na Literatura Contemporânea: Uma Leitura de Salman Rushdie, Margaret Atwood, Robert Coover e Nalo Hopkinson (crit). *Abusões*, 8 (1) 2022, 184–215.

Crane, Hart (1899–1932)

Bratton, Francesca. *Visionary Company: Hart Crane and Modernist Periodicals* (crit). Edinburgh: Edinburgh U P, 2022.

Gill, Jo. Hart Crane: The "Architectural Art" (crit). *Modernism/Modernity*, 29 (Jan. 2022), 1–25.

Parkinson, Thomas. *Hart Crane and Yvor Winters: Their Literary Correspondence* (corr; crit). Berkeley: U California P, 2022.

Starčević, Mirko. Weldon Kees and the Poetic Landscapes of Despair (crit). *Acta Neophilologica*, 55 (1–2), 2022), 61–72.

Dell, Floyd (1887–1969)

Noe, Marcia. *Three Midwestern Playwrights: How Floyd Dell, George Cram Cook, and Susan Glaspell Transformed American Theatre* (crit). Bloomington: Indiana U P, 2022.

Derleth, August (1909–1971)

Freeman, Austin M. *Theology and H.P. Lovecraft* (crit). Lanham, Md.: Lexington Books, 2022.

Dorn, Edward (1929–1999)

Connors, Carrie. *Laugh Lines: Humor, Genre, and Political Critique in Late Twentieth-Century American Poetry* (crit). Jackson: U P Mississippi, 2022.

Dos Passos, John (1896–1970)

Dabney, Lewis M. *Soul Mates of the Lost Generation: The Letters of John Dos Passos and Crystal Ross* (corr). Charlottesville: U Virginia P, 2022.

Klein, Sascha. The Roar of Modernity: Metropolitan Soundscapes and the Making of the Modern Subject in Dos Passos' *Manhattan Transfer* (crit). *Revista Canaria de Estudios Ingleses*, 84 (2022), 69–82.

Shaheen, Aaron. From Vorticist Dreams to Futurist Nightmares: John Dos Passos's Novels of the 1920s (crit). *Arizona Quarterly*, 78 (Win. 2022), 1–28.

——— and Rosa María Bautista-Cordero, eds. *John Dos Passos's Transatlantic Chronicling: Critical Essays on the Interwar Years* (crit). Knoxville: U Tennessee P, 2022.

Dreiser, Theodore (1871–1945)

Bowman, Daniel. Horsepower: Animals, Automobiles, and an Ethic of (Car) Care in Early US Road Narratives (crit). *Journal of American Studies*, 56 (Oct. 2022), 613–34.

Dunbar, Paul Laurence (1872–1906)

Chaudron, Patricia. Paul Laurence Dunbar and the Naturalism/Dialect Poetry Divide (crit). *Texas Studies in Literature and Language*, 64 (Fall 20220, 257–83.

Jarrett, Gene Andrew. *Paul Laurence Dunbar: The Life and Times of a Caged Bird* (biog; crit). Princeton, N.J.: Princeton U P, 2022.

Leslie, Alex Zweber. Race, Region, and the Black Midwest in the Dunbar Decades (crit). *American Literary History*, 34 (Sum. 2022), 449–76.

Dylan, Bob (b. 1941)

Arnoff, Stephen Daniel. *About Man & God & Law: The Spiritual Wisdom of Bob Dylan* (crit). NY: Morgan James Publishing, 2022.

Domínguez, Freddy Cristóbal. *Bob Dylan in the Attic: The Artist as Historian* (crit). Amherst: U Massachusetts P, 2022.

Falco, Raphael. *No One to Meet: Imitation and Originality in the Songs of Bob Dylan* (crit). Tuscaloosa: U Alabama P, 2022.

Hampton, Timothy. Records of a Confident Man (crit). *American Literary History*, 34 (Win. 2022), 1503–12.

Marcus, Greil. *Folk Music: A Bob Dylan Biography in Seven Songs* (biog; crit). New Haven: Yale U P, 2022.

Nogowski, John. *Bob Dylan: A Descriptive Critical Discography and Filmography, 1961–2022* (bibl; crit). 3rd ed. Jefferson, N.C.: McFarland & Co., 2022.

Portelli, Alessandro. *Hard Rain: Bob Dylan, Oral Cultures, and the Meaning of History* (crit). NY: Columbia U P, 2022.

Stewart, Jon. *Dylan, Lennon, Marx and God* (crit). Cambridge: Cambridge U P, 2022.

Trudeau, Stephanie, ed. *The Dylan Tapes: Friends, Players, and Lovers Talking Early Bob Dylan* (I). Minneapolis: U Minnesota P, 2022.

Wilson, Rob. Transfiguration as a World-Making Practice: From Norman O. Brown to Bob Dylan (crit). *Boundary 2: An International Journal of Literature and Culture*, 49 (Aug. 2022), 99–116.

Eiseley, Loren C. (1907–1977)

Cheng, Qianqian. *Loren Eiseley's Writing across the Nature and Culture Divide* (crit). Lanham, Md.: Lexington Books, 2022.

Ellison, Harlan (1934–2018)

Nguyen, Josef. Reconsidering Lost Opportunities for Diverse Representation (crit). *American Literature*, 94 (Mar. 2022), 73–102.

Erdrich, Louise (b. 1954)

Allan, Samantha. Memory at Work: Domestic Archives in Documentary Poetry by Women of Color (crit). Ph.D. Dissertation, U Texas Austin, 2022.

Jacobson, Kristin J. Pregnant Possibilities in Recent Climate Fiction by Ward, Lepucki, Lee, and Erdrich (crit). *MELUS*, 47 (Win. 2022), 148–71.

Jameson, Elizabeth. American Borderlands: Reflections on Margins, Mainstreams, and Alternatives (crit). *Canadian Review of American Studies*, 52 (Aug. 2022), 105–25.

Minhas, Nabeel Ahmed and Ghulam Murtaza. Preservation of Native American Culture: An Analysis of Louise Erdrich's *Tracks* (crit). *Pakistan Journal of Humanities and Social Sciences*, 10 (1) 2022, 191–98.

Smith, Jeanne Rosier. *Writing Tricksters: Mythic Gambols in American Ethnic Fiction* (crit). Berkeley: U California P, 2022.

Sparks, Angela. Kinship Ecology and the Bildungsroman: The Child-Animal Relationship in Louise Erdrich's *The Birchbark House* Series (crit). *Textual Practice*, 36 (Mar. 2022), 404–21.

Eugenides, Jeffrey (b. 1960)

Potier, Jérémy. Banlieues d'Amérique: Poétique d'un Lieu Commun (crit). Thèse de Doctorat, Université Toulouse-Jean Jaurès, 2022.

Ferris, Joshua (b. 1974)

Dix, Hywel. Unfilled Vocations in Contemporary American Fiction (crit). *Textual Practice*, 36 (Jan. 2022), 40–57.

Field, Eugene (1850–1895)

Bredehoft, Thomas A. Eugene Field, Wynkyn de Worde, Medievalism, and Authenticity (crit). *Medieval Perspectives*, 36 (2022), 85–107.

Fitzgerald, F. Scott (1896–1940)

Alexander, Jeanne M., comp. Current Bibliography (bibl). *F. Scott Fitzgerald Review*, 20 (2022), 287–302.

Bloom, James D. "In Uniform and at Moral Attention": From F. Scott Fitzgerald to Philip Roth (crit). *F. Scott Fitzgerald Review*, 20 (2022), 206–18.

Bryla, Martyna. Rewriting the American Dream for the Trump Era and Beyond in Gary Shteyngart's *Lake Success* (2018) (crit). *Atlantis: Revista de la Asociación Española de Estudios Anglo-Norte-americanos*, 44 (1) 2022, 145–63.

Cobb, Cam. "Who's This Welles?": Pat Hobby's Take on Hollywood Celebrity Culture (crit). *F. Scott Fitzgerald Review*, 20 (2022), 190–205.

Curnutt, Kirk and Sara A. Kosiba, eds. *The Romance of Regionalism in the Work of F. Scott and Zelda Fitzgerald: The South Side of Paradise* (crit). Lanham, Md.: Lexington Books, 2022.

Donaldson, Scott. *Fitzgerald and the War between the Sexes* (crit). University Park: Pennsylvania State U P, 2022.

Fahy, Thomas. "A Night at the Fair": Popular Culture and the Influence of the Pan-American Exposition on F. Scott Fitzgerald (crit). *F. Scott Fitzgerald Review*, 20 (2022), 159–77.

Gottlieb, Madeline. "Watch Out or These Other Races Will Have Control of Things": Witnessing Race and Racial Witnessing in *The Great Gatsby* (crit). *F. Scott Fitzgerald Review*, 20 (2022), 27–42.

Hazelgrove, William Elliott. *Writing Gatsby: The Real Story of the Writing of the Greatest American Novel* (crit). Essex, Conn.: Lyons Press, 2022.

Krsteva, Marija. *Towards a Theory of Life-Writing: Genre Blending* (crit). NY: Routledge, 2022.

Kruse, Horst H. Sizing up Zelda Sayre: Covert Strategies of Indictment in Fitzgerald's "A Full Life" (crit). *F. Scott Fitzgerald Review*, 20 (2022), 178–89.

Mastandrea, Martina. *F. Scott Fitzgerald on Silent Film* (crit). Leiden: Brill, 2022.

Messenger, Chris. Joseph Conrad's Major Fiction and *Tender Is the Night*: Part Two: *Lord Jim, Nostromo, Victory, The Secret Sharer*, and What F. Scott Fitzgerald May Have Learned for the Novel's Form and Narration (crit). *F. Scott Fitzgerald Review*, 20 (2022), 97–120.

Milică, Iulia Andreea. Fashionable Flappers: Constructing Femininity in F.S. Fitzgerald's "The Offshore Pirate" and "The Ice Palace" (crit). *Revista Canaria de Estudios Ingleses*, 84 (2022), 97–116.

Miljković, Marija. Women's Drive for Power: Women and Cars in Selected Works of F. Scott Fitzgerald (crit). *Književstvo*, 12 (2022), 45–57.

Noonan, Mark J. Financing Fitzginnegan: Joycean Influences and Similarities in the Works of F. Scott Fitzgerald (crit). *F. Scott Fitzgerald Review*, 20 (2022), 121–58.

Senn, Farrah R. F. Scott Fitzgerald's Flappers: Supplanting the Pious Mother Figure with the Modern Irish Idea (crit). *Journal of the Georgia Philological Association*, 11 (2022–2023), 71–89.

Sieweke, Lara Rodríguez. Fitzgerald's "Winter Dreams" in Two 1922 Magazines: An Intermedial Nostalgic Reading (crit). *F. Scott Fitzgerald Review*, 20 (2022), 43–96

Smith, Lauren. "A Boat against the Current": *The Great Gatsby*'s Nick Carraway and Compulsory Heterosexuality (crit). *Sigma Tau Delta Review*, 19 (2022), 172–78.

Steenis, Jacob. Responding to *The Great Gatsby*: Can the Reading Process Itself Reinforce Racist Assumptions? (crit). *F. Scott Fitzgerald Review*, 20 (2022), 1–16.

Fitzgerald, Zelda Sayre (1900–1948)

Curnutt, Kirk and Sara A. Kosiba, eds. *The Romance of Regionalism in the Work of F. Scott and Zelda Fitzgerald: The South Side of Paradise* (crit). Lanham, Md.: Lexington Books, 2022.

Krsteva, Marija. *Towards a Theory of Life-Writing: Genre Blending* (crit). NY: Routledge, 2022.

Kruse, Horst H. Sizing up Zelda Sayre: Covert Strategies of Indictment in Fitzgerald's "A Full Life" (crit). *F. Scott Fitzgerald Review*, 20 (2022), 178–89.

Franzen, Jonathan (b. 1959)

Jiao, Min, Jing Yang, and Jingcheng Huang. Overpopulation and Cognitive Mapping of Freedom: Johnathan Franzen's *Freedom* (crit). *Neohelicon: Acta Comparationis Litterarum Universarum*, 49 (June 2022), 385–401.

Potier, Jérémy. Banlieues d'Amérique: Poétique d'un Lieu Commun (crit). Thèse de Doctorat, Université Toulouse-Jean Jaurès, 2022.

Pourjafari, Fatemeh and Leila Baradaran Jamili. *Ethical Narratives: Reauthorization of Authorial Agency and Articulation of Authenticity in Post-Postmodern Novels* (crit). Krefeld: Pirmoni, 2022.

Varsava, Jerry. The Clashing of Liberties: Fraught Environmentalism in Franzen's *Freedom* (crit). *ISLE: Interdisciplinary Studies in Literature and Environment,* 29 (Fall 2022), 771–97.

Gaiman, Neil (b. 1960)

De Vita, Novella Brooks. Conversations with Creatives: Interview with Neil Gaiman (I). *Journal of the Fantastic in the Arts,* 33 (3) 2022, 92–116.

Marchese, David and Mamadi Doumbouya. Neil Gaiman Dreams in Color (I). *New York Times Magazine,* 7 Aug. 2022, 28–33.

Weinstock, Jeffrey Andrew. *A Critical Companion to Neil Gaiman's* Neverwhere (crit). Cham, Switz.: Palgrave Macmillan, 2022.

Gardner, John (1933–1982)

Hiortdahl, Sandra. *Grendel Recast in John Gardner's Novel and* Beowulf (crit). Newcastle upon Tyne: Cambridge Scholars Publishing, 2022.

Glaspell, Susan (1876–1948)

Noe, Marcia. *Three Midwestern Playwrights: How Floyd Dell, George Cram Cook, and Susan Glaspell Transformed American Theatre* (crit). Bloomington: Indiana U P, 2022.

Tabur, Şemsettin. The Spatiality of Violence in Susan Glaspell's *Trifles* (crit). *Journal of American Studies of Turkey,* 57 (Spr. 2022), 93–110.

Haldeman-Julius, Marcet (1887–1941)

Barrett-Fox, Jason. *Untimely Women: Radically Recasting Feminist Rhetorical History* (crit). Columbus: Ohio State U P, 2022.

Hamilton, Virginia (1934–2002)

Austin, Sara. Images of Horror: Black Childhood as a Site of Resistance in Visual Media (crit). *Journal of the Fantastic in the Arts*, 33 (1) 2022, 9–38.

Selden, Sarah. Harlem Renaissance or Momentary Aberration? An Analysis of the Newbery's Progress toward Racial Inclusivity (crit). *Children's Literature Association Quarterly*, 47 (Sum. 2022), 134–56.

Hansberry, Lorraine (1930–1965)

Beall, John. Teaching Gwendolyn Brooks's Poetry and Lorraine Hansberry's *A Raisin in the Sun* (crit). *Midwestern Miscellany*, 50 (Spr. 2022), 12–19.

Carr, Gregory S. Interrogating Whiteness in Bruce Norris's *Clybourne Park* (crit). *Theatre Symposium*, 29 (2022), 64–72.

Fleming, Julius B., Jr. *Black Patience: Performance, Civil Rights, and the Unfinished Project of Emancipation* (crit). NY: New York U P, 2022.

McClendon, Blair. Radical Acts: The Many Lives of Lorraine Hansberry (biog; crit; rev). *New Yorker*, 97 (24 Jan. 2022), 65–69.

Moran, James. Boucicault—O'Casey—Hansberry: Tracing a Line of Influence (crit). *Nineteenth Century Theatre and Film*, 49 (Nov. 2022), 165–81.

Schwartz, Benjamin. The Unfinishedness & Untimeliness of *A Raisin in the Sun* (crit). *Texas Studies in Literature and Language*, 64 (Win. 2022), 396–415.

Shields, Charles J. *Lorraine Hansberry: The Life Behind* A Raisin in the Sun (biog; crit). NY: Henry Holt, 2022.

Winstein-Hibbs, Sarah. Otherwise Charisma: James Baldwin and the Black Queer Archive of Civil Rights Historiography (crit). *American Quarterly*, 74 (June 2022), 295–315.

Harrison, Jim (1937–2016)

Busnel, François. *Jim Harrison, Seule la Terre est Éternelle* (biog; crit). Paris: Gallimard, 2022.

Hassler, Jon (1933–2008)

Lauck, Jon K. Goths and Visigoths: Jon Hassler and the Midwestern Moral Universe (crit). *Middle West Review*, 8 (Spr. 2022), 89–96.

Hayden, Robert (1913–1980)

Engstrand, William. A Vernacular of Resistance: Endurance and Resistance in the Middle Passage (crit). *Journal of Ethnic American Literature*, 12 (2022), 27–37.

Wall, Joshua Logan. *Situating Poetry: Covenant and Genre in American Modernism* (crit). Baltimore: Johns Hopkins U P, 2022.

Heinlein, Robert A. (1907–1988)

Greenham, Ellen J. *After Engulfment: Cosmicism and Neocosmicism in H.P. Lovecraft, Philip K. Dick, Robert A. Heinlein, and Frank Herbert* (crit). NY: Hippocampus Press, 2022.

Hemingway, Ernest (1899–1961)

Allen, Edward. Hemingway's Impressions: Learning to Voice the Classics in the Early Journalism (crit). *Symbiosis*, 26 (2) 2022), 151–71.

Baker, Mark Allen. *A Guide to Hemingway's Key West* (biog). Charleston, S.C.: History Press, 2022.

Barnes, David. Hemingway's British Accents (crit). *Symbiosis*, 26 (2) 2022, 173–86.

Beall, John. Hemingway's Marlin and Pound's Canto 40 (crit). *Hemingway Review*, 41 (Spr. 2022), 120–29.

Buchholtz, Mirosława and Dorota Guttfeld. *Ernest Hemingway in Interview and Translation* (crit, I). Cham, Switzerland: Springer, 2022.

Cain, William E. No Explanations: Hemingway on the Making of Decisions (crit). *Hemingway Review*, 41 (Spr. 2022), 49–74.

Carver, Beci. Waugh's Hemingway (crit). *Symbiosis*, 26 (2) 2022, 131–49.

Chakravertty, Tania. *Ernest Hemingway and the Fluidity of Gender: A Socio-Cultural Analysis of Selected Works* (crit). NY: Routledge, 2022.

Christian, Timothy. *Hemingway's Widow: The Life and Legacy of Mary Welsh Hemingway* (biog; crit). NY: Pegasus Books, 2022.

Cirino, Mark and Michael Von Cannon. *One True Sentence: Writers & Readers on Hemingway's Art* (crit). Boston: Godine, 2022.

Cirules, Enrique. Ernest Hemingway and the Faded Fame of Antonio Gattorno (crit). *Hemingway Review*, 42 (Fall 2022), 85–95.

Coutinho, Léo and Hélio Afonso Ghizoni Teive. "But Man Is Not Made for Defeat": Insights into Ernest Hemingway's Dementia (biog). *Arquivos de Neuropsiquiatria*, 80 (Jan. 2022), 97–100.

Dubey, Poonam. *The Novels of Ernest Hemingway: A Thematic Study* (crit). Kanpur: Vanya Publications, 2022.

DuBose, Michael D. *True at First Light* and *Under Kilimanjaro*: The African Book in Two Parts (crit). *Hemingway Review*, 42 (Fall 2022), 50–67.

Dumm, Brian. Enantiosemy and Transcendental Homelessness in Herman Melville's *Moby-Dick*, Ernest Hemingway's *In Our Time*, and Michael Ondaatje's *Warlight* (crit). Ph.D. Dissertation, George Washington U, 2022.

Evans, Robert C., ed. *Critical Insights:* The Old Man and the Sea (crit). Ipswich, Mass.: Salem Press, 2022.

Fenton, Jamie. "A Certain Amount of Windowpane Trouble": Injury, Censorship and Style in Hemingway's London Writing (crit). *Symbiosis*, 26 (2) 2022, 211–34.

Hahn, Thomas Edward. Benjamin Percy and Queer Ecomasculinities: Ideas of the Short Story from Hemingway to the Present (crit). Ph.D. Dissertation, St. John's U, 2022.

Hays, Peter L. Nuns Help Hemingway with Tale and Piece of Tail (biog). *Hemingway Review*, 42 (Fall 2022), 96–102.

Heaney, Emma. Stare, Flaunt: Seeing Trans Femininity in Literary Modernism (crit). *Modernism/Modernity*, 24 (June 2022), unpaginated.

Hemingway, Brendan and Stephen Adams, eds. *Dear Papa: The Letters of Patrick and Ernest Hemingway* (corr). NY: Scribner, 2022.

Herlihy-Mera, Jeffrey. Ernest Hemingway, A Cuban Exile (crit). *Hemingway Review*, 42 (Fall 2022), 80–84.

———. Hemingway's Shadow across the Literary Cultures of Cuba (crit). *Hemingway Review*, 41 (Spr. 2022), 75–86.

Kennedy, J. Gerald, ed. *Ernest Hemingway* In Our Time (crit). NY: W.W. Norton, 2022 (Norton Critical Editions).

Krsteva, Marija. *Towards a Theory of Life-Writing: Genre Blending* (crit). NY: Routledge, 2022.

Kurlansky, Mark. *The Importance of Not Being Ernest: My Life with the Uninvited Hemingway* (biog; M). Coral Gables, Fla.: Books & Books Press, 2022.

La Rocque, Lance and Lisa Narbeshuber. Addressing Modernity from the Woods: Utopian Counter-Discourses in "Big Two-Hearted River" (crit). *Hemingway Review*, 42 (Fall 2022), 15–34.

Lansky, Ellen. All Aboard: Reading, Writing, and Drinking with Ernest Hemingway (crit; M). *English Language Notes*, 60 (Apr. 2022), 139–49.

Larson, Kelli A. and Steve Paul, eds. Current Bibliography (bibl). *Hemingway Review*, 41 (Spr. 2022), 150–60.

———, eds. Current Bibliography (bibl). *Hemingway Review*, 42 (Fall 2022), 118–30.

Le Bihan, Adrien. *Autopsie d'une Rancœur: Hemingway Alias Argo contre Général Leclerc* (biog). Espelette: Cherche Bruit, 2022.

Marín Ruiz, Ricardo. The Influence of Cubism in Hemingway's Conception of Bullfighting in "The Capital of the World" (crit). *Hemingway Review*, 42 (Fall 2022), 35–49.

Marrone, Claire. Revisiting and Rereading Hemingway's *A Moveable Feast* and McLain's *The Paris Wife* (crit). *Hemingway Review*, 41 (Spr. 2022), 19–30.

Ng, Lay Sion. Toward a Politics of Cure: Jake Barnes's Embracing of Otherness in *The Sun Also Rises* (crit). *Hemingway Review*, 41 (Spr. 2022), 31–48.

Norris, Marcos Antonio. Ernest Hemingway's "The Short, Happy Life of Francis Macomber" and *Death in the Afternoon* (crit). *Studies in the American Short Story*, 3 (1–2) 2022, 18–34.

Peón Casas, Carlos A. Hemingway in Cuban Contexts: Revisiting Reaches of His Imagination (crit). *Hemingway Review*, 41 (Spr. 2022), 87–99.

Rix, Alicia. "Horn Knowledge": Knowingness in Hemingway and Kipling (crit). *Symbiosis*, 26 (2) 2022, 187–209.

Rodríguez Pazos, José Gabriel. Hemingway en Español: Las Traducciones de *The Sun Also Rises* (crit). *1611: Revista de Historia de la Traducción*, 16 (2022), unpaginated.

Qabaha, Ahmad. Travel and Imperialist Nostalgia in Ernest Hemingway's *Green Hills of Africa* (crit). *International Journal of Arabic-English Studies*, 22 (1) 2022, 167–80.

Stephens, Gregory. Fathering under the Influence: Hemingway's Representation of His Sons in "Bimini (crit). *Hemingway Review*, 41 (Spr. 2022), 100–19.

Thurston, Michael, ed. *Ernest Hemingway* The Sun Also Rises (crit). NY: W.W. Norton, 2022 (Norton Critical Editions).

Tyler, Lisa. Aestheticized Slavery: Blackamoor Jewelry in Hemingway's *Across the River and into the Trees* (crit). *Arizona Quarterly*, 78 (Win. 2022), 29–53.

West, Kevin R. Why Things Happen and Why They Don't: Causality and Contingency in "The Snows of Kilimanjaro" and "One Reader Writes" (crit). *Hemingway Review*, 41 (Spr. 2022), 130–35.

Will, Barbara. The American Red Cross and the Making of Ernest Hemingway (biog; crit). *South Central Review*, 39 (Spr. 2022), 20–38.

Yanagisawa, Hideo. Hemingway's Roadmaps in Cuba: "The Strange Country" as a Postwar Road Narrative (crit). *Hemingway Review*, 42 (Fall 2022), 68–79.

Howells, William Dean (1837–1920)

Ball, Andrew. *The Economy of Religion in American Literature: Culture and the Politics of Redemption* (crit). London: Bloomsbury Academic, 2022.

Harner, Christina Henderson. The 1893 Columbian Exposition and the Utopian Dreams of Edward Bellamy, William Dean Howells, and W.T. Stead (crit). *Nineteenth-Century Contexts*, 44 (Feb. 2022), 89–109.

Kolding, Isaac. *A Hazard of New Fortunes* and Political Speech (crit). *American Literary Realism*, 54 (Win. 2022), 120–34.

Wegener, Frederick. Talking "Horse" and "House" in The Rise of Silas Lapham (crit). *American Literary Realism*, 54 (Win. 2022), 95–119.

Hughes, Langston (1902–1967)

Anderson, Austin. Literary Alibi: The Consumption of African American and Dalit Literatures (crit). *The Comparatist: Journal of the Southern Comparative Literature Association*, 46 (Oct. 2022), 134–55.

Fernández-Alonso, Alba and María Amor Barros-Del Río. Gender and Race in Langston Hughes' Poetry of the Spanish Civil War (crit). *Journal of Gender Studies*, 31 (6) 2022, 671–83.

Gerland, Oliver. Race and Power in *Pullman Car Hiawatha*: A Teaching Approach (crit). *Thornton Wilder Journal*, 3 (July 2022), 56–65.

Henry, Zoë. Syncopating Commemoration: On the Legacy of Langston Hughes (crit). *Modernism/Modernity*, 15 (Dec. 2022), unpaginated.

Hofer, Matthew. *Omnicompetent Modernists: Poetry, Politics, and the Public Sphere* (crit). Tuscaloosa: U Alabama P, 2022.

Jordan, Joseph P. "You Think / It's a Happy Beat?" Hughes's "Dream Boogie" (crit). *CEA Critic*, 84 (Nov. 2022), 234–39.

Kang, Nancy. The Homoerotics of "Negrotarian" Patronage in Langston Hughes's "The Blues I'm Playing" (crit). *Twentieth Century Literature*, 68 (Mar. 2022), 75–100.

Kernan, Ryan James. *New World Maker: Radical Poetics, Black Internationalism, and the Translations of Langston Hughes* (crit). Evanston, Ill.: Northwestern U P, 2022.

Munshi, Auritra. "Blacks Are Beautiful. And Ugly Too": Moving beyond the Racial Barrier and Foregrounding Resistance in Langston Hughes' Poetry (crit). *Postcolonial Interventions*, 7 (June 2022), 105–33.

Parlett, Jack. *The Poetics of Cruising: Queer Visual Culture from Whitman to Grindr* (crit). Minneapolis: U Minnesota P, 2022.

Tiwari, Bhavya. World Poetry: Comparing Poetic Worlds in Translation (crit). *Comparative Literature Studies*, 59 (2) 2022, 217–40.

Williams, Justin R. From Langston Hughes to Black Studies: Higher Education through the Lens of Black Poets (crit). Ph.D. Dissertation, U Memphis, 2022.

Hurst, Fannie (1885–1968)

Molloy, Deborah Snow. Performative Public Health in Fannie Hurst's "T.B." (1915) (crit). *Short Fiction in Theory & Practice*, 12 (Oct. 2022), 169–83.

Kirk, Russell (1918–1994)

Peralta, Camilo. "Delight in Horror": Charles Williams and Russell Kirk on Hell and the Supernatural (crit). *Mythlore*, 41 (Fall 2022), 127–42.

Lane, Rose Wilder (1886–1968)

Sandefur, Timothy. *Freedom's Furies: How Isabel Paterson, Rose Wilder Lane, and Ayn Rand Found Liberty in an Age of Darkness* (biog). Washington, D.C.: Cato Institute, 2022.

Larsen, Nella (1891–1964)

Fowler, Doreen. Racial Repression and Doubling in Nella Larsen's *Passing* (crit). *South Atlantic Review*, 87 (Spr. 2022), 1–18.

Fuleihan, Zeena Yasmine. The Fancy Girl Episteme: Tracking the Legacy of Master-Slave Rape in the Evolution of the Tragic Mulatto Trope (crit). *The Comparatist: Journal of the Southern Comparative Literature Association*, 46 (Oct. 2022), 124–33.

Joyner, Alec. The Laughing "No": Interpellation, Expression, and Laughter in *Quicksand* (crit). *MELUS*, 47 (Fall 2022), 24–47.

Kim, Seohyun. Joy or Vexation: Respectable Motherhood and the Trope of Childhood in Nella Larsen's *Passing* (crit). *College Literature*, 49 (Sum. 2022), 373–99.

Kreiser, Annie Elizabeth. Respectability Politics in Nella Larsen's *Passing* (crit). *Sigma Delta Tau Review*, 19 (2022), 161–66.

Montero Román, Valentina. Race, Gender, and "Real Brains": Interrogating Unreliability in Nella Larsen's *Passing* (crit). *Modern Fiction Studies*, 68 (Sum. 2022), 219–47.

Wyatt, Jean. Doublings and Dissociation in Nella Larsen's *Passing* and Helen Oyeyemi's *Boy, Snow, Bird* (crit). *Angelaki*, 27 (June–Aug. 2022), 182–98.

Laughlin, Clara (1873–1941)

Cusack, Christopher and Lindsay Janssen. "'Tis Yourself Is a Skeleton": Deathbed Scenes and Ethnic Identity in Irish-American Short Fiction, 1895–1910 (crit). *Irish Studies Review*, 30 (Feb. 2022), 1–15.

Leiber, Fritz (1910–1992)

Bracken, Christopher. The Animism of Belief: How to Merge with Others (crit). *New Formations: A Journal of Culture/Theory/Politics*, 2022, 104–05, 159–82.

Leonard, Elmore (1925–2013)

Rausch, Andrew J. *Perspectives on Elmore Leonard: Conversations with Authors, Experts and Collaborators* (crit). Jefferson, N.C.: McFarland & Co., 2022.

Leopold, Aldo (1886–1948)

LeBlanc, Antoine Boudreau, Cécile Aenishaenslin, and Bryn Williams-Jones. Looking for the Missing link Between Bio and Ethics (crit). *Canadian Journal of Bioethics / Revue Canadienne de Bioéthique*, 5 (1) 2022, 103–18.

Smith, Laura. *Ecological Restoration and the U.S. Nature and Environmental Writing Tradition: A Rewilding of American Letters* (crit). Cham, Switz.: Palgrave Macmillan, 2022.

Le Sueur, Meridel (1900–1996)

Nelson, Paul D. Bob Brown: "Paint What You See" (corr). *Ramsey County History*, 57 (Sum. 2022), 14–26.

Lewis, Sinclair (1885–1951)

Ball, Andrew. *The Economy of Religion in American Literature: Culture and the Politics of Redemption* (crit). London: Bloomsbury Academic, 2022.

Bowman, Daniel. Horsepower: Animals, Automobiles, and an Ethic of (Car) Care in Early US Road Narratives (crit). *Journal of American Studies*, 56 (Oct. 2022), 613–34.

Davis, Greg. Exploring Zenith: Narrative Technique in *Babbitt* (crit). *Midwestern Miscellany*, 50 (Fall 2022), 56–63.

Gottlieb, Robert. On Main Street (biog; crit). *New York Times Book Review*, 2 Jan. 2022), 1, 18–20.

Killough, George. Sinclair Lewis's Display of Language Failure in *Babbitt* (crit). *Midwestern Miscellany*, 50 (Fall 2022), 16–24.

McLaughlin, Robert L. Inside Looking Out, Outside Looking In: Group Affiliation and Disaffiliation in *Babbitt* (crit). *Midwestern Miscellany*, 50 (Fall 2022), 25–35.

Márin Gómez, Isabel. The Spanish Translation of *Babbitt* and Freedom of Expression in the Art and Culture of Spain (crit). *Midwestern Miscellany*, 50 (Fall 2022), 64–77.

Paladin, Nicola. Fascism, Populism and the Myth of the American Revolution in 20th Century US Literature (crit). *Oltreoceano: Rivista sulle Migrazioni*, 19 (2022), 103–10.

Parry, Sally E. The Man Nobody Knows: George Babbitt and Religion (crit). *Midwestern Miscellany*, 50 (Fall 2022), 36–45.

Potier, Jérémy. Banlieues d'Amérique: Poétique d'un Lieu Commun (crit). Thèse de Doctorat, Université Toulouse-Jean Jaurès, 2022.

Richards, Shaun F. "Our Ideal Citizen": Boosterism as Pride and Prejudice in Sinclair Lewis's *Babbitt* (crit). *Midwestern Miscellany*, 50 (Fall 2022), 46–55.

Lindsay, Vachel (1879–1931)

Gelmi, Caroline. Vachel Lindsay and the Primitive Singing of the New Poetry (crit). *Journal of Modern Literature*, 45 (Win. 2022), 99–117.

Ma, Ling (b. 1983)

Atasoy, Emrah and Thomas Horan. Prayer Had Broken Out: Pandemics, Capitalism, and Religious Extremism in Recent Apocalyptic Fiction (crit). *Studies in the Novel*, 54 (Sum. 2022), 235–54.

Cherniavsky, Eva. Cultural Studies Revisited: Determinate Conditions and the Depressive Position (crit). *American Literary History*, 34 (Spr. 2022), 54–66.

Muenchrath, Anna. Making and Reading World Literature in a Pandemic: Global Logistics in Ling Ma's *Severance* (crit). *Journal of World Literature*, 7 (2) 2022, 184–201.

Schaab, Katharine. Misogyny Survives the Apocalypse: The Collapse of Reproductive Justice in Emily St. John Mandel's *Station Eleven* and Ling Ma's *Severance* (crit). *Women's Studies*, 51 (Jan.–Feb. 2022), 1–17.

Malcolm X (1925–1965)

Finley, Stephen C. *In and Out of This World: Material and Extraterrestrial Bodies in the Nation of Islam* (crit). Durham, N.C.: Duke U P, 2022.

Thompson, Mark Christian. *Phenomenal Blackness: Black Power, Philosophy, and Theory* (crit). Chicago: U Chicago P, 2022.

Mandel, Emily St. John (b. 1979)

Atasoy, Emrah and Thomas Horan. Prayer Had Broken Out: Pandemics, Capitalism, and Religious Extremism in Recent Apocalyptic Fiction (crit). *Studies in the Novel*, 54 (Sum. 2022), 235–54.

Faber, Christine. *The Unsettled State of America: Contemporary Narratives of Home and Mobility in Times of Crisis* (crit). Hildesheim: Georg Olms Verlag, 2022.

Roy, Wendy. Trauma and the Ethics of Literary Culture in the Time of Pandemic: Emily St. John Mandel's *Station Eleven* and Saleema Nawaz's *Songs for the End of the World* (crit). *Studies in Canadian Literature/Études en Littérature Canadienne*, 47 (1) 2022, 50–72.

Schaab, Katharine. Misogyny Survives the Apocalypse: The Collapse of Reproductive Justice in Emily St. John Mandel's *Station Eleven* and Ling Ma's *Severance* (crit). *Women's Studies*, 51 (Jan.–Feb. 2022), 1–17.

Marquart, Debra (b. 1956)

Marquart, Debra. An Interview with Iowa's Poet Laureate, Debra Marquart (I). *Middle West Review*, 8 (Spr. 2022), 112–23.

Monroe, Harriet (1860–1936)

Mather, Jeffrey. Poetry in the World: Harriet Monroe's China Travels (crit). *English Studies*, 103 (June 2022), 574–85.

Morrison, Toni (1931–2019)

Ahmed, Alshaymaa Mohamed. *Comparative Postcolonialism in the Works of V. S. Naipaul and Toni Morrison: Fragmented Identities* (crit). Lanham, Md.: Lexington Books, 2022.

Baker, Courtney R. Mothers, Daughters, and the Lash: Mourning the Mother Tongue in Toni Morrison's *A Mercy* (crit). *Meridians: Feminism, Race, Transnationalism*, 21 (Oct. 2022), 334–49.

Brier, Evan. Unliterary History: Toni Morrison, The Black Book, and "Real Black Publishing" (crit; pub). *American Literature*, 94 (Dec. 2022), 651–76.

Cholant, Gonçalo. *Reconfigurations of the Bildungsroman: Taking Refuge from Violence in Kincaid, Danticat, Hooks, and Morrison* (crit). Berlin: De Gruyter, 2022.

Cobo Piñero, Rocío. Beyond Literature: Toni Morrison's Musical and Visual Legacy for Black Women Artists (crit). *Feminismo/s*, 40 (2022), 27–51.

Coser, Stelamaris. African Diasporic Connections in the Americas: Toni Morrison in Brazil (crit). *Feminismo/s*, 40 (2022), 53–78.

Cullhed, Sigrid Schottenius. Procne in Toni Morrison's *Beloved* (crit). *Classical Receptions Journal*, 14 (Jan. 2022), 89–103.

Dawson, Adam. "We Knew We Were Being Watched": Adultification and Coming of Age in Jacqueline Woodson's *Another Brooklyn* (crit). *Studies in American Fiction*, 49 (Spr. 2022), 99–118.

De Vinne, Christine. Place Names in Toni Morrison's *The Bluest Eye*: A Literary Landscape of Racism (crit). *Names: A Journal of Onomastics*, 70 (3) 2022, 1–11.

Goldberg, Jesse A. The Unspeakable Whiteness in Whitman's Democracy: Empire and the Limits of American Literature (crit). *College Literature*, 49 (Fall 2022), 652–81.

Goldstein, Philip. *The Theory and Practice of Reception Study: Reading Race and Gender in Twain, Faulkner, Ellison, and Morrison* (crit). NY: Routledge, 2022.

Goulimari, Pelagia. Shredding, Burning, Tunnelling: Modernity, *Mrs. Dalloway, Sula* and My Grandparents circa 1922 (crit). *Angelaki*, 27 (June–Aug. 2022), 163–81.

Howard, Matthew M. Race, Place, & Space: Historicizing Blackness & Mobility (crit). Ph.D. Dissertation, U Washington, 2022.

Hu, Jun. The Face of the Other in *Home* (crit). *Explicator*, 80 (Jan.–June 2022), 14–18.

Jacques, Wesley. Toward a Minor Lit: Reading Power in Douglass, Caulfield, and Breedlove (crit). *Children's Literature Association Quarterly*, 47 (Fall 2022), 267–85.

Kiguwa, Peace. Phantom Love: Affective Politics of Love in Toni Morrison's *Love* (crit). *Women's Studies Quarterly*, 50 (Spr.–Sum. 2022), 33–48.

Le, Anh. "My Legs Go Softly and the Heart Is Stretching to Break": The Slave's Quest for Desire in Toni Morrison's *A Mercy* (crit). *Sigma Tau Delta Review*, 19 (2022), 155–60.

Lillywhite, Austin. What Is Telling? The Racial Dimensions of Narrative and Cognition in William Faulkner's *Absalom, Absalom!* And Toni Morrison's *A Mercy* (crit). *Modern Fiction Studies*, 68 (Win. 2022), 728–48.

Makonnen, Atesede. Seeing Whiteness in the Nineteenth Century and Beyond (crit). *Victorian Studies*, 64 (Win. 2022), 254–58.

Mondal, Ayan. Toni Morrison, "Whiteness" and the New History of Race in America: A Critical Overview (crit). *Postcolonial Interventions*, 7 (June 2022), 69–104.

Nardi, Paola A. "They Lived There Because They Were Poor and Black": Spatial Injustice in Toni Morrison's *The Bluest Eye* (crit). *Journal of African American Studies*, 26 (Dec. 2022), 401–12.

Okonkwo, Christopher N. *Kindred Spirits: Chinua Achebe and Toni Morrison* (crit). Charlottesville: U Virginia P, 2022.

Oyebade, Olufemi. African-American Utopian Literature: A Tradition Largely Lost and Forgotten, yet Pertinent in the Pursuit of Revolutionary Change (crit). Ph.D. Dissertation, Temple U, 2022.

Pak, Yumi. "Say, Who Owns This House?": US Violence, Indebtedness, and Care in Toni Morrison's *Home* (crit). *MELUS*, 47 (Sum. 2022), 127–46.

Perera, Nirshan. How Toni Morrison Helps My High School Students Understand Dickens (crit). *Victorian Studies*, 64 (Win. 2022), 270–75.

Plate, Liedeke. Portrait of the Postcolonial Intellectual as a Wise Old Woman: Toni Morrison, Word-Work, and *The Foreigner's Home* (crit). *Transnational Screens*, 13 (Aug. 2022), 96–110.

Pollak, Alec. Toni Morrison's *Their Eyes Were Watching God* (crit). *MELUS*, 47 (Spr. 2022), 107–29.

Schottenius Cullhed, Sigrid. Procne in Toni Morrison's *Beloved* (crit). *Classical Receptions Journal*, 14 (1) 2022, 89–103.

Simões, Bárbara. *Fantasmas da Escravidão: Memória do Trauma em Romances do Brasil, de Angola e dos USA* (crit). Curitiba, P.R.: Appris Editora, 2022.

Smith, Jeanne Rosier. *Writing Tricksters: Mythic Gambols in American Ethnic Fiction* (crit). Berkeley: U California P, 2022.

Spatzek, Samira. *Unruly Narrative: Private Property, Self-Making, and Toni Morrison's* A Mercy (crit). Berlin: De Gruyter, 2022.

Sundman, Alice. *Toni Morrison and the Writing of Place* (crit). NY: Routledge, 2022.

Szolc, Magda. Violence and Rejection: The Hegemony of White Culture and Its Influence on the Mother-Daughter Relationship in Toni Morrison's *The Bluest Eye* (crit). *Polish Journal of English Studies*, 8 (1) 2022, 25–42.

Tawfiq Hamamra, Bilal. Deconstructing Wo(man) and Animal Binary in Morrison's *The Bluest Eye* (crit). *ANQ*, 35 (July–Sept. 2022), 223–25.

Vaughn-Manley, Tracy. Pens and Needles: Toni Morrison, Quilts, and Community (crit). *Journal of Ethnic American Literature*, 12 (2022), 38–55.

Verdelle, A.J. *Miss Chloe: A Memoir of a Literary Friendship with Toni Morrison* (biog; crit; M). NY: Amistad Press, 2022.

Walker, Rafael. Ernest Gaines's The Tragedy of Brady Sims: A Final Nod to Toni Morrison (crit). *Arizona Quarterly*, 78 (Spr. 2022), 1–25.

Zhou, Quan and Li Zou. Warning Objects: A Psychogeographical Survey of the Early American Landscape in Toni Morrison's *A Mercy* (crit). *ANQ*, 35 (Oct.–Dec. 2022), 478–87.

——— and Qiping Liu. Agentic Things and Traumatized People in Toni Morrison's *The Bluest Eye* (crit). *Journal of Modern Literature*, 45 (Spr. 2022), 106–20.

Mueller, Lisel (1924–2020)

Schirrmeister, Benno. *Poetik der zweiten Sprache: Die Lyrik der deutsch-amerikanischen Dichterin Lisel Mueller (1924–2020): mit drei Essays der Autorin* (crit). Trier: Wissenschaftlicher Verlag Trier, 2022.

Muir, John (1838–1914)

Smith, Laura. *Ecological Restoration and the U.S. Nature and Environmental Writing Tradition: A Rewilding of American Letters* (crit). Cham, Switz.: Palgrave Macmillan, 2022.

Mukherjee, Bharati (1940–2017)

Agarwal, Shilpi. *Exploring Diasporic Sensibilities in the Short Fiction of Bharati Mukherjee and Chitra Banerjee Divakaruni* (crit). Jaipur: Yking Books, 2022.

Bain, Maitry Mohan. *The Fiction of Bharati Mukherjee and Chitra Banerjee Divakaruni: Cultural and Traditional Perspective* (crit). New Delhi: Intellectual Publishing House, 2022.

Crespo Gómez, Ana María. Approaching "Home" in Bharati Mukherjee's *Darkness* (crit). *International Journal of English Studies*, 22 (1) 2022, 23–40.

Maxey, Ruth. "Indiascape": Bharati Mukherjee's Engagement with E.M. Forster, Herman Hesse, and R.K. Narayan (crit). *Postcolonial Text*, 17 (4) 2022, unpaginated.

Naqvi, Farha Fatima. *Gender Identity and Displacement in the Novels of Bharati Mukherjee* (crit). Lucknow: CaveMark Publications, 2022.

Nguyen, Bich Minh (b. 1974)

Oh, Seung Ah. The Black-Eyed Child in the *Little House* Books and Asian American Adoption in Bich Minh Nguyen's *Pioneer Girl* (crit). *ANQ*, 35 (Apr.–June 2022), 182–85.

Norris, Bruce (b. 1960)

Carr, Gregory S. Interrogating Whiteness in Bruce Norris's *Clybourne Park* (crit). *Theatre Symposium*, 29 (2022), 64–72.

Norris, Frank (1870–1902)

Dawson, Jon Falsarella. *Combating Injustice: The Naturalism of Frank Norris, Jack London, and John Steinbeck* (crit). Baton Rouge: Louisiana State U P, 2022.

Oates, Joyce Carol (b. 1938)

Anand, Aswathi Velayathikode and Srirupa Chatterjee. Overcoming Daddy: The Daughter's Rite of Passage in Joyce Carol Oates' Late Novels (crit). *Critique*, 63 (3) 2022, 296–308.

Horvath, Dorota Olivia. *Nietzsche and Joyce Carol Oates: Nietzschean themes in the Wonderland Quartet* (crit). Washington: Academica Press, 2022.

Phelan, James. Character as Rhetorical Resource: Mimetic, Thematic, and Synthetic in Fiction and Non-Fiction (crit). *Narrative*, 30 (May 2022), 256–63.

Smith, Namara. Popcorn and Stale Plush (rev). *London Review of Books*, 44 (10 Feb. 2022), 39–40.

Zhou, Xinshuo and Quan Wang. "A New Race of Immortals": A Posthumanist Reading of "Poe Posthumous; or, the Light-House" (crit). *Journal of Literary Studies/Tydskrif vir Literatuurwetenskap*, 38 (3) 2022, unpaginated.

Oliver, Mary (1935–2019)

Peterson, John. "Ten Lamps of Fire": Transforming the Darkness in Mary Oliver's *Thirst* (crit). *Religion and Literature*, 54 (Aut. 2022), 61–76.

Olsen, Tillie (1912–2007)

Herring, Scott. *Aging Moderns: Art, Literature, and the Experiment of Later Life* (crit). NY: Columbia U P, 2022.

Ostenso, Martha (1900–1963)

Vis-Gitzel, Janice. The Plants are Plotting: Political Orders in Ostenso's *Wild Geese* (crit). *Canada and Beyond: A Journal of Canadian Literary and Cultural Studies*, 11 (2022), 95–113.

Paretsky, Sara (b. 1947)

Lassner, Phyllis. "The Dark Path Back": Investigating Holocaust Memory in Sara Paretsky's Novel, *Total Recall* (crit). *Studies in American Jewish Literature*, 41 (2) 2022, 144–64.

Parks, Gordon (1912–2006)

Leers, Dan, et al. *Gordon Parks: Pittsburgh Grease Plant, 1944/1946* (crit). Pleasantville, N.Y.: Gordon Parks Foundation, 2022.

Piercy, Marge (b. 1936)

Bassett, Caroline. *Anti-Computing: Dissent and the Machine* (crit). Manchester: Manchester U P, 2022.

Powers, Richard (b. 1957)

Avignon, Nathalie. *Musique et Abolition du Temps: Figures d'un Idéal dans le Roman Contemporain* (crit). Paris: Éditions Classiques Garnier, 2022.

Day, Timothy Ryan. The Forest for the Trees: The *Umwelt*, the Holobiont, and Metaphor in Richard Powers' *The Overstory* and Shakespeare's *Macbeth* (crit). *Ecozon@: European Journal of Literature, Culture and Environment*, 13 (2) 2022, 119–38.

Deluca, Laura. Temporality in *The Overstory* by Richard Powers (crit). *Explicator*, 80 (July–Sept. 2022), 78–80.

Fernández-Santiago, Miriam. *Orfeo*: A Posthuman Modern Promethius. Uncommon Powers of Musical Imagination (crit). *Anglia: Zeitschrift für Englische Philologie/Journal of English Philology*, 140 (3–4) 2022, 591–606.

Googasian, Victoria. Feeling Fictional: Climate Crisis and the Massively Multi-Protagonist Novel (crit). *New Literary History*, 53 (Spr. 2022), 197–216.

Laguarta Bueno, Carmen. Richard Powers's *Generosity: An Enchantment* (2009): Transhumanism, Metafiction and the Ethics of Increasing Human Happiness Levels through Biotechnology (crit). *Atlantis: Revista de la Asociación Española de Estudios Anglo-Norteamericanos*, 44 (2) 2022, 222–38.

Lötscher, Christine. Ökopassionen: Plädoyer für eine neomaterialistische Lektüre von Kinder- und Jugendmedien im Anthropozän (crit). *Jahrbuch der Gesellschaft für Kinder- und Jugendliteratur-forschung GKJL*, 2022, 13–24.

McMain, Emma M. and J.T. Torres. Understories and Upside-Downs: The Pedagogical Misanthropy of *The Overstory* and *Stranger Things* (crit). *ISLE: Interdisciplinary Studies in Literature and Environment*, 29 (Win. 2022), 1145–66.

Murray, Jessica. Using Critical Animal Studies to Read Climate Change Fiction: Literary Reflections and Provocations (crit). *English Academy Review*, 39 (2) 2022, 67–78.

Na, Zhang. *Posthuman Becoming Narratives in Contemporary Anglophone Science Fiction* (crit). Newcastle upon Tyne: Cambridge Scholars Publishing, 2022.

Schoene, Berthold. *Aborealism*, or Do Novels Do Trees? (crit). *Textual Practice*, 36 (Sept. 2022), 1435–58.

Staes, Toon. Minds, Mapping Minds, Mapping Minds: Reading the Complex Minds of Richard Powers's *The Echo Maker* (crit). *Critique*, 63 (2) 2022, 190–203.

Stewart, Garrett. *The Metanarrative Hall of Mirrors: Reflex Action in Fiction and Film* (crit). London: Bloomsbury Academic, 2022.

———. Open-Circuit Narrative: Programmed Reading in Richard Powers (crit). *Novel: A Forum on Fiction*, 55 (Nov. 2022), 547–65.

Purdy, James (1914–2009)

Snyder, Michael. *James Purdy: Life of a Contrarian Writer* (biog; crit). NY: Oxford U P, 2022.

Putnam, Samuel (1892–1950)

Szuberla, Guy. Samuel Putnam: Desperately Seeking (Chicago) Modernism (biog; crit). *MidAmerica*, 49 (2022), 37–48.

Ramanujan, A. K. (1929–1993)

Patil, G.G. A.K. *Ramanujan's Contribution to Indian English Literature* (crit). New Delhi: Authorspress, 2022.

Richardson, John (1796–1852)

Godeanu-Kenworthy, Oana. *Between Empire and Republic: America in the Colonial Canadian Imagination* (crit). Lanham, Md.: Lexington Books, 2022.

Rivera, Tomás (1935–1984)

Quesada, Sarah M. *The African Heritage of Latinx and Caribbean Literature* (crit). Cambridge: Cambridge U P, 2022.

Robles, Francisco E. Communal Imagination and the Problem of Allegory in Tomás Rivera's … *Y no se lo tragó la tierra* (crit). *Twentieth Century Literature*, 68 (Mar. 2022), 53–74.

Robinson, Marilynne (b. 1943)

Brown, Patricia. What's Love Got to Do with It? Christianity, Africanism, and Privilege in Marilynne Robinson's *Jack* (crit). *Christianity & Literature*, 71 (June 2022), 208–22.

Douglas, Christopher. Christian White Supremacy in Marilynne Robinson's Gilead Novels (crit). *Christianity & Literature*, 71 (June 2022), 190–207.

Gardner, Thomas. *Lyric Theology: Art and the Doctrine of Creation* (crit). Waco, Tex.: Baylor U P, 2022.

Horton, Ray. Seeing in "the Darkness, Visible": White Supremacy and Original Sin in Marilynne Robinson's *Jack* (crit). *Christianity & Literature*, 71 (June 2022), 223–43.

Iacovetti, Christopher. "Entering into God's Point of View": Marily McCord Adams and Marilynne Robinson on the Practice of Christian Forgiveness (crit). *Religion and Literature*, 54 (Aut. 2022), 21–38.

Leise, Christopher. Marilynne Robinson's "Long Puritanism" and Forms of Structural Racism (crit). *Christianity & Literature*, 71 (June 2022), 156–71.

Scott, Grant F. Keats, *Housekeeping* and the Poetry of Mourning (crit). *European Romantic Review*, 33 (Apr. 2022), 229–45.

Smith, James K.A. Making the Truth: Fiction as Theology in Marilynne Robinson's *Jack* (crit). *Christianity & Literature*, 71 (June 2022), 244–56.

Spencer, Caleb D. and Abram Van Engen. Interview: Robinson on Robinson after *Jack* (I). *Christianity & Literature*, 71 (June 2022), 257–60.

Sykes, Rachel, Anna Maguire Elliott, and Jennifer Daly, eds. *Marilynne Robinson* (crit). Manchester: Manchester U P, 2022.

Van Engen, Abram. Della's Rage: Race and Religion in Marilynne Robinson's *Jack* (crit). *Christianity & Literature*, 71 (June 2022), 172–89.

Roethke, Theodore (1908–1963)

Hirsch, Edward. Contact: Theodore Roethke, "Cuttings" and "Cuttings (Later)" (1948) (crit). *Michigan Quarterly Review*, 61 (Win. 2022), 21–31.

Sandburg, Carl (1878–1967)

Quinley, John W. *Discovering Carl Sandburg: The Eclectic Life of an American Icon* (biog). Hendersonville, N.C.: Mt. Camp Books, 2022.

Simak, Clifford D. (1904–1988)

Jazbec, Milan. Clifford D. Simak's *Way Station*: In the Diplomatic Service of the Galaxy (crit). *European Perspectives*, 13 (Apr. 2022), 131–60.

Simic, Charles (1938–2023)

Kremžar, Nina. Transnationalism in American Poetry (crit). *Acta Neophilologica*, 55 (1–2) 2022, 33–48.

Smiley, Jane (b. 1949)

Berger, Jacob C. Three Daughters, Two Stories, One Tragedy: Ownership and Incest in William Shakespeare's *King Lear* and Jane Smiley's *A Thousand Acres* (crit). *CEA Critic*, 84 (Mar. 2022), 1–12.

Carden, Mary Paniccia. National Families and Private Companies: Narrative Structure and Economies of Exchange in Jane Smiley's *The Last Hundred Years Trilogy* (crit). *Critique*, 63 (3) 2022, 371–84.

Vander Ploeg, Scott. A Thousand Acres of King Lear: Reading Shakespeare through Smiley (crit). *CEA Critic*, 84 (Mar. 2022), 42–49.

Stegner, Wallace (1909–1993)

Stewart, Matthew D. *The Most Beautiful Place on Earth: Wallace Stegner in California* (biog; crit). Salt Lake City: U Utah P, 2022.

Stockman, Farah (b. 1974)

Lauck, Jon K. An Interview with Pulitzer-Prize Winning Journalist, Farah Stockman (I). *Middle West Review*, 8 (Spr. 2022), 109–11.

Stowe, Harriet Beecher (1811–1896)

Arfan, Shmoon and Smarika Pareek. The Subaltern Treatment of the Characters of *Uncle Tom's Cabin* and *The Lonely Londoners* (crit). *Literature & Aesthetics: The Journal of the Sydney Society of Literature and Aesthetics*, 32 (2) 2022, 334–46.

Black, Christopher Allan. Vesey and Gordon's Righteous Insurrection: The Legacy of Denmark Vesey's Natural Rights Revolution in Harriet Beecher Stowe's *Dred: A Tale of the Great Dismal Swamp* (1856) (crit). *Rocky Mountain Review*, 76 (2) 2022, 177–94.

Coleman, Dawn. Fathers, Mothers, Saints, Martyrs: Religion as a Lineage of Belief (crit). *Modern Language Quarterly*, 83 (Dec. 2022), 481–97.

Cook, Jonathan A. *Moby-Dick* and *Uncle Tom's Cabin*: Separate Spheres, Parallel Worlds (crit). *Amerikastudien/American Studies*, 67 (3) 2022, 329–51.

Corbo, Christopher. The "Topsification" of *Uncle Tom's Cabin* (crit). *Theatre Symposium: A Journal of the Southeastern Theatre Conference*, 29 (2022), 120–32.

D'Amico, Luella. Visions, Saints, and Sacraments: *Uncle Tom's Cabin* and Catholicism (crit). *Women's Studies,* 51 (Sept. 2022), 661–81.

D'Amore, Maura. Episodic Storytelling: Theorizing Seriality in the Undergraduate Literature Classroom (crit). *Pedagogy: Critical Approaches to Teaching Literature, Language, Composition, and Culture*, 22 (Oct. 2022), 395–414.

Donnelly, Andrew. Stowe's Slavery and Stowe's Capitalism: Forced Reproductive Labor in *Uncle Tom's Cabin* (crit). *Women's Studies*, 51 (Sept. 2022), 647–60.

Downes, Kathleen. Sick Sympathies: Pathological Affect in Stowe's *Dred* (crit). *Women's Studies*, 51 (Sept. 2022), 633–46.

Hampton, Sharifa. Writing to Right the Spirit of Adoption: The Adoptive Mother / Savior in Harriet Beecher Stowe's *Uncle Tom's Cabin*, Harriet E. Wilson's *Our Nig*, and Frances Ellen Watkins Harper's *Moses: A Story of the Nile* (crit). *Amerikastudien/American Studies*, 67 (3) 2022, 353–77.

Kojima, Naoto. Before Realism: The Great American Novel and the Forms of Nationhood, 1851–1882 (crit). Ph.D. Dissertation, SUNY Albany, 2022.

Margolis, Stacey. As the World Turns; or Against Methodology (crit). *American Literary History*, 34 (Spr. 2022), 256–66.

Shaw, Amber. "There Are Two Views Often": The Epistolary Friendship of Harriet Beecher Stowe and Elizabeth Gaskell (crit). *Women's Studies*, 51 (Sept. 2022), 682–98.

Stratton-Porter, Gene (1863–1924)

Schnurr, Ryan. "The Wealth They Drew to the Surface": Gene Stratton-Porter on the Leading Edge of Petromodernity (crit). *MidAmerica*, 49 (2022), 49–63.

Suckow, Ruth (1892–1960)

Becker, Molly. Talking American in the Midwest: Linguistic Diversity and Authenticity in the Twentieth-Century United States (crit; lang). *Journal of American Studies*, 56 (Feb. 2022), 65–86.

Vizenor, Gerald (b. 1934)

Andrews, Tarren. The Afterlives of Crisis: Harold and Custer on the Slipstream (crit). *Exemplaria: Medieval, Early Modern, Theory*, 34 (3) 2022, 260–66.

Rasmussen, Birgit Brander. Native American Literature, 901 AD? A New Reading of the Battiste Good Wintercount (crit). *PMLA*, 137 (Mar. 2022), 279–94.

Stewart, Anne. *Angry Planet: Decolonial Fiction and the American Third World* (crit). Minneapolis: U Minnesota P, 2022.

Vonnegut, Kurt (1922–2007)

Doss, Michael. Political Feelings: Objects-in-Process in the American Novel, 1963–2013 (crit). Ph.D. Dissertation, U Delaware, 2022.

Farrell, Susan. American Fascism and the Historical Underpinnings of Kurt Vonnegut's *Mother Night* (crit). *Journal of Modern Literature*, 46 (Fall 2022), 141–57.

Jarvis, Christina S. *Lucky Mud & Other Forma: A Field Guide to Kurt Vonnegut's Environmentalism and Planetary Citizenship* (crit). NY: Seven Stories Press, 2022.

Laufert, Wayne. *Behaving Decently: Kurt Vonnegut's Humanism* (crit). Washington, D.C.: Humanist Press, 2022.

McDonald, Frances. *Posthumorism: The Modernist Affect of Laughter* (crit). London: Bloomsbury Academic, 2022.

Saggers, Emma. *Carnivalesque Inversion in the Fiction of Kurt Vonnegut* (crit). NY: Peter Lang, 2022.

Whitehead, Julia A. *Breaking Down Vonnegut* (crit). Hoboken, N.J.: Jossey-Bass, 2022.

Walker, Margaret (1915–1998)

Graham, Maryemma. *The House Where My Soul Lives: The Life of Margaret Walker* (biog; crit). Oxford: Oxford U P, 2022.

Wallace, David Foster (1962–2008)

Affede, Giulia. *Always on the Verge of Being Found Out: Transitional Phenomena and the Re-Emergence of the Self in David Foster Wallace's Fiction* (crit). Fano: Aras Edizioni, 2022.

Andrew, Laurie McRae. *The Geographies of David Foster Wallace's Novels: Spatial History and Literary Practice* (crit). Edinburgh: Edinburgh U P, 2022.

Baggio, Guido. *Filosofia e Patologia in D.F. Wallace: Solipsismo, Noia, Alienazione … e Altre Cose (Poco) Divertenti* (crit). Torino: Rosenberg & Sellier, 2022.

Brick, Martin. It Skips a Generation: Spirituality in David Foster Wallace and James Joyce (crit). *Christianity & Literature*, 71 (Mar. 2022), 78–96.

Delazari, Ivan and Jason S. Polley. "Popping into Your Mind's Eye": Covert Multimodality in David Foster Wallace's "The Soul Is Not a Smithy" (crit). *Style*, 56 (4) 2022, 413–32.

Dulk, Allard den, Pia Masiero, and Adriano Ardovino, eds. *Reading David Foster Wallace between Philosophy and Literature* (crit). Manchester: Manchester U P, 2022.

Hayes-Brady, Clare, ed. *David Foster Wallace in Context* (crit). Cambridge: Cambridge U P, 2022.

Judy, Ron S. Acting Natural: Television and David Foster Wallace's Metaffective Fiction (crit). *Textual Practice*, 36 (Nov. 2022), 1832–49.

Prout, Matt. Art or Shit: Value, Sincerity, and the Avant-Garde in David Foster Wallace (crit). *Journal of Modern Literature*, 45 (Spr. 2022), 72–89.

Roache, John. Reading, Investment, and Guarantee: *The Pale King* and the Authority of the Modern Literary Archive (crit). *Textual Practice*, 36 (May 2022), 643–74.

Sircy, Jonathan. "Hiding in Plain Sight": Seeing and Forgetting Reality in David Foster Wallace's *Oblivion* (crit). *Christianity & Literature*, 71 (Dec. 2022), 601–18.

Wohlmann, Anita. *Metaphor in Illness Writing: Fight and Battle Reused* (crit). Edinburgh: Edinburgh U P, 2022.

Ware, Chris (b. 1967)

Feroli, Teresa. Reading Post-Slavery Subjectivities in Chris Ware's *Jimmy Corrigan: The Smartest Kid on Earth* (crit). *Texas Studies in Literature and Language*, 64 (Spr. 2022), 63–88.

Samson, Jacques and Benoît Peeters. *Chris Ware: La Bande Dessinée Réinventée* (crit). Brussels: Les Impressions Nouvelles, 2022.

Wilder, Laura Ingalls (1867–1957)

Jameson, Elizabeth. American Borderlands: Reflections on Margins, Mainstreams, and Alternatives (crit). *Canadian Review of American Studies*, 52 (Aug. 2022), 105–25.

Oh, Seung Ah. The Black-Eyed Child in the *Little House* Books and Asian American Adoption in Bich Minh Nguyen's *Pioneer Girl* (crit). *ANQ*, 35 (Apr.–June 2022), 182–85.

Woodward, Abigail S. Planted in the Shadows: Centering Sexual Violence in *Prairie Lotus*, *Little House on the Prairie*, and Oliver Optic's *Hope and Have* (crit). *Children's Literature Association Quarterly*, 47 (Fall 2022), 250–66.

Wilder, Thornton (1897–1975)

Bryer, Jackson R. Teaching Thornton Wilder's Plays (crit). *Thornton Wilder Journal*, 3 (July 2022), 19–29.

Bucker, Park. The Chimes at Christmas: Directing/Teaching *The Long Christmas Dinner* (crit). *Thornton Wilder Journal*, 3 (July 2022), 76–84.

English, Mary C. Wilder on Teaching (crit). *Thornton Wilder Journal*, 3 (July 2022), 1–6.

Gerland, Oliver, III. Race and Power in *Pullman Car Hiawatha*: A Teaching Approach (crit). *Thornton Wilder Journal*, 3 (July 2022), 56–65.

Grace, Sherrill. "Pay Attention!": Thornton Wilder's Correspondence with Timothy Findley: A Literary Friendship (corr; crit). *Thornton Wilder Journal*, 3 (Oct. 2022), 149–76.

Gunn, Tony. The Universe within Four Walls: Performing *Pullman Car Hiawatha* in the Classroom (crit). *Thornton Wilder Journal*, 3 (July 2022), 101–08.

Hall, Ann C. The Act of Interpretation: Teaching *Shadow of a Doubt* (crit). *Thornton Wilder Journal*, 3 (July 2022), 45–55.

Hallquist, Terryl W. *Mozart and the Gray Steward* in the College Classroom (crit). *Thornton Wilder Journal*, 3 (July 2022), 66–75.

Hecht, Stuart J. What I Learned from *Our Town*: A Director's Memoir (crit; M). *Thornton Wilder Journal*, 3 (July 2022), 85–100.

Hischak, Thomas S. *The Thornton Wilder Encyclopedia* (biog; crit). Lanham, Md.: Rowman & Littlefield, 2022.

Konkle, Lincoln. Teaching *The Bridge of San Luis Rey* and Wilder's Other Novels (crit). *Thornton Wilder Journal*, 3 (July 2022), 7–18.

Longacre, Wesley. Recent Thornton Wilder Research and Scholarship (bibl). *Thornton Wilder Journal*, 3 (Oct. 2022), 240–49.

Martocello, Charles. *The Skin of Our Teeth* and New Jersey: A Historicist Reading of Wilder's Use of Setting (crit). *Thornton Wilder Journal*, 3 (Oct. 2022), 200–19.

Olmert, Michael. "You Can Teach It": *Our Town*, Our Students, and "Noticing" (crit). *Thornton Wilder Journal*, 3 (July 2022), 30–44.

Regen, Haas. Wilder's *The Long Christmas Dinner* and Broadway's *Birthday Candles*: Interviews with Playwright Noah Haidle and Director Vivienne Benesch (crit; I). *Thornton Wilder Journal*, 3 (Oct. 2022), 220–30.

Rojcewicz, Stephen J., Jr. *Thornton Wilder, Classical Reception, and American Literature* (crit). Abingdon, Oxon.: Routledge, 2022.

Ullom, Jeffrey. *The Emporium*, Adapted and Completed: An Interim Report (crit; D). *Thornton Wilder Journal*, 3 (Oct. 2022), 231–39.

Vowels, Grace. *Heaven's My Destination*: Thornton Wilder, Artifice, and Camp (crit). *Thornton Wilder Journal*, 3 (Oct. 2022), 177–99.

Williams, Tennessee (1911–1983)

Arnaut de Toledo, Luis Marcio. A Fase Japonesa de Tennessee Williams em *The Day on Which a Man Dies: An Occidental Noh Play* (crit). *Todas as Letras: Revista de Língua e Literatura*, 24 (Jan.–Apr. 2022), 1–16.

——— *Nem Loucas, Nem Reprimidas: O Confronto Contracultural da Mulher com o Mainstream nas Late Plays de Tennessee Williams* (crit). São Paulo: Alameda, 2022.

———. A tragédia moderna em *The Demolition Downtown* e *Some Problems for the Moose Lodge*, de Tennessee Williams (crit). *REVELL: Revista de Estudos Literários da UEMS*, 2 (32) 2022, 519–46.

Chapman, Matthieu. A Stained *Glass Menagerie* (crit). *Theatre History Studies*, 41 (2022), 30–33.

Chen, Kewei. Queer Attachments in Tennessee Williams' "Portrait of a Girl in Glass" (crit). *Explicator*, 80 (July–Sept. 2022), 142–46.

Grogan, Bridget. The Balcony Scene: Class, Descent and Spatial Metaphor in *A Streetcar Named Desire* (crit). *ANQ*, 35 (Oct.–Dec. 2022), 468–70.

Panda, Ram Narayan. Deconstructing Gender in Tennessee Williams' *A Streetcar Named Desire* (crit). *International Journal of Languages and Culture*, 2 (Dec. 2022), 33–36.

Qi, Shouhua. *Culture, History, and the Reception of Tennessee Williams in China* (crit). London: Palgrave Macmillan, 2022.

Schvey, Henry I. *Blue Song: St. Louis in the Life and Work of Tennessee Williams* (biog; crit). Columbia: U Missouri P, 2022.

Willson, Meredith (1902–1984)

Cabaniss, Mark. *Miracle of* The Music Man*: The Classic American Story of Meredith Willson* (biog; crit). Lanham, Md.: Rowman & Littlefield, 2022.

Wilson, Lanford (1937–2011)

Allen, Chadwick. *Earthworks Rising: Mound Building in Native Literature and Arts* (crit). Minneapolis: U Minnesota P, 2022.

Winters, Yvor (1900–1968)

Parkinson, Thomas. *Hart Crane and Yvor Winters: Their Literary Correspondence* (corr; crit). Berkeley: U California P, 2022.

Woolson, Constance Fenimore (1840–1894)

Van Slyck, Phyllis. Henry James's "Poor Sensitive Gentlemen" and the Quest for Meaning (and Happiness) in Three Late Tales: "The Altar of the Dead," "The Beast in the Jungle," and "The Jolly Corner" (crit). *Henry James Review*, 43 (Fall 2022), 252–67.

Wright, Richard (1908–1960)

Al-Sarrani, Abeer Abdulaziz. The Anticipation of the Black Aesthetic in Richard Wright's Work (crit). *Journal of Language, Literature and Culture*, 69 (Apr. 2022), 34–47.

Chase, Greg. *Wittgenstein and Modernist Fiction: The Language of Acknowledgment* (crit). London: Anthem Press, 2022.

Kihara, Kenji. "I Don't Own Any Property": Richard Wright's *Native Son* and Rhetoric of Possession (crit). *Arizona Quarterly*, 78 (Spr. 2022), 27–50.

Norris, Keenan. *Chi Boy: Native Sons and Chicago Reckonings* (crit; M). Columbus, Ohio: Mad Creek Books, 2022.

Ouédraogo, Serge Lazare. Richard Wright's Protest Writing : The Expression of Dispossession and Non-Conformism (crit). Thèse de Doctorat, Université de Lyon, 2022.

Zitkala-Ša (1876–1938)

Özkan, Hediye. The Politics of Reconciliation: Revolutionary Leadership of Zitkala-Ša for Indian Education and Cause (crit). *Papers on Language and Literature*, 58 (Spr. 2022), 202–20.

Pal, Virender. Tearing into the Web of Lies: Identity Narratives of Zitkala-Ša (crit). *Integrated Journal for Research in Arts and Humanities*, 2 (Jan. 2022), 1–4.

Sarker, Sonita. *Women Writing Race, Nation, and History: N/native* (crit). Oxford: Oxford U P, 2022.

Library of America Editions

Fitzgerald, F. Scott. *The Great Gatsby, All the Sad Young Men and Other Writings, 1920–1926.* James L.W. West III, ed. NY: Library of America, 2022. [no. 353].

Michael Kim Roos

Winner of the 2025 MidAmerica Award
for distinguished contributions to the study of midwestern literature

and

Ana Castillo

Winner of the 2025 Mark Twain Award
for distinguished contributions to midwestern literature

These awards will be presented at the Society's 53rd annual meeting, Kellogg Hotel and Conference Center, Michigan State University, May 29–30, 2025.

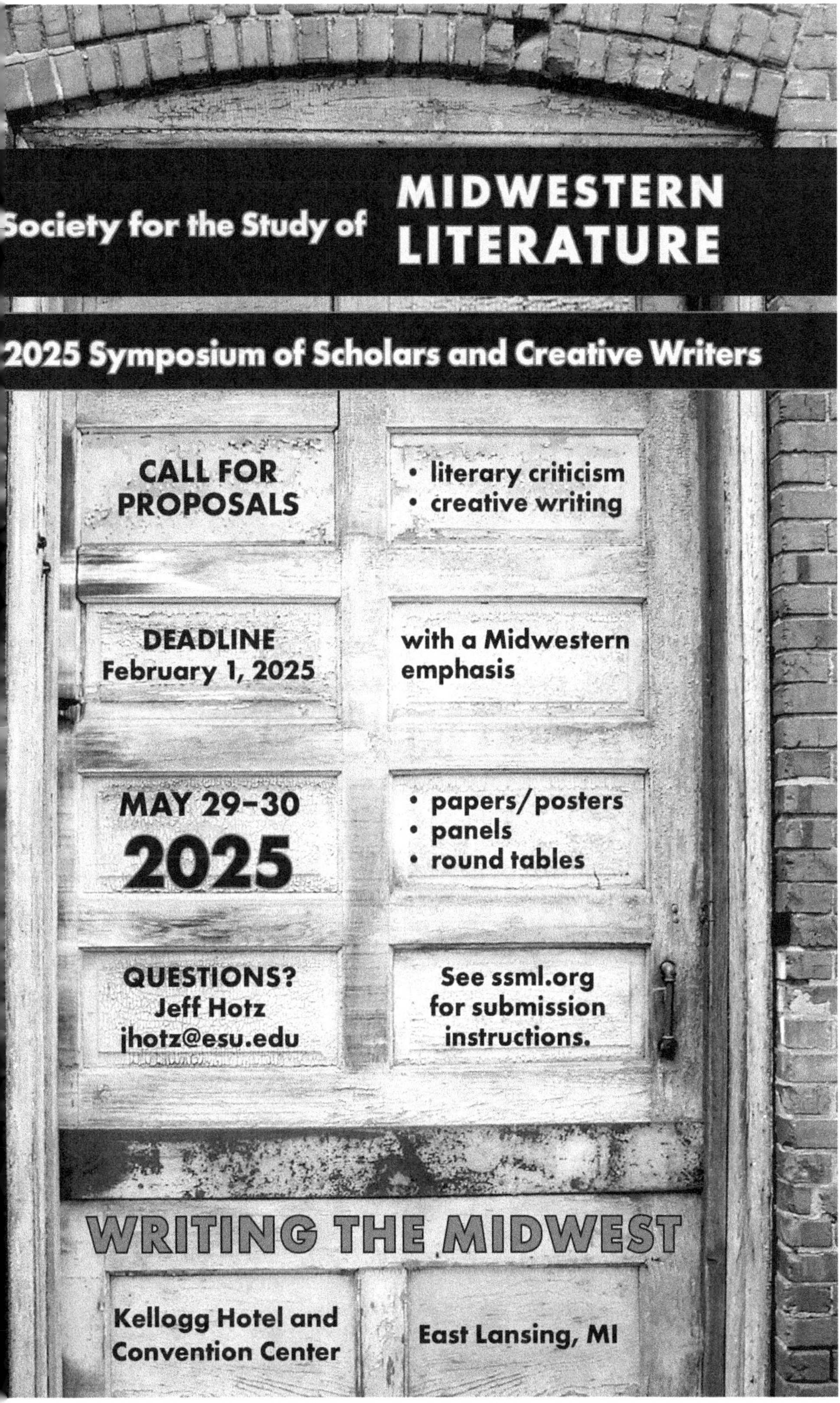

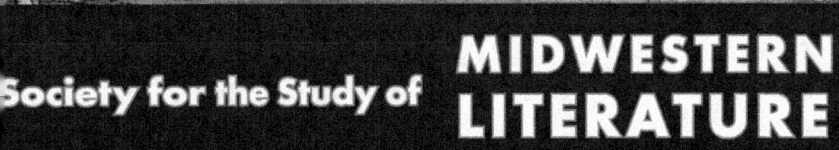

Society for the Study of MIDWESTERN LITERATURE

2025 Symposium of Scholars and Creative Writers

CALL FOR PROPOSALS

- literary criticism
- creative writing

DEADLINE
February 1, 2025

with a Midwestern emphasis

MAY 29–30
2025

- papers/posters
- panels
- round tables

QUESTIONS?
Jeff Hotz
jhotz@esu.edu

See ssml.org for submission instructions.

WRITING THE MIDWEST

Kellogg Hotel and Convention Center

East Lansing, MI

CALL FOR PROPOSALS

1925 was a banner year for Midwestern literature. Important novels published that year include F. Scott Fitzgerald's *The Great Gatsby*, Willa Cather's *The Professor's House*, Ernest Hemingway's *In Our Time*, Theodore Dreiser's *An American Tragedy*, and Sinclair Lewis's *Arrowsmith*. To celebrate the 100th anniversary of this important year, the Society for the Study of Midwestern Literature invites essay proposals for a special issue of its peer-reviewed journal *Midwestern Miscellany* on the topic of "Midwestern Literature in 1925," to be edited by Scott Emmert (University of Wisconsin Oshkosh). Proposals may focus on the famous novels of 1925 or texts / authors that have been overshadowed by Fitzgerald, Cather, Hemingway, Dreiser, and Lewis.

Proposals should be no more than 300 words and should include a brief critical bibliography. Completed essays should be between 3,000 and 5,000 words. Contributors must be member of SSML before publication.

PROPOSAL DEADLINE	ESSAY DEADLINE
January 1, 2025	August 1, 2025

Send proposal and short CV to Scott Emmert (emmerts@uwosh.edu). Please also indicate if you would like your proposal to be considered for a special panel at the 2025 Symposium of the Society for the Study of Midwestern Literature (May 29-30, East Lansing, MI).

NEED SOME INSPIRATION? LESSER KNOWN TEXTS PUBLISHED IN 1925

Bess Streeter Aldrich, *The Rim of the Prairie*
Sherwood Anderson, *Dark Laughter*
Lorna Doone Beers, *Prairie Fires*
Earl Derr Biggers, *The House Without a Key*
Thomas A. Boyd, *Samuel Drummond*
Louis Bromfield, *Possession*
Hallie Quinn Brown, *Tales My Father Told*
Edgar Rice Burroughs, *The Moon Men*
Edgar Rice Burroughs, *The Red Hawk*
Floyd Dell, *This Mad Ideal* and *Runaway*
John Dos Passos, *Manhattan Transfer*
Geoffrey Dell Eaton, *Backfurrow*
T. S. Eliot, "The Hollow Men"
John T. Frederick, *Green Bush*
Ruth Gaines-Shelton, "The Church Fight"
Zane Grey, *The Vanishing American*
John Herrmann, *Foreign Born*

Emerson Hough, *The Ship of Souls*
Langston Hughes, "The Weary Blues"
Alain Locke (ed.), *The New Negro*
Archibald Macleish, *The Pot of Earth*
Walter J. Mullenburg, *Prairie*
Martha Ostenso, *Wild Geese*
O.E. Rolvaag, *Giants in the Earth*
Helen Hooven Santmyer, *Herbs and Apples*
James Stevens, *Paul Bunyan*
Gene Stratton-Porter, *The Keeper of the Bees*
Ruth Suckow, *The Odyssey of a Nice Girl*
Ruth Plumly Thompson, *The Lost King of Oz*
Jim Tully, *Jarnegan*
Carl Van Vechten, *Firecrackers: A Realistic Nove*
Glenway Wescott, *Natives of Rock*
Harold Bell Wright, *A Son of the Father*
Little magazines: *Poetry, The Midland,* etc.